12.99 ✻

I0996799

Cutting
Confidential

Cutting Confidential

True confessions and
trade secrets of a
celebrity hairdresser

Shaun Lockes

Copyright © Shaun Lockes 2007
Illustrator copyright © Jacqueline Bissett 2007

The right of Shaun Lockes to be identified as the author
of this work has been asserted by him in accordance with
the Copyright, Designs and Patents Act 1988.

First published in Great Britain in 2007 by
Orion Books
an imprint of the Orion Publishing Group Ltd
Orion House, 5 Upper St Martin's Lane,
London WC2H 9EA

1 3 5 7 9 10 8 6 4 2

A CIP catalogue record for this book is
available from the British Library.

ISBN-13: 978 0 75287 536 1

Printed in Great Britain by
Clays Ltd, St Ives plc

The Orion Publishing Group's policy is to use papers that
are natural, renewable and recyclable and made from wood
grown in sustainable forests. The logging and manufacturing
processes are expected to conform to the environmental
regulations of the country of origin.

Every effort has been made to fulfil requirements with regard
to reproducing copyright material. The author and publisher will
be glad to rectify any omissions at the earliest opportunity.

With thanks to the following magazines and newspapers
for the statistical information: *Creative Head*, *Frizz*,
Salon Business and *The Times*.

To the thousands of clients whose hair I've done in the last 25 years for giving me such a fun job, enriching my life and enabling me to live my dream.

SHAUN LOCKES

The names in this book have been changed to protect the innocent and not so innocent. Shaun Lockes is a fictional name for a real-life London hairdresser. All the incidents recounted in this book happened in real life but have been condensed into one day for dramatic effect.

Chapter 1

7.30 a.m. Client —
a royal residence

*I*t's a nightmare of an early start today. That means getting to the salon and packing my session bag before I can even get started on my way to my royal client. I should have done it last night so I could go straight from home, but then again, I want to get in and make sure everything is OK. I don't want any distractions this morning, like worrying about the salon.

I check my watch – I have a passion for them, most hairdressers do – and realise I'd better step on it. Today I am sporting my brand-new white-gold Cartier American Tank, all sixteen grand's worth. The watch fetish might be considered a tad flashy, but I can't wear rings as they'd interfere with my cutting, and the subtle bling of a good watch doesn't seem too footbally. In fact, it makes me feel the bollocks. Hairdressers are often lumped together in the style stakes with footballers – with Porsches sometimes being referred to as hairdressers' or footballers' cars – or they share the opinion that we're morphed together in the intellectual department, renowned for our lack of brain power, which is probably true in some cases. I like to think I have a little more going for me than the odd get-rich-quick footballer, yet I'm conscious of the comparison.

£4.7 billion per annum is spent in UK hair salons, beauty salons, barber shops and grooming establishments.

Crucially, I rush to the window to check out the weather. Fine, drizzly rain: every hairdresser's – and paying client's – nightmare. As Peter Kay would say, 'It's the sort of rain that goes *right* through you.' Yeah, and right through my bloody blow-dry. Mental memo: remember to pack extra-strength hairspray and don't forget frizz-control root-booster for blow-drying. I could do without battling the elements – I've really got to pull it out of the bag today and get it perfect. I feel the stress levels start to rise.

What to wear? I need to look casual yet cutting edge (pardon the pun), as I'm doing a photo shoot later and my PR wants me in shot. In fact, she wants a picture of me and my celebrity to put in her reference library. It's cheesy, but I have to oblige, and so does my celeb client.

There's no such thing as a free lunch – or blow-dry three times a week. I decide on a brightly coloured stripy shirt, funky cufflinks and some de-stressed jeans. I know what you're thinking, but we hairdressers dispensed with the leather trousers years ago, or at least most of us did. Actually, they were very practical for cutting hair in, as the cuttings slid off the leather and you didn't get all the hair in your boxers like you do with certain trouser-wear, particularly my fine wool Prada's.

Stressed by my increasing lateness, I dash out into the traffic and try and hail a cab, buying myself a little thinking time.

I remember watching the film *Shampoo* as a young lad, thinking what a fabulous life a hairdresser had – this sought-after, charming man given adoration all day. No doubt some of my clients see me in that light. It would be remiss of me not to grudgingly admit that the Warren Beatty comparison is not unflattering. Every hairdresser enjoys a little ego-massage now and again and it's a nice little fantasy for my frustrated-house-wife clients to indulge in if they fancy me; which the majority used to, although the greying hair, ever-so-slightly expanding waistline and increasingly lined, if still cheeky smile may be putting a few off these days.

Jimmy, the cleaner, is polishing the mirrors when I arrive. He's a crap cleaner and sometimes I don't know why we have him, but he's been with us for so long I'm convinced he'd still turn up every day even if we got rid of him. And therein lies his strength: he turns up every day. At my stage of the game the last thing I want to go back to is mopping the salon floor. I've had more than enough of that over the years, thank you very much.

I blast myself with the hairdryer to dry my hair off from the drizzle, tweaking some styling wax through my new cut. I'm prone to a spot of vanity – it comes from looking at yourself all day while talking to your clients through the mirror – but even I worry when I catch myself unconsciously pouting as I apply the product and sort my hair out, thinking that if any one of the staff saw me doing it they'd mercilessly take the piss for a week.

I show Jimmy a patch of hairy skirting board that's been seriously bothering me near my styling section. Hair has the amazing ability to travel in the atmosphere and stick to everything when it's wet, particularly after cutting, and it's not long before an easily missed corner looks like Julia Robert's armpits on a bad day. Not conducive to paying attention to your client – my wandering eyes are all-too-easily distracted by poor housekeeping, and little observations like this don't enhance the feel-good factor and service experience if the client were to notice. Thankfully, most of them don't, and I wouldn't be doing my job properly if they did. They're more interested in buying into some of my hair magic.

> The most important thing a woman can have — next to talent, of course — is her hairdresser.
> Joan Crawford

I check the salon light bulbs, even though I'm running late, and point out a few to Jimmy that have blown since yesterday. He smiles and nods. He knows me well enough to know he has to get it sorted before I come back to my chair later. Silly little things like blown bulbs mean the world to me as they spell out a poorly managed business. I'm a stickler for making sure the salon looks perfect, but then it's not surprising seeing as it's my name above the door. My clients are wearing my brand 24/7 as it's my designer label that is metaphorically stitched into their hair. It's all about standards, and not just on a technical level, the salon's appearance is crucial, too. Keeping the standards up and bettering them – having the most gorgeous chairs, the most high-tech equipment, the best staff, the best coffee and the most talked-about salon. Constantly striving to be the best in one of the most celebrity-driven, fame-obsessed, cut-throat businesses in the world. Hairdressing isn't as fluffy as it's often portrayed; it's dog-eat-dog. Every salon is only as good as its staff, and its success lives and dies by its client base. No good salon owner can afford to lose a client, and least of all over something as trivial as a dirty skirting board.

My assistant arrives. She's late, and she knows it, but I don't bollock her. There isn't time. We've got to move ourselves if we're not going to keep our most important client waiting. She checks my session bag – my hairdresser's Tardis is how I often describe it. It has to cater for every eventuality and cope with any demand I throw at it. It has to have clairvoyant qualities, to be able to adapt at whim to any demanding client, any photographic session (inside and out, as all the elements may be chucked at us) or any flighty, mercurial magazine editor's ideas. It has to cope with horrendous circumstances – fine hair, thick hair, great hair, shit hair, no hair – hence the rainbow of different-coloured hair wefts and pieces in every length and texture, all ready to give any A-lister the illusion of lustrous, thick locks that hundreds of normal women will aspire to. Many a model revered for their crowning glory has no more than a carefully tended set of extensions. Just catch those caught-off-camera pictures in the trashy celeb mags where a gust of wind has made the glue visible.

My bag contains rollers of every size and variety – heated and Velcro – styling irons; curling tongs of varying barrel widths; every product known to man – but only those of my chosen manufacturer, of course – pins and grips, both in five different matching hair colours, pin-curl clips; crocodile clips; clippers; taperers; neck-hair trimmers; my favourite hairdryer diffuser; mobile hood dryer; scissors; thinning scissors; slicing scissors; tail combs; cutting combs; a plethora of brushes – pure bristle, nylon and mixed, mainly from Italy – and a needle and thread. Not for me, but for sewing in troublesome hats, bridal veils and tiaras. Other oddities include talc (if no time to shampoo), glitter spray (just in case), and a variety of extension leads (there's never a power point where you need one – hairdressers' sod's law No 1). I have, on an outdoor magazine shoot, been known to rewire the electrics on a park fountain in order to plug in my Carmen rollers.

Q: Why are hairdressers so unpopular?
A: Because they're always talking behind your back.

Finally, my toothbrush. Not for my pearly whites but because it is perfect for spritzing with hairspray to tidy up fine new hair growing and tufting around the hairline – lethal for spoiling an otherwise perfect chignon or some very close photographic work and it saves a fortune in studio retouching.

We cross-check our list like an airline captain and first mate as we re-pack the bag. This almost daily ritual is largely due to theft and my own dizzy creativity. On a shoot, when the

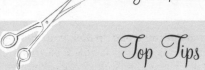

Top Tips

On looking after your hair

* When you wash your hair, think of it as a delicate pashmina and you will start to get an idea of how you should treat it. Hair grows approximately 1.5 cm per month, so to get it past bra-strap length, it could take well over six years, although most hair only has a lifespan of four years (hence some women never seem able to get past this level). Aged hair needs careful treatment – think of the amount of tugging, brushing and pulling, let alone colour or heat damage you subject the ends of your hair to daily! Don't be rough with it, as aged hair will be weaker. Be as kind as you can to the mid-lengths and ends.
* Cleanse and condition with top-quality products, whose ingredients are not harsh and will protect your hair and colour. They will really make a difference to how your hair looks and feels, and as they are concentrated you will use less so they can be more economical.
* Rinse your hair for two minutes – time yourself. Hair will shine beautifully if rinsed really well.
* The hair is made up of sections. The outside, protective layer (the cuticle) is where external damage takes place (from heat, styling irons, etc). This layer is like overlapping fish scales or roof tiles and will only shine if the scales are lying flat. This is what conditioner does when it is smoothed on – it flattens the cuticles. Sometimes damage is so severe, the inside (cortex) is damaged too – this is the internal structure of the hair, so hair will break and split.
* Damaged hair will not be smooth as the cuticles are ruffled or the overlapping scales are missing. This will make hair look fluffy and can result in the hair splitting. Split ends that aren't cut can cause further damage by travelling up the hair shaft, so never think that you'll get your hair longer by not cutting them off.
* If you leave product residue in your hair, it will 'steam' when you blow dry it. This means either you haven't rinsed properly or there is a build up through overuse of products, particularly silicone-based products, which build up on the hair – keep usage to a minimum.
* Less is more. Try to stick to the golden rule: one styling product is all you should use. If you use too many you

will overload your hair and it could end up dull, limp and lifeless.
* The internal section of the hair (cortex) is where all chemical and technical processes take place – ensure you look after this by never repeating processes over the same hair, i.e. ensure colour applications are made to the roots only, refreshing the ends only when necessary or if faded.
* Damaged cortex makes hair sensitised and porous. Hair should have a natural elasticity – if you stretch it to a third of its length when wet it should return to its original length when dry. If it doesn't have this elasticity, the cortex is damaged.

music is blaring and I'm getting into the swing of things, I'm prone to leaving things lying around. Make-up artists can be notoriously light-fingered, too, hence the constant replenishment required. This is predominantly down to the on-going battle for supremacy between hairdressers and make-up artists. It's like the Anglo-French relationship of cordial hatred. Make-up artists are very often trained hairdressers, too, and are therefore natural reserves if the hairdresser fails to shift their arse out of bed and make it to the studio, so they are a tad chippy about their expertise being over-shadowed by the often tardy, Diva hairdresser. That and their annoyance at not being able to bill for an extra service should the snipper fail to materialise.

One way of exacting revenge for their comparative lack of renown is to fail to return the coveted brush they borrowed from you, or a much-admired styling product. I have walked away from shoots with such depleted stock I ended up starting a new session bag from scratch. The more bitchy ones will spitefully attempt to get their own back by trashing your work with the not-very-careful placing of an Alice band when they re-touch the make-up during a shoot break.

Happy that we can cover every eventuality, even the shitty weather, we clamber into a cab, trailing the bag behind us.

I have managed to summon a quintessentially British cabbie, who shouts, 'Where to, Guv?' through the sliding glass panel.

Momentarily taken aback when I mention our regal destination, I think he vaguely recognises me – I wouldn't expect him too, really, middle-aged men aren't really my target market and I'm sure he's never had any inclination to watch one of my makeovers on daytime TV, unless he's been laid up with a bout of man 'flu. It doesn't take long for his curiosity to get the better of him and he asks me what I'm up to there today. We chat for a while and he tells me some stories about the people he's had in the back of his cab with loose and distant connections to various members of 'the Firm'. He asks me whether I ever did Princess Diana's hair, and I confide that it is my biggest regret that I never did; my one dream that can never come true.

98 per cent of unhappy salon clients don't complain — they switch salons.

He chats about a few celebs that he's now remembered he has dropped off at the salon and asks what they're really like, another question that has a tendency to bring me out in hives. If the truth about some of them got out, I wouldn't want it sourced back to me. So I tell him they are lovely and down-to-earth, as this is what he wants to hear. It's my job to be discreet. After all, clients tell their hairdressers everything, and my celebrity clients are no different, for all their egomaniacal, insecure, fucked-up, loveable ways.

Switching off from his constant stream of banter, we drive through the mounting traffic and it dawns on me, as it often does, that it is me – little old me, the nervous, somewhat cack-handed apprentice that was, the insecure fresh-from-school boy – who has grown into a top hairdresser and turned himself into a brand.

I am Shaun Lockes, the 'Snipper to the Stars', the 'Celebrity Crimper', the 'Hair Genie' – the media persona (or is it monster?) I have worked tirelessly to create, yet today I hardly feel like it. I fleetingly question whether I can even live up to it. The insecurity sweeps over me like a wave of nausea, the responsibility is suddenly overwhelming. There is no hiding place. This is a very important day, and my work will be scrutinised by relentless celebrity magazines and the critical eye of my peers. It makes me want to run away into a corner to work in a small, pressure-free suburban salon, away from the glare of the public or anyone else's watchful eye. Yet the buzz is in some ways addictive. I have a love/hate relationship with my adrenaline, I decide. While my vulnerability may seem touching, it's an expense I can ill afford and I have to big myself up mentally if I'm going to get through the next hour.

I defy any top hairdresser not to acknowledge this once in a while; but they never would – they couldn't be seen to, even if they would grudgingly admit it to themselves. Hairdressing is so out there, so in your face – your work isn't open to artistic interpretation as there is no in-between, only success or failure. Get it right and hordes of women will be cutting the picture out of magazines and taking it into salons up and down the country and you'll be hailed as a genius by the beauty press for creating such a must-have look. Get it wrong and you'll end up in the so-bad-a-look columns in every celebrity magazine going, much to the enjoyment of your rivals. Not only will you lose some hard-won editorial praise, but the custom of the original client, too. It's a win/lose situation and there is no middle ground. People will either love it or hate it. Every top hairdresser would admit to this fear of cocking up, if we weren't so generally full of self-belief, otherwise known as public relations crap. The word crap leads me to ponder that this fear of a bad-hair day is like having a Ratner moment. We all work far too hard building up our image to risk that. We hope today's papers are tomorrow's fish

Fabric softener

Essential if a bad apprentice tangles long hair at the backwash and it's matted into clumps that can only be cut out. It's also great for hair extensions.

and chip wrappers, but in our hearts we know that a bad hair-do can live on for ever. Remember the photos of Cherie Blair opening the door after her first morning in Downing Street? Or seeing the photos of Posh's hair-extension-induced bald patch before she sensibly removed them and went for her Pob (Posh bob)? Or Madonna's frighteningly receding, wig-covered hairline?

I've had my share of hair disasters – take the society bride whose wedding was featured in a celebrity magazine. I still cringe at the thought of it. My first celebrity wedding and I made the stupid mistake of overindulging on the Jack Daniel's the night before – mainly due to nerves – and not being compus mentus at 6 a.m. the next morning when I got up for work. Not really a bridal-hair expert at that time, I was understandably nervous when my PR breezed in and informed me that not only was I to be hairdresser to the bride at the celebrity wedding of the year, but my work was going to be featured in a celebrity magazine as a front cover and inside story. She'd just secured the notoriously tight-fisted bridegroom, who's a tad on the penny-pinching side, a lucrative deal with the powers-that-be in return for the usual behind-the-scenes pictures, and that included preparing his wife-to-be. After three wedding trials at the salon till late into the evening during the preceding weeks, on the day itself I drove down to the country, where the event was taking place, still hungover, arriving at 7 a.m. to wake up the bride.

Instead of nursing my burgeoning headache with a gentle hair of the dog or my tried-and-tested pick-me-up of a sachet of Resolve mixed with Dioralyte – try it, it works a treat – upon arrival I was asked to spruce up a visiting rock star whose CD I'd just been playing in my car.

As everyone's eyes were going to be on the bride, I was worried that my intricate chignon would tumble just as she was saying 'I do' while being 'papped' from every angle, so I decided to sew in her veil with some blonde-coloured cotton. She looked horrified, until I assured her that it was the only way to guarantee perfect hair and that I would take it all out afterwards.

So hard was I concentrating on the security of her veil, I overlooked my normally vigilant eye on the hair front – the hangover hardly helping me to be as diligent as usual in my curling technique.

Her up-do consisted of curly face-framing tendrils, which, to my horror, started to uncurl before my very eyes and hang limply and lifelessly before she had even finished saying her vows. As the champagne flowed, it became increasingly impossible to drag her away from the photographers and well wishers, not only to rescue her hair but also my reputation as her bad-hair day unfurled to all the A-listers and media frenzy present.

Nowadays, with a decade of celebrity experience under my belt, I would have no hesitation in whisking her into a private room to rectify any hair mistakes pronto, whether she wanted

HAIR FACTS

Hair grows in cycles called anagen, catagen and telogen. **Anagen** is the active, growing stage (which lasts for approximately five years). **Catagen** is the static stage, where the hair is ready to loosen from its bulbous root (this lasts for approximately two weeks). **Telogen** is the resting stage, where the hair is no longer growing but does not fall out. Once it has finished growing, hair will fall out two to three months after it has effectively died. The old hair is pushed out and the new one growing underneath it in the hair shaft starts to push up.

to come or not. I now have the confidence not to put my name to anything less than perfection. Looking back, I was far too star-struck and in awe of the occasion to put my professionalism first. That was a steep learning curve, and one I wouldn't want to repeat.

My assistant smiles at me nervously, thankfully oblivious to the resurgence of my past insecurities and the racing pulse that their reminiscence has evoked. I smile faintly, while mentally persuading myself they will never be repeated. I am her mentor and it is crucial that she believes in me. I try always to display an artistic confidence and a swagger of nothing-fazes-me arrogance, even if I'm not feeling it. I need to bolster my 'Can do, will dazzle' attitude, as much for myself as her.

There are 35,000 salons in the UK, with over 10,000 in London alone.

No doubt she is smiling through her own sense of pride, too, and it's a great feeling that I still share, even now after several visits. It's quite something to be invited into a royal residence, and we both know it. She texts her mum quickly to pass on the good news to her friends and family, and I remember how I did exactly the same thing. Monarchist or republican, it's a defining moment in your life to get to the other side of a royal household. No doubt she watched those royal fly-on-the-wall documentaries, just as I did as a child with my parents, never daring to dream that one day I might be on the inside.

The attack of nerves passes, thank God, as it always does. I take a deep breath and have a squirt of Bach's Rescue Remedy, relieved that my hairdressing stage fright has left the building. My assistant looks at me questioningly, until I pass it off as breath freshener. Regaining my composure, I remember how many of the other crimpers, otherwise known as my peers, would love to have a royal as a client, and will have their PRs straight onto the royal powers-that-be if I screw up. This is incentive enough to get my shit together mentally and concentrate on what I'm going to do.

It's a well-known fact that good hairdressers leave their problems at home and immerse themselves fully in their clients. As my camp old stylist used to say to me when I was training, 'It's a stage out there, darling, and you're the leading lady. Nobody wants to book a misery guts!' He was right, but having a public persona can be tiring when you don't feel like turning on the charm. Putting on a bright, sunny face is hard enough on days when you're feeling quiet and reflective, but there is more to hairdressing than that. Over the years, a good hairdresser will cultivate the vital skill of being able to connect with any person on any level. It's the knack of being able to adapt not only your conversation, but also your personality. I may be talking to the landed gentry one moment and a flashy Essex housewife the next. I could be cutting the hair of a famous actor in the morning and a student nurse who's saved up for six months to book a haircut with me in the afternoon. And as intriguing and interesting as all that is, it's ultimately quite draining. It's the knack of pretending to be fascinated by people even if you're not.

Fortunately, most hairdressers are extremely nosey and more than a little gossipy, so being fascinated isn't normally that difficult. This is inevitable considering we spend all day fishing into people's lives and looking for clues. Ask the right questions and get the right answers and I can normally deliver knock-out results hairwise. Miss a clue and I'm scuppered. For instance, there is no point in giving somebody a couture, high-maintenance haircut that needs daily blow-drying if I fail to find out they swim every day and only blow dry their hair on special occasions. So we dig and delve to establish just who we've got sitting in our chairs, and more importantly what they want, and we only have about an hour to find out all this information and perform a hair miracle.

Then there's the physical side – the risk of developing varicose veins from standing on your feet all day, and the likelihood of suffering from dermatitis during your training due to the constant, relentless amount of shampooing your poor hands are subjected to while you finish your three-year apprenticeship. I wouldn't call that glamorous: going to bed with red, swollen, bleeding mitts smothered in E45 and wrapped in cotton gloves. Or covered in plasters for the duration of your crimping career because your same-place cut is reopened every day by a nick from your excruciatingly sharp scissors. Most hairdressers have very scarred fingers and knuckles in the spot where they hold the hair while cutting. They also don't cut with their index finger and thumb, but their ring finger and thumb, with real experts only moving the top blade, never both together – check it out next time you get a haircut.

A new hairdressing salon opened up right across the road from an established barber shop, with a big bold sign saying: WE GIVE £10 HAIRCUTS.
Not to be outdone, the older barber put up his own sign: WE FIX £10 HAIRCUTS.

People have some very strange perceptions about our business and the lightweight image it has. It's perceived as being all fluff and nonsense, but it's far from it. It's quite unique, in its quirky, serious, yet frivolous way, and it is bloody good fun, for all its bad points. If you are lucky enough to work with some great people, and my team are, there is a bizarre irresistibility to hairdressing. It is a deliciously bitchy, wonderfully funny, irreverent, racy, pacy, saucy, creative and inspiring industry. Rather like a real-life *Carry On* film or a saucy seaside postcard, in some respects. And, it must be said, there's some good money to be made out of it, particularly if you do make it to the top. Lightweight it certainly isn't. In fact, it's a multi-million-pound industry that deserves to be taken seriously.

We arrive at our regal address, and my now-familiar face is ushered in by the guard, who even greets me with a cheery 'Good Morning' and flatteringly remembers my Christian name.

As I tread the hushed corridors to my client's suite, I think of how much I would love not to have to follow the footman but go off and explore the rabbit warren of rooms. The royal residence is actually surprisingly fusty. The whole place looks, it has to be said, in need of a little refurbishment and my ever-critical eye is drawn to the odd exposed pipe and dated plumbing, which in my modern house would never be on show.

Most hairdressers fancy themselves as wanna-be interior designers and the two are seemingly inextricably linked. I even get on my own nerves with my constant attention to detail, finding I can never just relax in a bar or restaurant without wanting to assess how the architect has hidden the air-con ducts or how ambient and atmospheric the lighting is. Salon lighting needs to be particularly well chosen: good enough (and bright enough) for the stylist to work in, particularly in the colour area, but ultra-flattering to the client. Blue-toned harsh lights, à la late-night burger bar, have to go as they are ageing, interfere with colouration and make clients look knackered, which makes my job ten times harder. If somebody is sitting there telling you how dreadful they look before you even start, it makes the task in hand of making them feel beautiful an uphill struggle.

The lighting should be ambient and soft in the cutting area, like the type you'd expect while having lunch with an old friend. Wherever you're colouring, though, it's vital that it's as close to natural daylight as possible. Ever walked out of a salon to find the colour you thought was so fabulous when you were sitting in the chair looks brash and brassy in the cold light of day? Now you see why it's so important. The chair itself should be comfortable, with a footrest, not just for their relaxation but also to keep clients stationary. No hairdresser wants to work on a moving target.

As I walk behind the footman, I find myself wondering whether anyone would be brave enough to get rid of the red and gilt décor everywhere – the corridors are lined with huge gold-framed paintings that continue into the distance like white lines on a motorway. It's hideously charming and exactly what you'd expect. It's also boiling hot. My royal client tells me that this is because the heating goes off in May and goes on in September, regardless of the temperature outside. I presume this happens in all the royal residences, but it appears to be the royal tradition.

We finally arrive at my client's suite of rooms, where I am announced by the butler and escorted through to the sitting room to wait. We start to unpack the bag, and I survey the power points in case I'm working in here today instead of the bedroom.

She casually plonks herself down on the sofa, hair wrapped in a towel. Mercifully, her make-up is done so there's no damage-limitation exercise to be conducted post-blow-dry. After a brief consultation and a quick look at her outfit, I set to work speedily, conscious of her appointment schedule. Getting someone's hair right is about communicating and it is crucial to have a clear idea of their aspirations. Giving someone a hairstyle that reflects her total look is about assessing her clothes and lifestyle as much as her hair and face shape. It's about making women believe that having beautiful hair will make them feel beautiful inside, too. And a royal client is no different from any other. Providing your stylist has a certain level of competence, I believe there's no such thing as a technically bad haircut, just a bad consultation. The difference with a top salon stylist is not just their cutting ability, but their wealth of knowledge at interpreting what their client wants and their vast experience in consultation skills. Ask the right questions and you can unlock the beautiful hair that's possible for every woman.

I like to think that the key to my success has been my ability to understand the complexities of women. Take a recent restaurant opening my PR dragged me along too – I am required to attend a certain number of these events in order to have a presence in the media. One of the most gorgeous socialites in Britain was there and I accompanied her after giving her a new look for the evening. Photographs of this woman do not do her justice, she is truly, strikingly beautiful, yet the following morning she called my mobile, asking me Snow-White-wicked-stepmother-style, who the most beautiful woman was.

> Gentlemen prefer blondes.... but gentlemen marry brunettes.
> Anita Loos (1925)

'Hi, Shaun, did you see the pictures in the *Mail* today?'

'Yes, somebody told me to have a look. It was a great evening–'

'Yeah, sure . . .

And my hair looked amazing. Thanks, darling. Yasmin is so stunning, such great bone structure . . .' Then, voice trailing, 'Do you think I looked beautiful?'

'The most beautiful. What did you think of the food?'

'Great. Great . . . Yasmin looked fab in that dress. She's just so skinny. Is she skinnier than me?'

'No. You're different shapes, you're more curvy and voluptuous – you looked sensational, especially your hair.'

'Voluptuous? You mean she is skinnier than me?'

I reassured her that she was the most beautiful in the land, but it saddened me how little self-confidence she had. Here I am selling a (hair) dream to ordinary, everyday women by doing women like her, but she doesn't possess half as much confidence as the work-a-day woman who tries to emulate her. One of life's delicious ironies, I suppose.

I wonder if my royal client has any of those nagging insecurities. It's too early to tell – I haven't been doing her long enough. I've changed her look a little, softening it, and she's had some grudging praise from the press, much to my relief, and hers, no doubt.

My assistant passes me my trusty tools, anticipating my every move without error.

It takes a long time to train up an apprentice, to get their mind in tune with yours and for them to anticipate your every whim. It's not just technical, it's emotional. I prefer to have a girl, and it helps if she's good-looking. It's not a pre-requisite, you understand, but it's all part of getting the image right. My current one is good, and I have no doubt she'll make it. She's already experienced things most hairdressers can only dream about, just as I did with my mentor, and its invaluable experiences like these that will help her become a much-better-than-average hairdresser. Coping with pressure, working in difficult conditions on shoots and home visits – in-salon is always the preferred option, just in case your session bag is missing an essential item – learning how to make hair look fluid and lustrous when it's been weather- and hat-proofed to within an inch of its life. But most of all, listening to me, just as I did with my mentor, and learning how to talk to people like this. People who, with my social upbringing, I shouldn't feel comfortable with. But I do, because I've learned how to. What to say; when to chat and when to shut the fuck up. A million text books could never teach you that skill; it's something you can only learn on the salon floor, by taking it all in like a sponge.

I can't ever remember wanting to be a hairdresser that badly. I didn't play with hair much as a child, fiddling around with friends or family or playing salons. I didn't even eat, sleep and breathe it during my training, like some of my contemporaries did, and still do. My mother was a hairdresser and she had her own salon before I was born, so no doubt hairdressing crept into my veins in the womb and buried itself there, waiting for me to discover it when I got older.

At school, I knew I couldn't go to sixth-form college as my parents were having financial difficulties and school fees were an expense they could do without. Not that I would have been A-Level material anyway – apart from Art, I wasn't really interested in academia. Being mildly dyslexic didn't help much, but I only ever felt happy when dealing with the creative and artistic side of the school curriculum. Circumstances sort of paved my destiny; it was time to leave school and what else could I do? College wasn't an option, I needed to earn my own money as things were very tight at home. I have, I think, an aesthetic eye, so it seemed natural to combine my soaring teenage testosterone levels with my desire for fun and adventure and make the move to London to become a hairdresser. It seemed to tick all the boxes: fun undoubtedly, I'd heard my mother tell me all her funny stories; meet women? (Of course, and with a little charm I could get laid, too). Creative? Artistic? (Yes, if I went for a top salon, as

220,000 staff are employed in the hair and beauty industry in the UK, 150,000 of whom are hairdressers.

my mother insisted, I could really learn from the masters, as she wished she had done).

It was hard for me to start as a hairdresser. I felt like I was breaking new territory by believing it to be more worthy than my school masters did. It just wasn't rated in those days and was barely classified as a career. It was a dead-end job for people considered too thick to do anything else. Yet look where it is today, and that's what I am most proud of. It's a respectable industry. It isn't poofy, or a gay domain, it's credible, hip and happening. Teenagers don't mock it any more, they think it's cool, even if their parents and schools have a different opinion. And I, in my minuscule way, have helped change that perception. Me and hundreds of other hairdressers like me.

Not every school leaver is going to be good at doing a manual job. Hairdressing is never going to attract the Einsteins of this world, and the chances of a hairdresser winning the Nobel Prize are slim, but let's not knock it any more. And it isn't just full of rent-a-chair self-employed stylists as it was when I was training, or mobile, freelance hairdressers, there is a wealth of

Q: What happens when a blonde develop Alzheimer's?
A: Her IQ goes up.

spin-off, credible careers to be had in the industry now, and lots of women are involved in the trade. It's a credible, viable, believable career to have in an industry whose profile is growing rapidly.

There was another reason for my career choice, though – namely, making money.

Having seen my parent's finances fall to pieces as they were approaching retirement, I vowed that would never happen to me. I still have an overwhelming dread of not being financially secure and stable. I live in abject and unfounded terror of losing my home, my business and all the things I've worked so hard to accomplish in order for that empty, insecure feeling to be banished to the back of my mind.

I do love hair, and feel I have found my true vocation – if a little by accident – but I love the women it's attached to more, and being a hairdresser seemed like a pretty fool-proof way to meet women. And believe me when I say I have met every kind of woman.

* * * *

Salons are very high-tech these days. We can text clients when they are due for an appointment, send them automatic birthday cards, build up a database of their colouring history, what services they spend their money on, how frequently they come and what shampoo they bought at their last visit. We can call them to ask why they've stopped coming and we can remind them that they need their legs waxed. There are machines that can speed up colour development, cutting the waiting time by half, machines to tear the thousands of meshes of foil a busy salon will get through that can be altered to fit each colourist's personal specification and even salt-blasting peel machines in the beauty rooms to rejuvenate skin and get rid of cellulite, but when it comes to the work itself, it's as traditional as ever.

Some of my schoolmates sneered and mocked me, calling me 'gay boy' when they discovered my chosen career path. I'm not, by the way, although there's no doubt that to be a good hairdresser you have to be in touch with your feminine side. Now those same friends marvel at my working day when we meet for a pint after work. I like to remind them how they took the piss out of my first £25 per week wage, when they all started on more than double that. Now, when I talk about my day styling and crimping some of the sexiest, most lusted-after women on the planet, their jaws drop in envy, much to my immense satisfaction.

Once I made the mistake of telling a particular renegade school buddy about an up-coming photographic assignment. Having been hounded relentlessly by his increasingly desperate attempts to meet the model I'd be styling, I kindly arranged for him to assist me on the shoot where his dream girl was being paid more than we both earn in a year to model the latest designer get-up. Of course, he was as much use as an ashtray on a motorbike, and she was intrigued and confused by my new apprentice's gobsmacked expression. Protocol dictates that you have to be cool (even when you feel hot) when models strip naked during outfit changes. I have learned to look the other way. My friend, however, did not. By the end of the day, the poor, bemused creature could only state how bloody disappointed he was to have taken a whole day off to look at a pair of gnat bites. 'I shan't be wanking over those any more, mate,' he reassured me. Back to quantity surveying, then, and fantasising about the MD's secretary two desks down.

I am proud of how far I have scaled the hairdressing heights. I have taken the gift of an above-average hairdressing ability (I'm not vain enough to consider myself a hairdressing icon, unlike some of my contemporaries) and worked my wily charm to nurture and grow it into the brand I am today. I refer to myself as a brand because, in this celebrity-obsessed consumer age, that was what I was told I needed to do by some very clever executives and influential magazine editors in order to truly make it. By definition, making it means:

Having your own salon – *check*

Having retail products bearing your name – *working on it*

Having a TV profile – *check*

Having an enviable client list – *check*

The ultimate goal is to build up that little list of magic ingredients and hope the big boys buy you out – selling your soul, not just your name. Yet even being able to tick all those boxes, here I am having an inexplicable attack of the don't-believe-the-hype jitters at a royal residence of all places.

* * * *

I blow-dry my regal client's hair section by section as we make polite small-talk. My assistant passes me various brushes and spritzes product onto the roots while I switch between cool and hot shots on my hairdryer in order to hold her style. Most hairdressers, even the male ones who don't possess the multi-tasking gene, have a unique ability to listen, chat, concentrate and think about something else while appearing completely engrossed in the conversation they are having with their client. It's a miraculous skill and deserves a David Attenborough documentary. I finish and show her the back.

Thank God she likes it. I am given the Royal nod of approval, relieved, as it is such an important occasion and the media will be out in force, and convinced it will stay put without resembling the normal royal-helmet look beloved by generations before her, I am satisfied that I have done my best. She leaves us to get ready for her official engagement. Her secretary will call mine to arrange her next booking, she informs me as she hurries out. The invoice will be sent discreetly to the lady-in-waiting for payment, as usual.

The average price of a service in these salons has increased by 90 per cent over the last 10 years (from £10 to £22).

The Firm could never be seen to be accepting favours, so everything is above board, even though I'd happily do her for free. The value of a royal seal of approval should not be underestimated. I like her more than I expected to – she's kind and sweet and tries to be informal, even if she is a tad reserved. This is, undoubtedly, born of necessity. The Firm has had their fingers burned too many times by trusting people outside their circle.

I have a sneaky look around her suite of rooms while my junior packs up the session bag. There are family photographs of familiar faces dotted around the drawing room, just like you would see in every home up and down the country. I find myself warming towards them: perhaps they are just like the rest of us, after all. I study the hotchpotch of mementoes and memorabilia from their well-documented travels, but these are their personal keepsakes and look very different from the version the public see. Careful not to be caught snooping, I get back to packing up my tools.

Once we're finished, we are ushered out by the butler, through the maze of corridors, and hail a cab outside.

I am papped as I get into the cab. This has started to happen a lot recently, the paparazzi sneaking a quick photo, as well as people asking for autographs, much to the howling amusement of my wife and family, let alone my old school mates who I meet up with at my local once a week. Paps hang

HAIR FACTS

When women are pregnant, the oestrogen levels in the blood increase dramatically, making the growing phase last longer, with fewer hairs entering the final, dying phase. Newer hairs continue to make their appearance and over the nine months of pregnancy hair gets thicker and thicker. This is when women are likely to report that their hair is thick and lustrous (this is where the term 'blooming' comes from). When their hormones return to normal, hair growth goes back to normal, so due to the resting stage, these hairs fall out two to three months later, reducing the hair's density back to its original thickness. For some women, hair may continue to fall out in this way for up to a year; however, this is rare. Breastfeeding can also alter the timing of the hair loss by delaying its onset.

around the salon like a pack of wolves, especially if they've had wind from secret sources that somebody special is being done inside. This can be very tricky. It's well-documented that many celebs lament their lack of privacy, only to be distraught should the press show lack of interest, their sometimes size-able egos getting the better of them. Most paparazzi run their schedules through private 'moles' and it took me a while to figure out who ours was. Of course, my celebrity clientele would be mortified if it was a salon insider, and my credibil-ity would be forever shot to pieces. They have to be able to trust and confide in their hairdresser, and any hairdresser who has the slightest understanding of women would know there are only certain times when it's acceptable to be photo-graphed, and coming into the salon in a grotty old tracksuit and trainers with no make-up isn't going to be one of them, especially for women whose image and appearance is their meal ticket. A papping session is fine if instigated by them – real pap pictures are often blurred, not like we see in the celeb mags, most of which have been carefully instigated by a PR whose client needs a little gentle exposure.

I decided that such was the seriousness of the matter, I had to give my entire staff a severe warning about the dangers of tipping off the press while conducting an investigation into who our indiscreet Judas was. My undercover detective work paid off. My salon manager put two and two together and got five. We were talking one day about the small, weasly-looking guy who sells the *Big Issue* beside the salon's local coffee shop. The manager told me how he would chat to him on his fag breaks, and how he would always ask who was in that day. Days later, we saw him taking a backhander from the local papparazzo and bingo!

'Should I have a go at him?' he asked.

'No way, we got two mentions in *Heat* last week. It's great publicity, and as long as it isn't one of us, my conscience is clear,' I told him, ashamed at my lack of morals, yet remorseless that I put my business first. Every journalist starts a conversation by asking, 'Who do you do?' and I know which side my bread is buttered. The press love it if you're doing 'the right people', and it doesn't do your profile any harm with the other hairdressing Holy Grail, Daytime and Breakfast TV. The producers of career-boosting makeover slots love to know who you've snipped.

At industry events, I have even noticed how I am sometimes followed around by what my wife calls 'the groupies'. These are the (very often pissed) hairdressers whose love of the Malibu and Pineapple affords them the confidence to re-invent themselves as the God of all hairdressers, the Papal equivalent of the cutting industry – The Mullered Critic. It's hard to swallow.

'I didn't like what you did to that girl off *Love Island*'s hair – it was shit,' they slur. 'Your latest photos were too avant-garde,' shouts another. I flash an uneasy smile and tell them how interesting I find their opinions, desperately looking to be rescued, while posing for yet another photograph that is destined to grace the wall of some hair salon staff room somewhere, only to have an arrow with the word 'Wanker!' drawn on by some smart-arse and pointed directly to my unknowing mug.

* * * *

*H*airdressing events are always piss-ups of the most unbelievable magnitude. Considering how a good percentage of the crème de la crème are ex-rehab, this is somewhat ironic. Most hairdressers know how to have a bloody good time, hence their regular attendance at AA and CA and their propensity to spend most of the evening making questionably frequent visits to the toilet. That, together with their contrived yet factual reputation for being largely a gay profession, leads to the phrase 'Charlie and the Chocolate Factory' to surmise their notorious nocturnal activity. Some of our breed even find it impossible to get through the normal working day without a little sustenance in the form of some nose candy. One hairdresser in particular, so the bitchy rumour goes, had his new salon designed specifically so his cutting station was positioned right next to the loo. And you thought they were thin because they don't have time for lunch.

The taxi arrives at the salon. My first job, after unloading our kit and caboodle, is to get my ass behind the desk and check to see who's made it in on time and who's pulled a sickie. By now, it's nearly 9 a.m. and there are already four clients waiting on the sofa. My receptionist is playing back the answer-phone and listening out for cancellations and the dreaded familiar tones of the staff, voices thick with BAFTA award-winning imitations of 'flu, bemoaning stomach cramps or a bout of that old chestnut, 'the dodgy curry'. If one of my seniors is off sick, the whole salon will be thrown into disarray. Their clients will have to be fitted into every-one else's columns and consequently we'll all be running late. Worse, if they are suffering from the aftermath of the weekend, they'll probably take two consecutive days off, even if on the second they're fit enough to work, just to make it look more credible – that makes it even more bloody frustrating.

Sickies are usually pulled on a Saturday or a Tuesday, as most hairdressers have Mondays off – many salons are still closed on a Monday – so it gives them a long weekend. It's even worse if there's a bank holiday, as those who normally have another day off in the week will throw caution to the wind and

> A man being asked what made him bald said, 'My hair.'
> Anon

sneak a day off either side to make it an extra long break. On a regular week, some party like mad on a Sunday night, especially the queens as Sunday night is busy on the gay club scene, and haven't fully recovered by Tuesday. The ironic thing is that most hairdressers don't realise that salon owners have worked all this out for themselves, and have a healthy scepticism of even the most ingenious excuse, especially if it falls near their day off.

Luckily my team slowly trickle in, some looking fresh-faced and some looking decidedly hung- over. I go and check the stereo for some inoffensive ambient music – mellow and relaxing to start the day. Music is one of my pet hates – if left to my staff I'd either get camp disco, rap or hip-hop. I frequently tell them the music is for the salon clients to listen to, not them. Most of our clients are between twenty- five and forty-five, some are career women, some housewives, some ladies who lunch and there are quite a few men, too. Mainly husbands of the ladies, although we do get a sprinkling of pop stars, actors and Premier Division footballers. And what they want is background Muzak to relax to, nothing too 'in your face'.

The juniors are busy getting their jobs done – there are gowns to launder, mirrors to polish, towels to fold, toilets to fill with anti-theft loo rolls (some of our aristocratic clients can be a tad light-fingered in the salon sundry department), basins to clean, roller trolleys to tidy, backwashes to stock with enough shampoo and conditioner to last the day. The stylists are supposed to clean out their own brushes, but very rarely do. That lowly task is left to the juniors. It's a rite of passage – they've served their time doing the shitty jobs, now it's somebody else's turn.

My receptionist puts a call through. It's my PR Meredith, asking me if I've seen today's *Daily Mail*. I send a junior down to the paper shop to grab a copy, while listening to her screeching delight as she tells me all about their article, the 'Top 10 Worst Hair Disasters', which mentions a few of my rivals and worse, some of their salons. Thankfully, we are spared the humiliation of making the list and I fleetingly delight in the mercy that has been shown my name, then feel guilty as I realise how easily it could have been me. Who is the journalist? Do I know her? My PR makes it her business to find out. We should get her in for a freebie – she sounds dangerous. You know the old saying, keep your friends close and your enemies closer.

Another call comes through, it's my Smashy- and Nicey-style great mate and bitterest rival, Lucas. We like/hate/love each other and tend to stick together at industry dos when we both realise that in comparison to some of the other arseholes in the business, we find each other tolerable.

He, unfortunately, has made Miss Bitchy's list and is mortified.

'She came in for a freebie last week and didn't tip anybody, the tight cow! She had £300's worth of highlights, facial, massage, manicure and pedicure and she then has the nerve to write that,' he moans. He's right, what a Megabitch. Some hard-nosed journalists don't have an inkling that one catty piece can destroy somebody's business and livelihood for ever. I suppose that's the risk we take in playing the PR game, it's always liable to work against you as well as for you. It's debatable as to whether Oscar Wilde was right about there being no such thing as bad publicity, I decide, listening to my mate slagging off his journalistic traitor.

It could have been me. I got off lightly, I decide. I am tempted to casually drop into the conversation that I cannot chat as I'm off to the *Morning Britain!* studios to do the much coveted makeover slot, but decide it would be pushing my luck to tempt bad Karma and kick a man when he's down.

Perhaps it's going to be a good day after all.

Six steps to beautiful hair — how to wash your hair properly

How often should you wash your hair? As often as it needs it, but remember, it's the styling afterwards with electrical equipment that is damaging, so bear this in mind if you decide to wash daily.

1. Prepare the hair

Brush the hair well using a gentle, real bristle brush like a Mason Pearson. Brushing out any tangles before you start will make shampooing it easier and ensure hair stays tangle free.

2. Wet the hair thoroughly

Thoroughly dampen all the hair. The water temperature should be just above lukewarm, so as not to stimulate the sebaceous glands.

3. Cleanse 1

Work one 50p-sized amount of good-quality shampoo through your hands and distribute evenly around the head. Emulsify — run a spritz of warm water over the head quickly to help shampoo work through the hair. Massage with Effleurage (smooth, circular) movements, with both hands working in tandem, and using the flat, spongy pads of your fingers, not the tips. Work around hairline, above ears and round to nape, then work from nape up to crown, from crown to fringe and repeat. Keep raking the hair through with your fingers so as not to tangle it. Rinse well.

4. Cleanse 2
Repeat above.

5. Condition
Smooth conditioner through mid-lengths and ends, working up towards roots if required (only on coloured or damaged hair). Do not put it on the roots (first few inches) and do not rub it in, smooth it down the hair shaft to flatten the cuticle (which makes hair shine). Work through/massage for one minute, in order for it to work. Do not comb through as it puts too much stress on weak, wet hair, but rake through and smooth with your fingers.

6. Rinse
Rinse for two minutes. Time yourself. All traces of product residue should be removed. Now you can comb through with a wide-toothed comb, working in steps up your hair, from the ends towards the roots — never the other way around, which makes the tangles worse. Towel dry well before styling.

Chapter 2

9.30 a.m. —
Morning Britain!
Studio, live makeover

I barely have time to unpack and repack my session bag before rushing off to the *Morning Britain!* studio for the sought-after live makeover slot. I was pushing it to try and cram two important sessions one after the other in my diary, but I could ill afford to turn either down.

One of my rivals is the resident hairdresser on the show, but fortunately for me he can't always make it, so whenever he's rumoured to be out of the country, there's a flurry of hairdresser's PRs calling up the production assistant offering the services of the rest of us, and the TV Hair Wars begin.

It may seem like there's a multitude of TV makeover shows requiring the skills of a celebrity hairdresser, but believe me they are few and far between. If you do manage to get a regular slot on another show, the chances are you'll blow your chance of a shot on prestigious breakfast/daytime shows – why would they want to use a hairdresser who has a profile on a rival show or channel? Every programme will want you to work exclusively for them, so allegiances need to be carefully planned. Do you sign up to a lesser channel or go on a satellite programme if there are no other offers on the table, and risk losing out on the few-and-far-between chances to do terrestrial morning slots? Most of us take what we can get, and once the resident slots are filled, there isn't much left over, which leaves a good percentage of us scratching around in the dirt, picking over the bones. Competition is fierce

47 per cent of clients have their hair coloured in a salon, but industry sources say that 72 per cent of the UK's female population colour their hair.

and if a new show is rumoured to be in production, the producers can normally have their pick of the bunch.

Luckily, mine seemed to be the most persistent PR to bombard the studio, so I am given the slot today. I know all eyes will be on me, not just the PRs of my rivals, and the rivals themselves who had no doubt tried to get in on the action by networking with any contacts they knew directly, but the producer and the production team, too.

I make a point of getting on well with the junior production assistants; they will be the producers of tomorrow, so it's foolish not to get them on side. They say everything in life is not about what you know, but who you know, and it certainly works like that in TV. Get pally with one of the production team: you never know what show they may be given five years down the line – they might even end up Daytime Controller of an entire station. And you knew them when they were sharing a packet of digestives with you while you were being barked at by a producer ten years earlier. That mindset has certainly paid off for me – most of my TV appearances have come through clients who are presenters or from people I worked with years ago.

I've never really understood why controllers seem so hell-bent on sticking to a supposedly winning formula. Somebody does a programme that is new and different, and because it works, every man and his dog jump on the bandwagon until the public become so sick and tired of it that they vote with their feet, or rather their remote

> I'm not bald –
> I'm just taller
> than my hair.
> Clive Anderson

controls. As much as I'm tired of reality TV, with its car-boot programmes, garden makeovers and property shows, the public's fascination with making people collapse into an uncontrollable heap when confronted with how terrible they look seems as vivid as ever. Thank God, because that's when I become one of the fairy godmothers that make Cinderella go to the ball. I weave my hair magic and somebody sheds tears of delight that she will no longer have a sour-puss of a face that turns milk into yogurt just by looking at it. Or at least that's what the director would like. The reality can be a little different.

I call my elderly parents from the cab and try to get them to switch on. I know how proud of me they are, and they'll boast about it to all the other residents in the sheltered accommodation flats where they live. I try desperately hard not to lose my temper as I repeat the channel and time to them for the third time. My assistant is sniggering cheekily, and I can't help but start, too. For a moment it takes my mind off the task ahead and calms my customary pre-TV jitters.

Today, as I walk onto the familiar set and am greeted by the show's two very nice presenters, it strikes me how nervous I still am. As much as I jump at the opportunity to seize the moment, I always have a terrible fear of the live slots. Once, I dried up on camera. TV folklore says it happens to everyone at least once, and it did to me. When asked what technique I was using for the cut I was in the middle of, my brain just shut down. No words would come out of my mouth, which felt like a sheet of builder's sandpaper. Luckily, I was rescued by the anchorman, who realised what was happening and I will always thank him from the bottom of my heart for saving my fledgling TV career. Thankfully, production teams don't tend to stay long on any one show, so after a short while my faux-pas was forgotten, even if my confidence on any one show was severely dented. The terror of this happening again never leaves me, although I am now far more experienced, and I am sure that I could cover my tracks if the stuff of my nightmares became a reality. Live TV is like doing a bungee jump – you wonder why you are putting yourself through the fear yet you know you'll feel amazing once you've done it.

The presenters must sense my nerves and dash over to say a cheery hello and put me at my ease. Kindnesses like these go a long way when you're feeling slightly sick and in need of a friendly face. I look at the tired old set and am reminded again of how tiny and scruffy it looks in real life. On telly it seems so much grander and more impressive, yet in reality the sofa is stained and cramped, the table scratched and there are mountains of wires and cables tucked under the rugs. The guests are being plastered in thick orange-coloured foundation to avoid them looking like Morticia Addams on camera. There are certain TV rules to abide by: never wear black or white (too draining), don't wear patterns (too busy) and never go without make-up. The camera puts on at least 20lb, so presenters always look trimmer in real life. As the arty hairdresser, I am allowed to go on without a suit, but they don't really like jeans, so the twenty pairs of trendy, Italian designer ones hanging in my wardrobe are normally out of the quest-ion. Because I've come straight from the royal residence – a fact I mention cas-ually – I'm allowed to get away with it. No doubt some eager researcher is going to drop that into the script and hope I won't get a bollocking from my regal client for not being discreet. Head spinning, I head off to the make-up rooms to get myself done and to look for my client.

I have been emailed a picture of today's makeover recipient and a little background detail on her, but as usual it's a blurred, drunken holiday snap of some woman with scraped-back hair that really doesn't tell me much about its length, texture or condition, or give me much idea of what to bring with me. Thank God for the

Tardis session bag. Most TV researchers don't consider it necessary to ask for a picture of the candidate's crowning glory in all its majesty, although they would if they were the one doing the cutting. I suppose I should be grateful for technology – before the days of email I wouldn't even have *got* a picture. I nervously glance around the studio, hoping to recognise her. I have some idea what I might do to her hair, but until I see and feel it, my plans will be guesswork.

I am taken through the myriad rooms in the TV centre by a young jobbing researcher wearing an earpiece and clutching a clipboard, which occasionally interrupts her and requires her to track down guests who have wandered away from the Green Room. She is chattering away about the show content and filling me in on the running schedule as we make our way to the makeover studio.

The frequency of visits to salons has dropped by 25 per cent over the last 10 years to an average of 8.8 times per year for women and 6.6 times per year for men.

Today's theme is women recovering from post-natal depression who have been nominated to get a new look by their presumably much-relieved husbands. I am dreading what might be in store – the raging hormones of pregnancy and childbirth, let alone any medication they may be on, does strange things to hair, so this could be asking for trouble.

As we arrive at the make-up room, my heart sinks as I catch sight of a small, ferrety looking woman who is anxiously poring over a copy of *100 Hairstyles* magazine. Her hair is every hairdresser's nightmare. It is so unbearably fine and greasy, not only the details of her skull but the contours of her brain are visible through it. It isn't hair, it's fucking down, I decide, my heart sinking to my boots. I have more hair on my arms than she has on her entire head. She's wearing it tied up at the side in some sort of ribbon. What the fuck am I going to do with her? She looks like a Yorkshire terrier. She looks up at me and smiles hopefully. I manage a weary smile.

'You're Shaun Lockes. I'm so thrilled to meet you. We're so excited about the makeover. Did they pass on the photo?'

'Yes,' I falter, 'Sorry, did you say we?'

'Yes, my daughter Sharon. She's in the loo. She's been through such a lot. She's really looking forward to having a new look.'

I'm beginning to think I am the luckiest man in the world when Sharon finally appears, vaguely recognisable from the very outdated picture I've been staring at for the last week.

Please God, let me have somebody easy! I mentally register my cosmic order and think about some of the women whose lives I've helped to change with Luciano, the camp Italian producer of a very popular, big-budget series on satellite. I am his new golden boy, and am currently filming a series of hair makeovers for him, although I'm careful not to let the team at *Morning Britain!* know that.

Appearing on this type of show is mentally exhausting, but also amazingly rewarding. In fact, in a way, they're becoming a bit of a passion of mine; especially when a truly appreciative recipient is genuinely thrilled with their new look, restoring my faith in the general public and the rest of humanity. Some even turn into very good and loyal clients – a double whammy in the success stakes. The results really can be life altering, which gives me great satisfaction and is a pleasure to see.

The trouble only comes when these women have unrealistic expectations about their haircut. Some women attach so much importance to their life-changing new look that they expect to lose a dress size, change their personality, become four inches taller, get a better sex life and radically reinvent themselves in the space of a single one-hour haircut. And the more I appear on the TV makeover shows, the more they seem to be booking me at the salon. It's draining to even attempt to achieve a 100 per cent satisfaction record with them. It's only hair, after all. I may be able to make them feel better about themselves, but I can't go to the gym for them or re-boot their love lives. How can I ever live up to what they expect of me?

What I mustn't do today is get demotivated and assume I'll get another Pauline.

Pauline was the supposedly grateful recipient of a makeover in *New Look – New Life*, and was a bloody nightmare. She may have looked Doris Day candy in her heartfelt 'before' slot, but she epitomised the worst aspects of these makeover candidates, with her expectations far exceeding reality. She thought that the makeover team were her passport to a new life that would instantly change everything without any effort on her part. She also had an opinion about everything, which she was chomping at the bit to share, and thought it was her job to bring me down a peg or two instead of letting *me* help *her*, by coming out with such withering crap as, 'I bet nobody tells you what they think of you like I do,' and, 'You think you're so hotshot, well, I'm telling you . . . you're not doing that to *my* hair.'

Some of these makeover-show women share one thing in common: part of the reason they are desperate for a new look is that they won't listen to any half-decent hairdresser trying to give them a new look. Pauline didn't 'do' short, nor medium, shoulder-length or long, come to think of it. She didn't want to be a blonde, brunette or redhead. She wanted to be

HAIR FACTS

Temporary hair loss can be caused by stress, shock, medication, hormonal changes and diet. Eating nutritious blood-producing foods like seeds, nuts, berries and dark fruit and vegetables like spinach, curly kale and avocado can help. Essential vitamins are zinc, Omega 3, 6 and 9, and vitamins D and C.

'an individual' and kept telling anyone who'd listen, particularly the crew, that Luciano, the presenter and I – and even the cameraman – were all 'oppressing her true personality'. If I was a psychoanalyst, I would bet that Pauline, who has probably never been given any attention by anyone in her whole life, was simply relishing all the focus being on her for a change. Luciano had already told me that some of these women drag out the filming for as long as possible, desperate not to return to their more ordinary lives. Pauline was rather daunted by my 'posh' upmarket salon and so behaved with deliberate obstinacy, concealing her overwhelming desire to let me make her look dramatically better than she did before. Worse, she was prone to visit with her three chavvy daughters and their butch, bulldog other halves, in order to feel comfortable. I can tell you, they may have put her at ease, but they had the opposite effect on me as they peered over my shoulder and wondering what Mum – tattooed on one of their arms – was going to look like when the 'new her' was unveiled.

Q: What's the difference between a dumb blonde and a supermarket trolley?
A: A supermarket trolley has a mind of its own.

Luciano told me firmly that he had reminded her, rather less gently than at first, that she had agreed to be on a makeover show and that involves letting people make her over. After all, he had over 45,000 applicants for the fifteen spaces he had for this series, and they're all having well over £70,000 of free work done. It's amazing how quickly even the most desperate common or garden housewife can act the diva once the cameras start rolling. It's us poor sods – the dentists (why are everybody's teeth so terrible?), the plastic surgeons, the life-coaches, and me, the hairdresser – who are giving up our time and expertise for free in return for a little publicity.

I knew Pauline was going to be trouble when she started emailing me photos of her cat, the contents of her wardrobe and her newly decorated living room. This was all so I could get a greater understanding of Pauline the inner woman before deciding on what style to give her.

'Where on earth did your researcher find her? Broadmoor? I need to be able to do something radical!' I told him, pre-empting the disaster that was going to become my day.

'Sorry, Shaun, I talk with 'er again – she need the one 'fing we not geev her, a, how-you-say, personality transplant,' he shrieked camply.

I was rather inclined to agree with him, envisaging one of my upset colourists storming off in a frustrated huff. 'I'm not going to be able to please that one – I'm warning you,' I told him.

The buzz a TV crew creates in the salon is great for business. The regular clients love a bit of filming going on – they seem to find it completely fascinating and are very impressed to be at such a happening salon, even if, for me, it can be akin to torture. Because, after all that hassle, there follows, of course, the *pièce de résistance*: the dreaded 'reveal' – the bit where I have my fingers (and everything else) crossed that I get a happy punter who thinks there hair is a work of genius. This hold-your-breath reaction will inevitably follow me around like an unwelcome smell until it fades from people's memories – thankfully rapidly in this disposable age.

But at least when a show is being recorded you have a little more time should you need it. On live TV, forget it. Time is the enemy. The live terrestrial shows run notoriously short of time, as producers have a weird mindset that they'd better have too much material to fill the programme than not enough, cramming in loads of 'items' and 'stories' they can then cut short, or worse, miss out altogether if they run out of time. Ever noticed how the frantic presenters end up shouting their 'closing goodbyes' and 'what's on tomorrows' over the rolling credits, practically breaking records for speaking quickly? And the live makeover slots are always the first to end up on the proverbial cutting-room floor.

As not enough time is ever allowed for these segments, or the length of the show isn't conducive to performing a life-changing stratospheric makeover, the before and after slots are sometimes carefully contrived. If we're lucky, we hairdressers get to take a good few snips and get cracking on the haircut before the punter is introduced at the start of the programme, leaving a nice long bit of hair around the front and sides, shown from a carefully chosen camera angle, designed to ensure it looks like we've yet to attack their hair. This is not because we can't do a haircut in the required time frame, but more that we have to allow for the make-up artist to do her thing. Then there's the fashion stylist to consider; they need to get the punter not only dressed, but baubled, bangled and beaded, too. The conscientious hairdresser also has to bear in mind that they will be dragged, screaming and kicking, back onto set at least five minutes before they are due to go live with the reveal, cutting their precious styling time even short-er. However, to be challenged with totally transforming some-body's look in such a short space of time is one of the aspects of my work that I relish and enjoy the most. It's a different technique than the one I use in the salon; I've acquired a knack of cutting some serious corners without compromising my artistic credibility. Now that's a challenge I feel I have con-quered and am proud of.

Sometimes, they cross over live to the make-over studio, where we have to look like we're relaxingly snipping away and doing our thing, all getting along famously. Then, at the end of the programme, when they've inevitably run out of time, it's time for the 'after' slot. This normally involves a frantic battle of wills to get some TV airtime between the makeover team, which is sometimes less like a team you'd imagine. The word 'team' implies some consideration for one another's feelings, whereas the jostling for attention that goes on can be more like a scene from *Braveheart*. If the make-up artist and fashion stylist run over and hog the airwaves with a detailed explanation of the colour palette they've chosen or a full-on description of the victim's genetic accoutrements, the snipper can be left with the scraps, and ends up talking over the voiceover for the next programme, with the carefully planned explanation of his cutting prowess lost between the presenters' voice-over link to the next item or the next set of adverts. All that stress, hard work and early start and I some-times hardly get a chance to sell myself to the viewing public, which is the whole point of the exercise.

You may wonder why any of us bother with TV at all, but the fact is it's the most powerful medium, by far, so the incen-tive is that the exposure you'll receive compensates not only for my loss of earnings – we don't always get paid for these appearances – but also the disappointment at my manners and politeness, which renders me unable to interrupt my chatter-ing colleagues to take over the treasured airwaves.

Normally, the shoot for record-ed series is done on a quiet day, or even when we're closed on a Sunday, as the noise of the hair dryers isn't conducive to the sound quality required by the boom man,

The average British woman spends nearly £37,000 on her hair during her lifetime.

which means bang goes my day off. On the rare occasions when we film in the salon on a working day, my entire column may need to be cancelled, usually at alarmingly short notice because the researchers are so manic they have no idea who is doing what to whom more than twenty four hours in advance, and are desperate to fit in with the plastic surgery, or wait for the poor victim to come round from recovery, which may not have gone as well as planned. Ditto for the columns of the technicians and other salon staff who are needed to colour hair, add extensions, wax legs, apply self-tan and full make-up and paint nails. The film crews don't seem to think it's important to turn up on time either. So while I may have cancelled my bookings for the allocated time slot and moved mountains to ensure my team are on hand at the agreed time, the crew may have a different agenda. The producer may over-run at the clothes shop filming Miss Makeover squeezing into some jeans for the first time in years, muffin-top hanging over proudly and resulting in a bout of tears – all TV heaven to catch on camera – so sod the hairdresser.

Tomato ketchup
Brilliant for removing the green tinge bleached hair gets when damaged by chlorinated water.

Not satisfied with me having to cancel my bread-and-butter business, leading to a double-stress week as I frantically try and find some non-existent gaps in my column to appease my regulars, the poor paying clients visiting on the day in question are politely told to shh while the new look is painstakingly explained: 'I decided to go for copper highlights to bring out Pauline's eyes' and 'I've razored the fringe to soften and define the hairline, etc.' to the presenter.

So, dear old Pauline could quite easily end up costing me several sleepless nights and still not give me the vital piece to camera required – the point of the whole bloody exercise – the crucial and all important 'I love it!'

If she does, the phones will ring off the hook the next day and I'll be fully booked with what we lovingly refer to as 'The Pilgrimage'. These are the viewers who are looking for a touch of transformation and will travel from all over the UK to find it. Ditto for the lifestyle gurus, the dentists, the plastic surgeons, etc. One appearance on a show like this can fully book their diary for a whole year and give them a credibility their competitors can merely aspire to. That's why we all do it, and that's what I have to frequently remind myself of, even though some of the recipients lead me to seriously question what the production team must have said in their ads, and where they place them (*Psychotic Weekly?*), to attract these people in the first place.

'The Pilgrimage' want it all – for as lovely and sometimes reverential as they are, they bring their pictures, they want a forty-minute consultation before you start and a radical, life-changing transformation. They want to leave the salon a new person. I don't blame them, as that is what they're buying into by watching these programmes, but I'm getting to the stage where doing four a day is too much, and maybe one a day is ample, however much I appreciate them, and however vital they are to the business. A lady I did the other day came all the way from Swindon with her mother. The pair of them hung on my every word. I swear that had I farted they would still be sitting there, gazing at me intently and even applauding. I jokingly told her I would need at least half an hour with a psychiatrist before tackling her image change.

Another one brought me in a photo of her dream hairstyle, which must have been taken from a porn mag. 'Which hair are we talking about here?' I couldn't resist asking. 'Muff or head?' Some people never cease to amaze you. There is indeed nowt so queer as folk.

I am what my mates jokingly refer to as a Z-list celebrity, and I tend to get quite a few of these Pauline-style dressing-downs from people, much to my astonishment. I am, I like to think, an all-round nice guy. I don't believe I am in any way special, just hopefully talented with the scissors and a good boss who's established a sound business and lived a few dreams for a couple of years. So I found it quite shocking when recently, at a friend's fancy dress party, a very bad Audrey Hepburn, more than a little worse for wear on the Cava, came over and pulled me off my chair in order to join in the 'Locomotion'. Much to my annoyance, as I was fending off a brewing row with my wife at the time, I staggered back to my seat and told her I would pass. Later on, she accosted me by the buffet table and told me she had followed my career and had always thought I was a nice bloke, until now. Now, she admonished me, I was 'up myself'. Who did I think I was, treating her like that? She'd had enough, she told me. She wasn't bloody Cruella de Ville and if one more person said she was, she'd swing for them; she was meant to be Audrey Hepburn from sodding *Breakfast at Tiffany's*. Was everybody blind? Bloody fancy dress, she mumbled, stumbling off towards the dance floor. Bloody arsehole celebrity hairdressers.

What did I do? I wondered, sneaking a Marlboro Light on the Portaloo steps, before she came zigzagging unsteadily back to me, holding on to her wonky tiara.

'And another thing, I watched you on that *Get a New Look* the other day. What did you do to that poor woman's hair? You ruined it. She was so *misunderstood*,' she shouted, before collapsing drunkenly into a heap of black velvet.

I pray that Sharon isn't going to give me any such trouble today.

'Hi, Shaun,' she greets me shyly after I introduce myself.

I start my consultation with the immortal words, 'Tell me about your hair.' I have learned over the years to ensure I ask open questions so my client cannot answer yes or no. It's especially good for the introverts or those who are a little backward in coming forward, which Sharon seems to be. Mum inevitably takes over: 'Well, Shorn, we've cut out some pictures from the magazines and we think Sharon should go for a . . . I can't believe we're meeting you . . . I've told all the girls at the factory . . . Here, Sharon, take a picture on the mobile . . . where's that magazine cutting gone?' she says, rummaging in her handbag.

Please don't say Meg Ryan, I think they always say bloody Meg Ryan . .

'. . . Meg Ryan! Won't it look fantastic?' says Mum, who's

fussing around like a Norland Nanny on speed.

'Sharon,' I gently question, 'is this what you want? Are you sure? How often do you wash it? How do you style it? Are you sure you want something so different?' I venture, looking at her shoulder-length, mousey-brown hair, which looks as care-worn and deflated as she does. With a mother like that, it's hardly surprising.

The rest of the team come in. One, Camp Frankie, is an old friend who I met on another makeover show. I'm pleased to see him as we spark off each other well on screen, so it's great that he's got the styling slot today.

'Didn't I see your ugly mug in *Hello!* magazine at that society wedding? Didn't they have Elton John there, playing the piano? Tell all,' he shrieks excitedly.

I've been to a few celebrity parties in my time, but nothing like that. It was off-the-planet. An A-list client had invited us to the wedding of their son at their country estate. Mrs Lockes was frantic about what to wear, and we were both a little nervous about mingling with such élite guests. I mean, this was one of the parties of the year, and from experience, any celebs we knew would be far too grand to mingle with the likes of us and would want to distance themselves from mere mortals at least ten rungs down the stardom ladder, even if they were all over me when they came into the salon.

The average woman spends £25 per month on shampoos and hair care products, and in excess of £300 a year on haircuts and colouring.

We drove through an enormous set of white gates, complete with security guards, flashing our invite nervously as if we weren't entitled to be there. We drove down a long gravel drive, winding though perfectly manicured lawns, for what seemed like an eternity, finally arriving at a beautiful mini White House, set in the breathtaking Buckinghamshire countryside. We stopped and were about to get out to allow the liveried security men to park up for us, thinking we were doing really well in knowing the form, when we were told, 'Please head on up to the main house, Sir, Ma'am'. Main house? Oh my God, we realised, this is just the gate house.

Embarrassed at our faux pas, we got back in and drove for another three minutes along the winding, torch-lit gravel drive. Then we saw it, a mansion of such magnitude it was surely the same size as one of the Queen's residences. We parked and joined the guests, who were all walking through a lilac, smoke-filled tunnel. When we arrived inside, we stopped dead in our tracks. There, in front of our eyes was a cross between Neverland and Willy Wonka's Chocolate factory. It was awesome. The theme of the party was Fairyland, and there were waterfalls, a lake, trees and a forest. The waiting staff were professional ballet dancers dressed in lilac tutus, pirouetting as they served us. The food was presented on lily pads – delicious little canapés of miniature-sized cod in batter and tartare sauce in baby ice-cream cones – the drinks were served from buttercup-shaped glasses. It was amazing. I'm a crap star-spotter, whereas Mrs Lockes never misses a celeb, so the whole evening was spent with her discreetly whispering into my ear, '*Look, Mick Jagger,*' and '*Bloody hell, it's Ivana Trump*' or, '*Behind you, check out the ice-cube-sized diamond in the black satin dress*'.

None of it could be caught on camera, because at events like these cameras are a no-no. Either because it's private and it's considered too crass and cheap to try and get pictures of famous people, or it's being covered by some celeb magazine as an exclusive and they are paying a fortune for it. That didn't stop Mrs Locks, who, spotting the lead singer of her favourite eighties band, bravely went up to him and asked if I could take a picture on her mobile. He was so out of his head he barely seemed to notice. Afterwards, she seemed very quiet. Eventually she told me that while she was posing with him, his notoriously lechy hand had made its way up her evening dress with a smarmy, 'Come on, don't tell me you didn't used to fantasize about me when you were a teenager.' To which she replied, 'Don't flatter yourself. It was the drummer I fancied. In fact, my mum said you had a face like a King Edward potato.'

'Talk about shattering your illusions,' she said afterwards.

The entertainment involved a series of acts so famous that Harvey Goldsmith would have killed for them all to be playing on the same bill. A ballet, a famous orchestra, a world-renowned opera singer, a household-name TV presenter to compère, and a Top-of-the-Bill pop star as a finale. And here they all were, exclusively serenading an audience of 350 carefully chosen guests. I have never seen so much wealth in one place at one time, and my watch fetish was on high alert as I scanned the room looking at a combined collection worth millions. The fact that I'd made it onto the guest list in my own right seemed quite something. 'It must have cost them well over a million,' you could hear some of the less-well-mannered guests gossiping (me included).

Frankie is enthralled and can't wait to be characteristically indiscreet and tell everybody, until we are interrupted by the arrival of the fearful Lydia, the make-up artist. She can be ruthless where air time is concerned, and if I'm not careful she'll overwhelm even Frankie's and my extrovert personalities. It won't be long before her trademark put-downs and stinging asides are getting to both of us.

Having sized up the competition, my attentions turn to Sharon, who still hasn't said a word and is looking increasingly white and pasty. Shit, I hope she doesn't faint. The studio lights are so blindingly bright and churn out a furnace of heat, so it's a distinct possibility.

'10 minutes to go, guys!' The researcher with the earpiece is back and it's time to get Sharon's hair prepped. I need to pre-wash it and rough dry it so she can go on air for the 'before' slot, then dampen it back down to cut it for the 'during' segment, and get ready to finish it for the 'reveal'. I set my assistant to work, slightly perturbed by Sharon's seeming detachment. Lydia and Frankie are busy showing Mum what make-up and outfits they have in mind. Shame she may not be able to keep any of it. Unbeknown to the viewers at home, sometimes there's no such thing as a free lunch unless the retailers are willing to 'gift it', or the clothes are bought by the station, so the beautiful outfits could be winging their way back across London by the time the credits roll, and Cinders might turn back into a pumpkin at midnight. At least my haircut will be a permanent reminder of her day at the studio, even if she may never be able to get it looking quite as good as it will today. I'm always conscious of giving the punter a haircut that will not only improve their look, but which they'll be able to cope with at home – for me that's the key to a great makeover.

Frankie gives me some Rescue Remedy as the countdown begins. I look up at the monitor from the makeover room, which is about 10 foot by 8 foot and boiling hot. I glance over at Sharon, who has just come up after being bent over the basin for her shampoo – more like a dunking as the basin is the size of a loaf of bread and is designed for hands only – and she seems to have some colour back in her cheeks. I have ten minutes, which would be wisely spent making some headway into the cut before I do it for real, so I leave the top long and start on the underneath, making sure the length hangs over my handiwork so it can't be spotted.

Through the monitor I can hear the opening music and then the presenter doing her intro. I can also hear the producer through my earpiece:

'Right guys, five, four, three, over to Shaun first, tell us about that gorgeous hair . . . two, one.'

'So, Shaun, what are you going to do with Sharon's hair?' I'm asked.

I waffle on about her face shape, hair texture and my planned cut, conscious that Lydia is breathing down my neck, ready to interrupt me should I pause, to tell the viewers about her make-up colours – which she does, for at least forty-five seconds. That's half poor Frankie's time gone. He shoots her a glare as the red light comes off the camera and our off-air position is confirmed by the next item on the monitor, showing some juicing-machine price comparisons.

'She's done it again,' whispers Frankie as he waltzes past me, bum clenched in fury, his now white knuckles scrunching a pale ivory chiffon blouse and two Mouret-style dresses into a ball of pent-up anger. But I have no time to listen; I desperately need to crack on if I'm ever going to get Sharon finished. I snip away as if my life depended on it, half listening to the incessant instructions being fielded through my ear-piece to the presenters by the producer.

'Sorry, Shaun, honey, but I'm simply going to have to insist that I start work on my canvas now,' Lydia drawls as she smiles through gritted teeth. I know it's impossible for her to apply her make-up when I'm working, so I beg another five minutes to get the outline done. I can work on the layers while Lydia does her bit, so I compromise.

The cut is taking shape and I breathe a temporary sigh of relief, at least until the researcher pops back and informs us

> A celebrity is any well-known TV or movie star who looks like he spends more than two hours working on his hair.
> Steve Martin

that we've got two minutes until the midway slot. I often get asked if I can do a truly good haircut in twenty minutes and I would have to say that I can, but to get it to the perfection we demand in the salon, a little more time is needed. I always invite the makeover subjects I do to stay back at the end of the show so I can go back over the cut afterwards, as I know it will be scrutinised once she heads back to her local salon. The perfectionist in me can never let a client leave without it being absolutely technically perfect and twenty minutes just isn't enough time.

'Five, four, three, two, Shaun, it's you first again . . . one.'

I explain the importance of texturising and layering and get a little technical before the presenter jollies me along by telling me how good she's looking already. Then it's Frankie who is busy extolling the virtues of this seasons' sling-backs, and I catch Lydia scowling as the producer tells us there's no time for her as the phone-in is about to start. Frankie smiles sweetly and it's not lost on Lydia. Nobody has had time to ask Sharon how she is, and I now have only ten minutes to finish her hair and style it, so her feelings are furthest from my mind.

The researcher has managed to escort Mum to the Green Room for a cup of tea and to get her out of the way while the filming is going on, much to our relief.

The time vanishes, and before I can reach for my wax to tease it into shape and polish her tousled new look, the researcher is back and it's time to leave the relative safe haven of the makeover room and head back to the studio to join the presenters. We gather at the side of the catwalk and prepare to sell ourselves and our abilities, not only to the watching viewers, but to the production team too.

Sharon steps out from behind the

curtain for the 'reveal' and, as is customary, the husband is brought on to give her a bouquet of flowers and tell her how amazing she looks. The crew all clap and cheer as the new Sharon is unveiled, and the presenter asks us to talk through what we've done. Luckily, I'm first again and flash a dazzling smile, working my charm and saying what a pleasure it's been to make Sharon over. Then Frankie tells the nation where they can purchase a new wardrobe just like Sharon's and finally Lydia bullshits on about how fabulous her colouring is and how the shape of her eyes have been accentuated.

Sharon is deathly quiet. Oh my God. What the fuck is she going to do? I find myself smiling demonically, hoping and praying that even if she faints, dries up or suddenly becomes uncharacteristically loquacious, she will, at least, love her hair.

'Sharon, what do you think of your new look? Your husband Dave says you look gorgeous, do you feel fantastic?' asks the presenter, clearly eeking it out due to the lack of response and desperate to hear those magic words.

Sharon starts to weep. Oh my God! We all freeze. Fuck Frankie, I think. It doesn't bloody matter if she doesn't like what you've done, you didn't design the bloody clobber, you only chose it. And sod you, Lydia, if she hates your make-up she can wash it off. But me? My fucking haircut? She can't stick her hair back on, can she?

My heart is pounding so violently, I'm convinced every viewer must surely be able to see it. Please, I beg, teeth flashing a fixed, tense, fake smile. Please . . . say something.

'It's my hair . . .' says Sharon, voice muffled with tears.

The pause is palpable, the silence deafening. My pulse is thundering into near-cardiac arrest.

'I never thought I would ever have hair this beautiful . . .' Sharon sobs onto the presenter's shoulder and my beaming relief is broadcast to a nation of old-age pensioners, women doing their ironing, students meant to be revising and grown men having a sickie.

'Well, I think that's one of the nicest makeovers we've ever done,' states the presenter. 'Well done, Shaun!'

I want to kiss Sharon right here and now.

Back in the Green Room, I re-check the cut and sign an autograph for Mum. I'm sure that the stress has lost me two stones in anxiety, but it's been worth it. My dad has even called my mobile to comment and the producer has mentioned that there may be some more slots coming up in the next few months, if I'm interested. Interested? I'd kill for them.

Heading back to the salon, the high of live TV begins to wear off. It's quite a come-down leaving the starriness of the TV studio and rejoining the real world. It doesn't feel half so good to be back in the cold light of day as I wait to restart my normal working routine.

Heading back to reality, I start to gear up for the day at the salon when I realise I don't even know what I've got scheduled. Frankie catches me up just as we're about to pull away and leans through the cab window.

'Shaun,' he pants. 'Forgot to tell you the gossip . . .' he catches his breath.

'Austin & Harte have split, and it's war. They're taking each other to the fucking cleaners. They've just opened that new salon, too, all one million quid of it. Apparently it's so acrimonious they're even fighting over the trading name. And they've just launched their products. The whole lot's gone tits up – the lawyers have been called in and it's already getting nasty.'

He pats his chest in an attempt to get his breath back and continues, 'Well, the whole of their staff are looking to move – I mean it, Shaun. Nobody can bear it there any more. They're all fully booked and their clients don't care which salon they move to, they've all said they'll follow. I've got the number of one of the senior colourists here, why don't you get in touch? I told him I'd be seeing you today and he's waiting for your call. Here.' He passed me a scrap of paper.

'Don't feel bad about calling him, Shaun, they've had it coming. You should hear some of the stories they've been telling. All he wants is for you to offer him the same deal as he has now. He's not trouble, I can tell you. He's been with them for years, never moved about, but he's had enough. He says it's like Omaha Beach over there. And wherever he goes, the rest are sure to follow. If he doesn't come to you, someone else will grab him, so jump in quick, he's just about to walk out, and he's got all his client's numbers . . .'

My mind's working overtime. Oh My God! £10k of regular, weekly turnover could be just about to walk out of their salon and into mine. And if I'm clever I could build on all that business – discount on the first visit for beauty therapy, half price on their first manicure. My eyes become two pound signs and I nearly forget to thank Frankie as the cab pulls away. I'll 'bunch' him tomorrow (send him his favourite flowers), I think, as I fold the number carefully and smile as I put it safely in my jeans' pocket.

10 things the hair ads don't tell you

1. Hair is technically dying from the moment it comes out of the follicle at the scalp. Therefore, ads promising vitality (meaning life) are scientifically ridiculous.

2. There is no cure for split ends. The only solution is to cut them off before they travel any further up the hair shaft and do more damage.

3. If your hair has been subjected to chemical or technical damage, there is no way you can 'repair' or cure it as the processes take place deep inside the cortex, and is irreparable. Even the most scientific of products can only mask the damage. Conditioners and even intense repair masques will only last until they are shampooed out, but they will make hair feel silkier.

4. Damage to hair by overuse of heat-styling equipment is the most prevalent, and straightening irons are the worst offenders. Using them daily can be lethal to your hair's condition. Also, your hairdryer should be held at least five inches away from your head — hold it directly on to your hand to see how hot it is if held too close and remember that your hair doesn't have any nerve endings like your flesh!

5. Cutting your hair regularly (every six

weeks) will not make it grow faster. It will, however, reduce the likelihood of split ends so your hair will look and feel healthier.

6. Shampoo your hair as often as you wish — some people need to wash their hair every day and others as little as twice per week. Take the time to cleanse and rinse hair properly and you will notice the difference.

7. Most shampoos are made of detergent, even the expensive ones, with fragrances and conditioning chemicals added. But good, gentle products will have reduced levels and make your hair feel much better. They will also be more concentrated so you will use less and they will last longer.

8. If you must colour your own hair, which I would never advise, then be sure that your application is on the root/re-growth area only, and be as accurate as possible. Overlapping of colour will result in colour 'banding' and you may end up looking like a stripy tiger, and damaging your hair to boot.

9. Serums and other 'glossing' products are actually made of silicone, which if it builds up on the hair can leave a nasty residue, so use sparingly.

10. Environmental damage from heating and air-conditioning can make hair look dull and lacklustre. Hair will always grow faster and be more lustrous in summer/sunshine months, but be careful to avoid sun, salt and chlorinated water damage.

Chapter 3

11.30 a.m.
client —
Mrs Affair

Once back at the salon, my early morning fades into oblivion as I realise that all the people here have been carrying on life as normal, totally unaware of my glorious makeover. For the second and last time that day, I unpack my session bag and start to contemplate my column – there's no time before one of the receptionists buzzes me to let me know 'my lady's in'.

This somewhat bizarre terminology is a hangover from the sixties, when hairdressers were called things like Mr Roger and Mr Gervaise when they were really christened rather less glamorous, showbizzy names. There was a silly and unfathomable habit of turning Christian names into surnames, so the women would be called Miss Pamela. Calling female clients *ladies* has become the hairdressing norm. You can always tell a new assistant when they come out with a normal phrase like, 'Your client has arrived for her appointment,' and get looked at like they've moved to Hairdressing La-La Land from Planet Normal and have yet to become fluent in the lingo. They are always called ladies and gents, instead of women and men. And, they are never 'here' but 'in'. It's written in the hairdressing Ten Commandments.

One of the miraculous things about hairdressers is their ability to remember crucial details about their clients by giving them labels. Hence my next client is Mrs Affair. Hanging a label on people is the easiest way of remembering something personal about them. Seeing as the average stylist will deal with over forty clients a week, and with over half only visiting every six weeks for technical work or cutting, the average salon has a huge database. That's one hell of a lot of people to remember, and names aren't always the easiest thing to recall.

In my current stable of clients I have:

Mr Closet Gayboy – a city banker who has a penchant for a bit of the other with the odd rent boy.

Mrs Boob Job – who has been sharing with me (metaphorically) the delights of her new silicone breasts following a very successful, confidence-boosting tummy tuck.

Ms Prozac – a newly divorced Mother, low on self-esteem as her husband ran off with the nanny, who enjoys confiding in me her new-found happiness since the discovery of legal prescription drugs.

Mrs Born Again – an Alpha Course Devotee who enjoys trying to convince me to believe in God and embrace my spiritual side during the course of her six-weekly haircuts.

Miss Uptight – an It-girl on the social scene who is more high maintenance than a set of mink bed linen.

Mrs Moneybags – a done-well-for-herself ex-PA from the Highlands, married to, and petrified of, a rich Russian who is so controlling she's unable to visit her local Starbucks without his permission.

Mr Turn-You-Gay – a very camp music-industry guy who fervently believes every heterosexual man is a closet gay and assumes that if he works hard enough on me he just might convert me to a same-sex relationship.

This might leave you wondering, and worrying, about how discreet your own hairdresser is. I can assure you they probably aren't – it's not normally in a hairdresser's genetic make-up to be devout and loyal to the secrets that make up your own personal emotional shrine. Every funny tale, every amusing ditty, every uncovered indiscretion, every deep-rooted insecurity you've confided is probably recounted to their colleagues in the staff room while their chair is still warm from your visit.

The confidentiality clause comes in because nobody will ever know it's really you, thus guaranteeing your anonymity. You will just be labelled, perhaps a little unflatteringly, maybe even mockingly, but always very wittily. It's a very detailed science, the labelling process, like an advanced form of people watching. And you will never, ever know what they've called you unless you get a look at the salon database, where there's sometimes a discreet coding to let the salon know your degree of difficulty, the state of your hair and possibly even your tipping prowess. There the very extreme few may be referred to as a:

NM – nightmare; a difficult client who everybody dreads doing.
PIA – pain in the arse.
TGA – tight as a gnat's chuff (a bad tipper).
FP – frizzy pubes hair that will leave you exhausted after wrestling through a blow-dry to tame it into shape.
Hammer Horror – A client with tremendously difficult hair.
A or M – Arthur or Martha; doesn't know if he/she is a dyke/gay.
LFHOF – late for her own funeral; somebody who is always late and manages to get away without paying the cancellation fee by coming up with some seriously dreadful excuses.
PSY – stands for Psycho; somebody who keeps changing their mind about what they want.
NUT NUT – worse than a PSY; this is somebody who is seriously in need of some help. Bound to be a serial nightmare and mentally unstable with it.
MSE – stands for Moose; a no-hoper in the looks department, who probably has terrible hair too.

If you are worried that you may fall into any of these categories, sneak a look at your colouring notes the next time you visit your salon and you may catch a discreet initial in the corner. If there isn't one, you'll be one of the nice ones, who are thankfully still in the vast majority. Even if you did fall into the very small minority that warrants this type of coding, any good salon would still be very grateful of your custom and welcome you with open arms.

Mrs Affair is ready and shampooed, sitting at my section.

Mrs Affair's not the one who has been indulging in some extra-marital activity; it's her husband who's the culprit. This long-running saga began when she sat sobbing in my chair, revealing that she had her suspicions, and we left it that she was going to hire a private detective to get some evidence. These wealthy women can't leave things to chance; they need to get their facts straight if a £6 million white stucco property in Knightsbridge, a picture-perfect ski lodge in Courcheval and a hillside summer holiday hideaway in St Tropez are at stake. Most of them haven't worked for years and are terrified at being left in a financial mess when they may have £30k of school fees to pay each year.

I'm grateful to see Mrs Affair in my section; the last thing I need after a stressful morning is one of our Nightmare PIA clients. The worst one is Mrs X. One of the most grating things about this woman is that she is always early for her 9 a.m. appointment. There's nothing more draining than a client arriving early for a booking, especially first thing. It leaves you no time to mentally set yourself up for the demands of the day. She marches in, seconds after the security alarm has stopped bleeping, demanding a café latte – 'Skinny with an extra shot and not too hot!' – before the poor barista has even wiped the sleep-dust from his weary eyes. There simply isn't time to ease gently and languidly into the day when she is chomping at the bit to get shampooed.

The average woman will spend nearly two full years of her life washing, styling, cutting and colouring her hair either at a salon or at home, taking an average of 41 minutes a day just to style it.

Nobody, including me, has the nerve to tell her to go away until opening time, so the stress levels start to rise before the day has even begun. Her stylist hasn't even arrived before she is pacing up and down the backwashes checking her Cartier watch every two seconds and screaming to get started. Juniors hide in the laundry room so they don't have to shampoo her and argue over whose turn it is. Then, when some poor bugger gets pushed out by the others to take their turn and see to her, everything is wrong – the water too hot or too cold, the massage technique too firm or too soft, the chair too uncomfortable. It's no better for the stylist – the rollers are too small or too large, the comb is pulling her hair, the magazines are too gossipy ('Why don't you have magazines for us intellectuals, like the *National Geographic*?' she barks. 'Why, are you in it as some endangered species?' I'm tempted to retort, which, of course, I don't.) The water is Highland Spring, not Evian, as listed in your menu, she informs me. Her croissant is too crumbly, her gown too static, the lighting above her mirror is 'Making me look dreadful' she states – I bite my lip as I hear this one. Her colour is too red/brown/gold – this varies depending on her mood – the toilet handwash is too drying – 'Please get Molton Brown next time' – the mirror in the toilet is too high, the flowers are making her sneeze. All this, and with the millions she clearly has in the bank, she doesn't tip. I'm not talking about tipping me – I consider myself very lucky to receive the odd tip – but my staff rely on their gratuities. And she doesn't tip any of them. Not even a quid to the junior. And she has a face like Rose West chewing an acid tab. And on her way out, after physically pushing other paying clients out of the way to grab her very expensive fur from the cloakroom, she proceeds to waste forty minutes with one of my poor receptionists, who will patiently book a complicated string of appointments dovetailing waxing, manicures, highlights, blow-dries and cuts, from now until Christmas, which she will, without fail, automatically cancel and remake once she gets home and checks her diary.

'That woman,' says whichever receptionist has been lumbered with her, 'is utterly draining,' as she slumps onto her computer, exhausted, deflated and customer-serviced out.

* * * *

I am very happy that I don't have to cope with Mrs X today, and am much more interested in my poor old Mrs Affair.

'Well, what news?' I ask, as I start snipping her overgrown locks back into their carefully designed shape, one eye discreetly on the clock, as always, so I don't run late all day.

'I've got him!' she shrieks excitedly.

She proceeds to tell me that not only is he having an affair with his secretary, but that she has video proof that her lawyer seems to think is pretty water-tight in securing the palatial family home in SW3.

I listen to the oldest cliché in the book being trotted out, one that I've heard a hundred times before: husband runs off with blonde bimbo just as let-herself-go-a-bit wife recovers from exhausting decade that is child-raising hell and was preparing to regain her libido, figure and dispense with her fatigue with much gusto.

'What are you going to do now?' I ask.

'What do you think I should do?' she asks wearily, sniffing through the tears.

'Why don't you give him a dose of his own medicine? You're looking good, you're an attractive woman, why not go for it? It could do wonders for your confidence,' I encourage.

She tells me she just might, with a sly smile.

I finish blow-drying her hair and send her out with not only a fabulous cut but a new lease of life.

* * * *

*A*fter a quick caffeine re-fuel, by way of a double-shot cappuccino, I return to my section and spot an envelope marked 'Shaun' tucked discreetly into my brush bag. It is hand-written and marked personal (I always dread those). It must be from Mrs Affair – she must have written it in the loo and nipped back to my chair while I was downstairs sorting out her bill.

I open it and read, *'Thanks for a fantastic haircut, I feel like a new woman.'*

Great, I think, satisfied that I've sprinkled a little of my hair magic in her direction, and given her back a little of her lost self-esteem.

I read on, *'I've been thinking about what we talked about and have decided to take you up on your offer – I'm ready if you are. I couldn't think of anyone better to embark on my affair with. Call me. x'*

The colour drains from my face. The feel-good factor subsides into a knotted, sinking cesspit that is now my stomach.

'Are you OK?' my salon manager asks, noticing my deathly pallor and gaping, shocked expression.

Not really, I say, and show him the note. I tell him I feel obliged to call her and gently tell her she's got the wrong end of the stick.

'Shit, now we'll never see her again. I mean, if you don't call her, she won't come back, and if you do, and tell her she's read you wrong, she'll be too embarrassed to come back,' he points out depressingly.

'Shame as she was a great client; she spent a fortune on products, she used the beauty rooms, everything. And she had her colour done once a month.'

'All right, don't rub it in, you bastard,' I shout after him, his shoulders hunching Dastardly and Muttley style while he tries not to let me see him chuckling.

Me and my big mouth.

*   *   *   *

Of course I know the reason why this has happened, and let's face it, before I got married I was shagging half of my clients. It was a great way to meet loads of up-for-it women. What better job for any young, healthy male with a voracious appetite for totty than to get intimate with twelve women a day? It's definitely one of the major advantages of choosing hairdressing as a career. And the reason I was so successful in the pulling department isn't due to my smoulderingly handsome looks – I should be so lucky – it's far simpler: I have learned to understand women. You couldn't fail to, talking to them day in, day out, and I love listening to them. Any man who has mastered the art of listening realises he has cultivated a powerful aphrodisiac. Who did Jen turn to when Brad left her? Her crimper. Kate tries to get Pete Doherty out of her system (ditto Sienna and Jude), and who do they go out and about with? Their hairdressers. We are a whole breed of Elton John's – everybody's favourite agony aunts.

This is, of course, much to my own wife's annoyance, who insists that I am totally incapable of listening to and understanding her in the way I do my clients. Fair cop, I have to agree. Listening to complicated, needy, sometimes neurotic women makes me very impatient when it comes to my own love life. The last thing I want to hear is how my wife feels when I've had a bellyful of empathising all day. Having said that, hairdressing is a great job – being paid to make women feel great about themselves and being revered and praised for my creativity isn't a bad way to earn a living. And even though I'm firmly ensconced in the Mars not Venus camp, most of the conversations I have with my female clients are a revelation in understanding the female psyche – handy information for any red-blooded male.

Women have some pretty fixed ideas about their hairdresser's sexuality. Some women prefer their hairdresser to be gay. If he is, it sort of uncomplicates matters, as there is no sexual *frisson* to spoil the relationship. Gay men seem to have an even better ability to get on women's wavelengths, as most gay hairdressers have a wicked, deliciously bitchy sense of humour which women adore. Many women feel safer with a gay man and enjoy the security of being able to relax with them.

Q: What do you call a blonde between two brunettes?
A: A mental block.

Other women pointedly require a female hairdresser to feel comfortable. Although there isn't, and shouldn't, be any difference between the sexes when it comes to ability, some women really buy into the 'Why would another woman *want* to make me look beautiful?' theory or the 'Only a man can truly know what makes a woman look sexy' school of thought. Others want to fancy their hairdresser and enjoy some sexual chemistry while they sit in the salon. This works both ways, as a lot of my straight male clients like going to my female stylists if they can't get in with me.

The trust element is crucial. Women are putting one of their most prized possessions, their crowning glory, in somebody else's hands. While most women can control the rest of their appearance – their make-up, their wardrobe, their weight – their hair, and how good it looks, is in the hands of another (literally). Ask any women who's had a hair disaster and they will recoil in horror at the thought of repeating such a humiliation, preferring epidural-free childbirth to the curse of a crop they're desperate to grow out or a colour disaster waiting to be corrected.

The other reason why many straight hairdressers meet their girlfriends or partners through 'the salon chair' is that hairdressing has sexual overtones. It's a touchy-feely job.

There is no other profession or service, other than medical ones, where you touch a client as intimately as we do. The head, scalp and neck are all erogenous zones, so touching these 'off-limits' areas can create a sexual *frisson*, which keeps many a handsome stylist fully booked the way cutting technique alone can't. Hair is sensuous, hair is mystical, hair is bloody important to most women, and somebody who can make hair fabulous has to hold a little sexual appeal. The majority of cancer victims who are clients will often tell me that the worst part of their illness and chemotherapy treatment is losing their hair. Hair is a symbol of womanliness and femininity, that's why most men who aren't part of the hairdressing fraternity will never understand how life-altering a good haircut can be. I have clients who say that if times are tough they will economise in every area of their life, except on the price of a good haircut. Of all the makeover shows I've been involved with, the hair normally gets the biggest response – forget the plastic surgery or the new wardrobe – despite the fact that the hair is usually the least expensive element of the transformation.

The average human hair can support nearly four and a half pounds in weight. To put this into perspective, if a human hair was as thick as a nylon rope, you could dangle a railway locomotive from it.

This is partly why I went into hairdressing; as my father pointed out, it's recession-proof. In difficult times, hairdressing rarely suffers as badly as other retail professions. Hair is an amazingly important part of how we feel about ourselves. Recent surveys suggest that long, shiny hair sends out two sexual messages: first, it releases more human pheromones into the air (the sex hormones that attract potential mates) and secondly, it denotes health, good genes and excellent fertility (rather like full lips, breasts and hips). No wonder ancient civilisations thought hair was a fertility symbol for women, while for men it was a sign of strength and virility. Ask most balding men whether they would want to win the lottery or have a full head of real, natural hair and hair will win every time. More women dread getting alopecia than they would a serious illness. Look at Gail Porter – hailed with a bravery award just for coming out about her stress-related hair loss.

Hair is such an integral part of how we look. It is so important that if a woman finds a good hairdresser she will only tell three out of ten of her friends, unwilling to share her 'find' whereas if she has a bad haircut she will tell seven out of ten, so determined will she be to ruin her once-trusted salon's reputation. Women are notoriously secretive about their hairdressers, and this must be due to the fact that they like to feel they own you during the time they're in your chair. They often don't want to contemplate all the other women's hair you do, and if you're clever, you'll make them feel like the only client you're doing all day. You will make them feel that their conversation is witty and sparkling, their company is scintillating and that they are possessed of a unique vitality and charm which you find captivating. This, coupled with the touching and emotional connection can lead to a stylist's column being as oversubscribed as a Robbie Williams concert.

Why else would clients like Mrs Affair confide only in me about her husband? She didn't tell another living soul. She trusts me to be far enough removed from her circle of friends to be discreet, yet to be there to provide an expert shoulder to cry on, some sound advice and to listen to her more intently than anybody else. Do it too well and they might even feel like you want to have an affair with them.

* * * *

I sift through the ten or fifteen messages in my in-tray, which as usual are a mixture of clients calling up to ask me to fit them in, or reps bypassing the security fence that is my team of receptionists and secretary to try and get me to endorse the latest gadget or gizmo set to 'transform the hairdressing world'. The chances are it won't – the only thing that has revolutionised hairdressing in the last decade is straightening irons, and I don't condone over-using them as I see the damage they cause to hair every day. This is why there's a massive increase in hair extensions, which reportedly has led to a worldwide shortage of real hair – people want the long lustrous locks that seem so unattainable with their own spindly ends, but they're probably only in such a state because of all this heat damage they've endured. One of my reception- ists is such a hot-iron junkie that she's locked her ceramic straighteners in the boot of her car in a desperate attempt to stop using them, cold-turkey style – and there are thousands of women like her.

I see a message to call an old mate, Kenny.

I trained with Kenny – he's now working at a salon in Mayfair and we keep in touch. I know if he calls it must be something gossipy, so I dial his number. Sure enough, he con- firms the rumour about the Austin & Harte – the media-dar- ling salon is about to go tits up because the owners are at each other's throats. One is furious about the other's increasing media profile and has thrown a hissy-fit, demanded to be bought out by his more popular partner. Now it seems they are soon to be ex-partners in real life too. This once loved-up gay couple is now so acrimonious that the two guys involved will only speak via their juniors and the staff; their clients, who ultimately pick up on everything, have all drifted away due to the nasty vibe.

In our profession, if you lose your staff, you lose your client- ele, and if you lose your clients you lose your business, hence the variety of strict clauses in hairdressing employment con- tracts across the industry. No salon owner can afford to see half their turnover walk out of the door, and just one busy stylist taking a hike can spark a chain reaction of catastrophic proportions. For instance, a busy colourist has a tantrum, throws the towel in and buggers off. He works closely with a particular stylist, who then decides that if the colourist has gone, some of his clients may follow, so he'd be better off going wherever they've gone. There follows the manicurist, the therapist, the receptionist and the junior. A whole clique of once-solid turnover walks out of the salon, never to be replaced. Those clients start telling their friends, and another new hairdressing empire is born. That only has to happen once or twice to a salon and it can go out of business overnight. It is the biggest dread of any salon owner, and the story behind every salon break-up in hairdressing history. Every hairdressing household name was once working for another salon owner, until they decided to go it alone, taking most of their colleagues with them. And the bigger the names involved, the more nasty the split.

> *Too bad all the people who know how to run the country are busy driving taxi cabs and cutting hair.*
> George Burns

Some journalists have even compiled hairdressing genealogy trees, finding links between all the celeb hairdressers dating back to their training days. Most interesting is to see who fucked who over and who's still not speaking decades later. Please God, I'm never going to be on the receiving end of that – the lawyers are the only ones who ever win.

Once we have covered the gossip in detail, Kenny jokes

about a client we share – she doesn't know that we know she cannot make up her mind between us, but we know she hovers between the two, leaving and then returning every couple of months. We call her Mrs Boomerang. There are lots of Mrs Boomerangs, disloyal women who like to, pardon the pun, chop and change their crimpers. They disappear off for six months then come back, sometimes with a different colour, never mentioning or explaining their absence, but expecting to resume business as usual. Men don't do it as much – we're far less complicated. I have some gents who I've been doing since I first started.

Some of the Mrs Boomerangs I know live in the country and come to London every so often for a top-notch haircut, then go back to their local salons to recover from the expense and have a couple of cuts – 'Follow the line of the cut please, Lorraine' until the shape has morphed into the average-looking cut they so wanted to avoid and they have to return to have their cutting template restored by a top stylist.

Do you get what you pay for? Mostly, yes – splashing out on a couture set of highlights and a fabulous cut is worth every penny. After all, hair is the only accessory you wear 24/7. My Auntie Shirley says, 'You can always tell a top salon by the way they colour,' and she's probably right. It takes years of experience to be able to weave a highlight and place a foil meshe perfectly to the root without getting the colour to 'bleed', let alone perform a colour transformation of say, dark brown to natural-looking blonde. And being able to blow-dry really well is a dying art, too. There is a generation of hairdressers coming up who don't actually know how to create silky, smooth straight hair without rough-drying and reaching for the straighteners, when getting hair sleek with a blow-dry will not only feel one hundred times more lustrous, it will last twice as long, too. Not many salons can do it properly any more. Chignons? Most local salons won't be able to give you the perfect up-do. These techniques are passed down the generations, and unless you are learning from a master, you'll be taught only the basics.

Are the celebrity hairdressers better than anyone at your local salon? On the whole, yes, they probably are, because of who trained them. Not always though. I have always found the expression, 'I'm looking for a really good cut' wholly amusing. Who would be looking for a bad cut? Yet can a punter tell a good haircut from a bad one? Not really, not technically. However, they do know whether they can manage it themselves or not, and a good cut should always be manageable.

One stylist who I apprenticed and who's now huge in Los Angeles did monstrously expensive haircuts, which at best looked like he'd cut them with a knife and fork, suffering from severe cataracts. His work was sniggered at and ridiculed by his salon peers, as clients were sent to pay extortionate bills with one side noticeably shorter than the other, truly believing he was a genius with the scissors. His self-belief and mountainous ego had the A-listers raving about his snipping prowess and over-hyped journalists begging for a session, and even now this PR legend provokes a fanfare whenever he pops back across the pond.

Not only has his conceit and arrogance grown with his bank balance, but his hairdressing skills are now so dire it's a joy to behold. He has actually got worse, at least when he was working in London he was working with some of the best in the business – British hairdressing is the best in the world by a long-shot – and a certain amount of that rubbed off. However, years of the 'American Way', coupled with his nails-down-the-blackboard mid-Atlantic drawl and atrocious cutting technique mean I wouldn't let him cut my nasal hair these days. How does he get away with it? He has a knack for changing people – drastically. Go for a trim and you'll end up with a slightly wonky Erin O'Connor elfin bob. Go for a new look and you could end up even more radically transformed. His self-belief is infectious – he commands attention – and his disciples follow him with a lobotomised, Stepford wife-type devotion.

I have heard him say to desperate women, 'You look bloody *awful* – I can make you look ten years younger instantly. Get her washed and take off her bloody *dreadful* eyeliner while you're at it,' growling at a bewildered junior in his Loyd Grossman meets Jack Nicholson hybrid accent. She returns to the chair to have her self-esteem destroyed further when she's told her colour is crap – 'Far too harsh, if you wanna be blonde you gotta be honey, Honey' – and her glasses are the wrong shape. Then, as he is cutting her hair, he reassures her by telling her how life-changing her new look is going to be as he hacks away with his meat-cleavers. Bingo, one transformed woman – even if her next stylist starts with the telling question, 'Um, who cut your hair last?' while he evens up the geometric bob whose mathematical angles would have Pythagoras reaching for the Valium. Therein lies the key – she never gets to know how unmanageable his cut was because he never cuts it the same twice. Hence, it's only when she goes back to Joe Public Snipper because Mr Superstar is too impossibly busy to fit her in that she realises how much easier, and safer, her revised cut is. She lives with it for another five years then goes back for a little more follicle torture from the hair master because she has read about his unrivalled prowess in a magazine and has forgotten not to believe the hype.

You have to hand it to him, though, his limited technique has had the fashionistas drooling for over a decade. After all, they tell themselves, he's just done so-and-so supermodel, so he must be good. 'Divine – heavenly cuts,' they write in their columns, while those of us in the know scratch our heads, bewildered at the praise. He's a clever, if not very talented, guy, and it's a severe case of the Emperor's New Clothes, if you ask me.

My very first hair disaster was because I was too nervous to do a restyle. Looking back, I was probably incapable, too, such was the hit-and-miss training I received. I suggested timidly that my very first paying, long-haired client go for a trim, only for her to complain to the salon manager afterwards that she'd come all the way from Kent and looked exactly the bloody same as when she came in. It took me a long time to get over this dent in my very fragile confidence, and it taught me a big lesson. Don't ever be afraid to go for it. Make your mark and be memorable. What do women want, especially when they visit you for the first time? Well, the very last thing they want is to look the same as they did at the beginning, particularly clients visiting a top London salon – and with over 10,000 of them to choose from, there's plenty of competition, so if you don't get it right, and be bold, somebody else will.

Q: What's black and blue and brown and laying in a ditch?
A: A brunette who's told too many blonde jokes.

So what of the standards up and down the country? Well, you may find the next Vidal Sassoon snipping away in your local high-street salon, but it would be rare. The most talented will inevitably find their way to the big cities, where no doubt their dream will be to open their own salon. Unfortunately, most hairdressers know as much about finances as Ronnie Kray knew about the Ten Commandments, so it can, and often does, end in disaster.

Kenny and I have managed to cultivate a rare thing in the hairdressing industry – we are friends first and competitors second. But considering his behaviour, I'm amazed that Kenny has made it or has any clients at all.

Kenny is renowned for his very cocky (literally) party trick. The first time I saw him do it I was a shy, awkward, gangly apprentice and my provincial eyes nearly popped out of my head.

He had asked me to shampoo the duchess, a starchy, stout, country squire-type member of the aristocracy who came every Wednesday for a shampoo and set. She was an old-fashioned, Queen Mother type of God-fearing woman, and you had to be mind-ful of your Ps and Qs in front of her – think Lady Bracknell from *The Importance of Being Earnest*. When I first washed her hair, ignorant of upper-class etiquette, I made the mis-take of calling her – 'Milady' like Parker from *Thunderbirds*, before being swiftly informed by Kenny that 'Your Grace' was a more appropriate form of address.

I applied her setting lotion, got the roller trolley ready and waited for Kenny to reappear from the staff room. He insert-ed row after row of perfectly wound rollers from the fringe towards the crown, while I passed him pins, careful to pick up any I dropped. In those days, salons did so many sets, our tight-arsed owners insisted we rummage through the hair clip-pings until we found them all. Kenny was happily working away until he reached the nape area, when he pulled up his stool and settled down to do the back.

While our aristocratic client sat, completely oblivious to what was going on behind her, with her head down, chin on her large mono-bosom and arms folded neatly in her lap, he unzipped his fly and rested his bare cock upon the stool while he carried on putting in her rollers. The slightly deaf duchess couldn't hear the muffled laughter from the rest of the stylists as she chatted on about the end of the season and the grouse up in Scotland. His exposed cock lay limp but magnificent on the stool, as if joining in the conversation, for the duration of her set.

I, on the other hand, was now incapable of passing him

anything and, with tears of laughter streaming down my face, found it impossible to stand still any longer, so decided to take my leave and run to the staff room and collapse, doubled-up, into a heap.

Thereafter, I begged Kenny to do his cock trick whenever the opportunity arose, so impressed was I with his anarchic, anti-establishment, but harmless gesture. His irreverent attitude sums up hairdressers at their best: eccentric, mad and so far off the wall they can cross the boundaries of decency.

When scrunch drying was à la mode, Kenny also had a penchant for tipping the clients head upside down – for volume, you understand – and thrusting them unknowingly towards his ever-ready crotch, as if they were giving him a blow-job. The simulated gasps and orgasmic facial expressions kept the whole salon floor amused, while he rocked the oblivious client's head to and fro towards his ball bag. 'Just giving you some extra joooosssh, darling, OK?' he'd shout, the noise of the dryer drowning out any laughter.

As shocked as I was by Kenny's antics, clients' behaviour can be far more appalling. Take the rock star wife. Her husband is one of the guitarists in a legendary rock band, and she has a penchant for exhibitionism in its worst form.

Every six weeks she sits in front of my full-length mirror wearing a leather miniskirt so short it should be categorised as a belt, exposing her shaven haven, Sharon Stone-style, for all to see. Of course, this is never mentioned, but the direction of my eyes tells her all she needs to know. I've clocked it, and she knows this, as she crosses and uncrosses her long limbs, checking out my gaze to ensure she hasn't lost her touch. As much as I really, really don't want to look at 'it' – only out of embarrassment, you understand – I can't stop my eyes straying, and she knows it. We play this little game every visit, and I'm sure the window cleaner, postman, milkman and delivery guy all get the same treatment. I think she's what you would term an exhibitionist, and I'll bet her husband has no idea how she gets her mid-week kicks.

She is one client I'd never want to do outside the safety net of the salon, but plenty of my staff would, which is every salon owner's nightmare as its a whole bank of undeclared income that they've invariably swiped from you. Every hairdresser, therapist, colourist and nail technician 'does their privates' – a portfolio of private clients – and before I owned a salon, so did I. 'Privates' are the curse of every salon owner, and the downfall of every salon's profit margin. You pay for all the marketing and PR, the brand positioning and the media hype, let alone the stock and utility bills, only to find that the new, hard-earned customers who have chosen to walk though your salon doorway may be poached by your own staff, cutting out the middleman – you. This is partly why there's such pressure on salon owners to provide amazing environments in which men and women can pamper themselves, so the good old-fashioned 'mobiles' can't compete.

Slipping your number to a client is a cardinal sin, and any good boss should whip your arse and chuck you out on your ear for doing it. If a client slips their number to the stylist, it's a much lesser offence, even though it's incredibly bad form – not cricket, as they say – that doesn't comply with salon etiquette and would very likely piss off the salon owner to such an extent he may send you and your custom packing. In this day of computer technology, don't be surprised to get a text from your salon if you stop coming, and be warned, big brother may be watching you. Of course, you may just have stopped coming because the customer service wasn't up to scratch, which it isn't for over 60 per cent of women visiting salons in the UK, who vote with their feet and move on. Why else do they leave? Because they feel they're not being listened to or that the hairdresser never suggests anything new.

But how do you move on? Leaving your hairdresser is like telling your other half they have bad breath: there'll never be a right time. It's a hideous, traumatic thing to go through, as delicate and emotionally complicated as parting from a dear friend or lover.

Statistics say that we change hairdressers on average every

three years. In my experience, the chop-and-change allegiance invariably starts with a sickie. For example, Mrs G has been coming to Stylist A for aeons. Stylist A is off sick, so Mrs G grudgingly moves to Stylist B, grumbling like hell and going mad about the disruption. Stylist B pays her an amazing amount of attention, like Stylist A did in the beginning when she first started going to him, and she feels a million dollars. Stylist B has a totally different take on her hair and she goes home to her friends and family, who all tell her she looks years younger.

The next visit approaches, and what does she do? Will Stylist A get upset when he sees her going to Stylist B? No, we lie, but of course he will – and the gay divas are the worst offenders. They smile sweetly but kick off in the staff room about how loyal she was until Stylist B 'nicked' her, because they will inevitably try not to blame the client, preferring to believe it's down to some cunning scheme concocted by their new enemy, thus sparking a staff-room stand-off between the two. It's like something out of a spaghetti western, and the client remains oblivious. Sometimes the client feels so bad, sensing the betrayal her new allegiance will inevitably cause and knowing how much their ex-stylist will be upset, that she comes to me for advice.

The average woman says 7,000 words per day, the average man 2,000. The average hairdresser must be getting on for 10,000!

'We don't have that sort of salon,' I lie.

'Stylist A won't be upset, I promise. All our clients move around and try different people, I can assure you,' I continue, telling a whopper of such magnitude I'm amazed that my nose doesn't grow like Pinocchio. Of course, she and I really know that what she is doing is comparable to a KGB defection.

'You know,' I suggest weakly, 'Stylist A is always off on a Tuesday, so you could come in then, if it makes *you* feel more comfortable.'

'So he *will* be upset,' she says, catching me out good and proper.

This is partly why I need to spend so much time on the salon floor, to gloss over any salon fall-outs, which can be as deadly as a nuclear winter. Most hairdressers tend to be extrovert, so there are bound to be some monumental personality clashes, or car crashes as I call them. A large salon can employ well over fifty staff, so that's fifty opinionated egos battling for a place in the salon pecking order.

Most salons have a 'feeding list' – an order of who gets given new clients first. This is why it pays dividends to be friendly with the receptionist, to ensure your column is never empty. Everybody naturally loses a small percentage of clients over time, so you need to be drip fed a steady supply of new ones. The top stylists will only work in salons where they can be sure to be given a bolster every now and then, so seeing a salon having a good source of new clients is reassuring. This is why I spend a fortune on PR and brand awareness, to ensure those new clients keep on coming. If someone is sitting on their arse in the staff room, I'm losing money. Not only that, but contrary to what you may think, the most tranquil, stress-free days are the ones when everybody is fully booked and there's no time for sitting in the staff room, bitching and getting demotivated. As we say when we have a solidly booked column, 'Bash 'em in and bosh 'em out.' Bliss.

I have read articles by leading journalists comparing leaving your hairdresser to ending a relationship. Women have written at length about how it feels to make that change. The vulnerability headily mixed with the thrill of something new. It can mark a departure not from just your hair, but from your old-look life to your new one, filled with promise and renewed vigour.

Of all the staff-room wars I have witnessed, the worst ones are because one stylist is envious of the devotion another stylist inspires in their clientele. Take Rene and Rodney, two seniors at the salon where I trained. If one was busy and the other wasn't, they'd fight like cats, screeching obscenities at each other and spouting forth viciously personal insults. I think underneath it all they were actually quite fond of each other, but one just couldn't bear to believe the other was more popular or more in demand.

Everybody has quiet days – it's the law of averages – just like everybody, good or bad, has busy days, but however loved you are, the quiet days will always get to you. What if you've lost your touch? What if nobody ever books you again? I know it's illogical, but I defy any hairdresser to deny it. Rampant, raging insecurity, low self-esteem and irrational doubt of your abilities take over, swamping you like a tidal wave. You must be crap. Nobody will ever recommend you again. The reception must have something against you. Who are they favouring instead? Which receptionist do you need to take out for coffee or butter up?

Hairdressers are unbelievably insecure. We have massive egos that need feeding and however loved we are by our clients, it's never enough. Somebody, you can't help but wonder, must be better and busier than you. I have some devoted clients, it has to be said. Indeed, I have clients who regularly travel to the UK just to see me, nobody else will do. Some I share with other stylists – transatlantic ones, for instance, have me in London and somebody else in the States. Colourists sometimes even pass technical notes between each other to let them know if a formula has changed. Yet I always worry that they prefer what my other half is doing, and no doubt my doppelgänger across the Atlantic thinks exactly the same.

Do we get upset if a client chooses a different hairdresser? Yes, we do. It's mortifying to see somebody who once thought you were the dog's bollocks defecting across the salon to another stylist, who may even be somebody you've trained.

The one saving grace for me is that at least they are still sitting in my salon and not somebody else's. It's when we lose them altogether that it really hurts.

This happened to me recently. A lovely woman, whose hair I'd been doing for over five years, just stopped coming. No card, no call, nothing. We'd been through her traumatic battle with breast cancer, her husband's stroke, her daughter's divorce, her grandson's dramatic birth, everything. She felt like my mother. I have no idea what happened and I'm too embarrassed to call. I don't want to make her feel awkward. I still quietly hope I'll get a Christmas card telling me that she has emigrated to Australia, so I can proudly inform my reception team, who from time to time asked me what happened to her, that it was nothing to do with me not being good enough for her. I've said it – I feel like a Woody Allen movie – there it is, my hang-ups blatantly laid bare for all to see. Leaving your hairdresser is basically telling him he's not good enough any more.

Contrary to this, a friend of mine who lives abroad recently went back to her hairdresser after a twenty-year absence. He was so thrilled to see her he sent her flowers and champagne the next day, even though by then he'd become a real success and owned three or four salons. It was the fact that she had returned to *him* that made him elated. See what I mean? You never get used to losing clients. I have more clients now than I have time for, so ultimately some leave because they're fed up of never being able to book me when they want me, but it still makes me feel low when I fall out of favour with clients who decide to move on. Hairdressers are a very proud bunch and it always hurts to see people go to someone else.

Sometimes, though, the decision is taken out of your hands.

It's every client's nightmare – they call their salon to book an appointment with their regular stylist only to discover they've vanished off the face of the planet. Offered an alternative stylist, the client is met with no explanation of their trusted one's disappearance, and a harsh, stony silence when they gently enquire as to their whereabouts. I'm often asked why this happens by mystified clients, who of course have no idea why disclosing a hairdresser's new salon location is akin to breaking the Official Secrets Act.

The fact is hairdressing is a labour-intensive industry and a salon's turnover is entirely due to the team of staff they have. If a stylist joins you with an existing clientele, it's expected that he'll take them with him when he leaves. However, if the talent is nurtured in-house, do the clients belong to the stylist or the salon owner? It's the ancillary takings a salon owner loses which have the most devastating effect, such as colouring, beauty, etc. which a client has done every time she visits the stylist. As many operators could suffer, you'll find that often all the salon staff remain tightlipped about the stylist's new location. It's treason, business-wise, not to.

The unofficial etiquette is that if the stylist leaves without informing his clients previously, taking their number or giving them his, he is obeying the loyal code of conduct a salon owner expects. Some clients get so frustrated by this malarkey they swear, shout and curse at the receptionists and threaten to create and go nuclear unless told where their stylist has gone. But I can't blame a salon owner for risking losing a client by not passing the information on when I know I wouldn't. If she were to book with another stylist in the salon they'd no doubt let it slip and help their ex-colleague get busy in his new home, unless, that is, they're ruthless enough to lie in order to keep the client for themselves . . .

The relationship we have with our clients is complex, even more than the one they have with their other halves, if some of the things they tell me are anything to go by.

Washing powder

Fantastic for removing artificial colour (if a little damaging to hair!)

* * * *

I often hear mothers in their forties bemoaning their sex lives or their husband's constant demand for one. Take the woman I did yesterday. While looking for some empathy from me, after telling me in no uncertain terms that her libido is virtually non-existent, I couldn't help sympathise with her poor husband. He'd booked a 'leave the kids at home, escape from it all and hopefully have a shag-fest' weekend break at an exclusive country hotel, totally oblivious to her plan of having a little R&R. While she looks forward to a weekend of pampering, in the build-up before she confides that the thought of getting laid is on her mind, but not for the same reasons as her husband. She thinks of avoidance tactics – a carefully cultivated strategy cooked up with her best friend.

'We have decided the best plan of action is to jump him as soon as the porter has dumped the bags,' she told me, 'giving him a good seeing to.'

'Why the rush?' I venture.

'To get it over and done with. I want to be left alone once I've fulfilled my conjugal obligation, free to relax and enjoy the spa facilities for the rest of the weekend without him pestering me for more sex,' she informed me, matter-of-factly.

I retort, 'So is that all he's going to get then, poor bugger? Talk about getting his hopes up.' I felt an overwhelming sense of duty to warn the poor bastard what he had coming. I decided better of it, though, thinking that one shag would be better than nothing.

As shocked as I can some-

* *Proportion of women worldwide with naturally blonde hair: 2 per cent*
* *Proportion of women in the UK with naturally blonde hair: 12 per cent*
* *Proportion of women in the UK with coloured blonde hair: 39 per cent*

times be by some of my clients' trusting revelations, I have learned never to cross that invisible line between a client and their hairdresser. Ultimately, if too much of their visit is spent discussing the complexities of the universe and not enough on their hair, they won't be happy. It's not always the hairdresser's fault, sometimes we get invited to socialise and get involved, and it always ends in tears for both sides. One famous TV icon I do told me from the start: 'Now, Shaun, I don't want to get too personal with you. The reason I'm here is that I allowed myself to get too involved with my last hairdresser and ended up with him moaning about his problems on my private number at all hours. I'd rather not even talk about anything other than my hair, right?'

You're the boss, I told her. And they always are.

The Mrs Affair experience leaves me wondering whether I should tone down the charm a little. Perhaps it was my fault – I must have led her to believe I was interested, mustn't I? – although I could hardly compare with the post-teen, hormonal, dog-on-heat approach I employed at the salon where I trained.

That couldn't be a more diverse environment. The salon was a hot-bed of love action, and the amazing thing was that everybody had keys. All the senior members of staff could work late and help themselves to any stock that took their fancy – great for their private work – and worse, use the salon dryer banks – the sofas where the clients would sit for hours – as a shag pad. I don't think one stylist hadn't christened those poor sofas. It was like a private knocking shop; we were all at it. Instead of asking the birds to come up and look at my etchings, it was far more impressive to say, 'Why don't we pop back and look at my salon?' I must have fulfilled many a secret client/hairdresser fantasy on our infamous casting couch.

Not that working with a load of gay men was the best thing in the world for practising my chat-up lines. There were only a few straight stylists, so when I got the chance to work with them, their pulling patter was a revelation. It was there that I established what was to become my modus operandi for the

next decade. As a junior you had two hopes – Bob Hope and
No Hope – of being attractive to a client, but as a stylist . . .

It would normally involve being an emotional shoulder to
cry on and gaining their trust by empathising with them as
they slagged off the 'boyfriend' – agreeing that it was selfish of
him to want to watch the European Cup when all she needed
was some TLC, a red rose left on her pillow from time to time
and a thoughtful gesture like being bought a little jewellery or
him doing the hoovering now and again. Of course, I knew
what women wanted from their other halves because I heard
it endlessly from my clients, however, I did feel more than a little guilty for ganging up on one of my fellow men, when I
knew deep down that I wasn't all that different. But hey, I was
never one to miss an opportunity.

This would often result in me saying, 'Would you like to
come and talk it through over a drink?' I would then turn on
my most sensitive, caring side, with the inevitable, 'Shorn, you
really *understand* women,' just as I took them in my arms.
Things often went from there, and the all-important couch
would get another pasting. Women found going into the salon
when it was closed irresistible: I suppose it's like shagging your
boss on the office desk.

If I knew a particular client was starting to fancy me, I'd
call mid-cycle between haircuts, on the pretence of asking the
name of a restaurant she may have recommended, or a club,
film, book or hotel we had talked about. The inevitable, 'How
are things with him?' would follow and then the drink invite.
I must admit, in my prime I juggled my 'close' female clients
around though I was always careful never to let them believe
we were in a mutually exclusive relationship.

Once I was totally floored when a client I fancied came in
for a haircut, told me it was over with her boyfriend and then
pretended to totally ignore my invite for a drink to 'talk about
it'. I was mortally embarrassed and my confidence took a real
pounding. It even crossed my mind that I would never again
mix business and pleasure. Had she heard me? Surely she must

have done? I pondered, unsure why she had dismissed my advances. Two days later, she called the salon.

'Hello, Shaun,' she said sheepishly. 'Is your invitation still on? I'd love to take you up on your offer of a drink . . .' My heavily breathed sigh of relief must have been audible; yet I never did get to the bottom of why she'd reacted that way. All I could fathom was that she must have chatted it through with her best friend and been cajoled into calling me. But, faith restored, the chat-up wheels were once again set in motion, and the bedpost notches continued to rack up.

Q: What do you call a brunette in a room full of blondes?
A: Invisible.

Exploring my sexuality in this promiscuous fashion never seemed reckless to me. After all, we're talking tens of clients, not hundreds. My goal of owning my own salon was all-consuming, so a little 'live hard, die young' mentality when it came to my sex life allowed me the sort of carelessness I was never able to enjoy in other parts of my youth. I was so focused and determined to make it that 'making out' seemed a great way to let off steam.

It can't be denied that spending so much time with the opposite sex taught me about the social complexities that become increasingly vital the higher up the social ladder you climb. Some of the wealthy young socialites that come to me, men and women alike, have a very particular code of dating ethics. For instance, one handsome young colt with a title dated another very sweet, and very eligible young heiress for years, only to call time just when everyone expected an engagement. These two lovebirds were gossip-column fodder season after season, with all of top London society waiting for the date to be set. She ticked every one of his social boxes, so I was surprised when he confided that he was reticent about going up the aisle with her.

'I'd never have married her' he told me bluntly, when I was cutting his hair shortly after the break-up, 'One look at her mother and I could see what she's going to end up like. I like 'em skinny, and she'll become far too pear-shaped for me.' So as much as this suave, man-about-town was attracted to her impressive inheritance, she was dumped over her figure – and not of the financial kind. The poor girl ended up in the Priory afterwards, before finally finding happiness with another well-placed Alpha male.

Not that I aspire to emulate the relationships of some of my famous clients. One TV presenter I know, who takes great pleasure in delving into the emotional lives of the people who appear on her show, is notoriously open about her celibate sex life, even though she and her partner are very 'loved up' in all other aspects of their life. They say you never know what goes on behind closed doors, although if anybody is likely to, it's the hairdresser.

As I walk through the salon to the reception to see who I've got next, I can tell from the hushed giggles that there's some juicy gossip about. By now, the salon bongo drums are beating with news of Mrs Affair's little misunderstanding. The sorry tale has spread through the entire staff room and I am being teased remorselessly by the wicked bastards I employ. Poor Mrs Affair, you see, never trust a hairdresser . . .

Salon etiquette

Tipping
If you are happy, you should leave a gratuity of between 10 and 20 per cent of the bill for each of the services you have had, i.e. to your colourist, stylist, therapist or manicurist. You are not expected to tip the salon owner, receptionist or any catering staff. You should always tip the junior if you've had a good shampoo/colour removal at least a couple of pounds. Juniors do not get paid very much and rely heavily on their tips.

Talking through the mirror
There are some clients who, very frustrat-ingly, will keep turning around to talk to you while you are doing their hair instead of talking to you via the mirror. Don't ever be tempted to do this — it will get on your hairdresser's nerves, interrupting their work and make for a less accurate haircut!

Mobile phones
Don't be tempted to natter away on your mobile at the backwash — it is supposed to be a relaxing, indulgent treat and mobiles are not de rigueur.

Give feedback
Most hairdressers get quite frustrated if they don't get positive (or negative) feed-back — let them know what they did right or wrong so they can get a better idea of

what you're looking for next time. Don't say it's fine if it isn't.

Colour formulas

Never ask your ex-salon for your colour formula. They will never (nor should they) give it to you if you decide to switch allegiance, so don't ask them (unless you are moving abroad, in which case it would be acceptable).

Asking for phone numbers

Ditto asking where your favourite stylist has gone or for his phone number. If he didn't tell you he was planning to leave, and give you his new contact details, switch to somebody who will value your custom a little more (unless he/she was booted out, in which case you should ask yourself why).

Keep your head still

Don't move your head around too much — allow the hairdresser to guide you with their hands. Same applies at the backwash. Keep your head still and let the shampooist work around your head — don't keep lifting it up or moving it.

Wear the right clothes

Don't come for an all-over ebony dye job in a pale pink cashmere roll-neck that you stubbornly refuse to remove and then complain that the salon has got tint on it. For colouring, no high neck lines or better still, remove your top altogether and let the salon gown you up properly.

Keep your mouth shut...literally!

Don't chatter away whilst your hairdresser is going over your cut with the scissors after blow-drying it. This crucial part of the 'finish' is when they are likely to razor and chop into it.

Set and agree boundaries

Agree that you will go no shorter than X or no lighter or darker than Y and you'll be halfway to getting your hairdresser to really understand what you want.

Do your gown up!

Not only to prevent your clothes from any technical or chemical damage, but to stop dangerous splinters from your haircut getting anywhere near your skin (sharp hair fragments can cause nasty boils).

Salon etiquette for men only

Be a new man

Don't make cheesy, sexist, old-fashioned innuendos while having a massage — you'll only make your therapist feel intimidated and think you are an old perve. It is perfectly acceptable to enjoy beauty treatments and be heterosexual — chill out. Also, remember your therapist may be alone with you in a dimly lit room, so don't make her feel uncomfortable by making any sexy grunting noises as you enjoy her massage.

At the backwash

Ditto here — as pleasurable as it is having your hair washed, and for most men it is one of the sole reasons they want to go to a good salon and not a barbers — no orgasmic noises or groans. Just keep quiet and let your poor embarrassed shampooist get on with their job.

On the pull

If you really fancy the junior/manicurist/ therapist, speak to the receptionist or salon manager first to see whether it would be worth calling them to ask them out. If they have a boyfriend, forget it. If you make a play for them and they get to hear about it, they may become 'unavailable' every time you call to book, and you may lose a good stylist/therapist!

Chapter 4

12.30 p.m. —
Interview with a journalist

Why do so many journalists and fashionistas have such stupid names? I wonder whether it is a prerequisite for the job as I prepare for an interview with Binty – what sort of name is that? – the latest beauty editor of *Dazzle* magazine. Meredith, my PR, calls to brief me.

'Haven't you read *Dazzle* yet? Really, you must keep up, Shaun – Binty Roxborough-Huff is writing all the key pieces now, and she's been going to Lucas's salon for years, but she hates the new cut he's given her so she's going to give you a try.' Great, Lucas has probably cut it so short, in an attempt to be life-changing and ground-breaking – all stylists do this, but particularly to journalists to make their mark – that there's bound to be bugger all I can do with it.

Lucas would probably tell me that Binty is a pain in the arse who never turned up for her appointments and doesn't tip anybody – journalists tend not to. The higher up the media food chain they get, the less likely they are to actually grace you with their divine presence and come in for an appointment, let alone tip after one. Sometimes they even commit the cardinal sin of 'sending their assistant', who turns out to be as relevant to building my PR profile as their grandmother's milkman's cat. The assistant is usually a jobbing Hooray Henrietta who is being paid a single-figure salary. The more prestigious the magazine, the crappier the pay, so you could argue that it's no wonder they don't tip. The real fashion bibles are never short of willing just-left-finishing-school applicants looking for intern placements. Their match-made-in-bank-balance-heaven husband-to-be enjoys saying, 'Of course, Araminta was a fashion journalist before she married me . . .' rather than admitting she was really an underpaid Girl

Friday, who spent her days visiting desperate-for-recognition designers, salons and spas by taking her pampered boss's unwanted invitations for appointments.

Meredith's not the only one to get angry when the booking goes to a stand-in because a whole day's complimentary appointments have gone to a well-connected debutante junior office girl whose journalistic talent could hardly be compared to Jeremy Paxman.

Talk about taking the piss. In fact, once a famous seventies modelling icon was scheduled in for the works – all complimentary of course – our PR had bigged up her visit to near panic status, so that even I was getting hot under the collar in anticipation of her presence. However, on the morning in question we had a phone call from her agent, informing us that she was feeling a little tired, but her mother was over in the UK staying with her for a few days, so would it be possible for her to come in her place?

It's great being blonde – with such low expectations, it's easy to impress. Pamela Anderson

My poor receptionists passed on the request, sensing impending trouble. All I can say was my answer consisted of two words – one that began with F and the other O – a firm and resounding no. The brazen audacity of some celebrities. Over the years, some of them have become so spoilt they've lost touch with any reality they may have had left.

Worse, they'll name-drop and complain about the last poor sod's generosity they were so kindly indulged with and then move on to the next willing victim – and there are plenty of those! In fact, they have their pick, which is why we all have to play the game, and they know it. The irony is that the readership figures for the glossies is a third that of the weekly, chatty middle-of-the-road housewife-and-knitting-pattern magazines. But it's the élite seal of approval we're after, the cachet of being the must-see hairdresser as endorsed by that important style magazine, and going after mass-market press might alienate the movers and shakers in the beauty industry. It's commerciality versus snobbery and brand positioning. The fact remains that we need them more than they need us, so the balance of power resides firmly with the press. Also, keeping up a profile by being in the right type of magazines is the only way of getting a product line and, more importantly, keeping one.

Having your own product line is the hairdressing Holy Grail and the next big thing to accomplish on my personal agenda. The retailers – and those include the high-street chemists as well as the multinational grocers – are as fast moving and cut-throat as a sewer rat. Think Pete Doherty waiting at the altar and you'll have some idea of how, shall we say, unpredictable they can be. Having a product line is another ulcer-inducing matter entirely.

Forget just coming up with the hairdressing goods; reinventing yourself as a brand; attempting to become, and remain, a media darling; dealing with a clientele; coping with, and keeping, dozens of staff and remaining at the top of your artistic and creative tree – the biggie is getting 'listed'. Your products have to:

* Appeal to our core customer, say the grocers
* Have a unique, ground-breaking 'concept', say the buyers
* Have beautiful, touchable packaging, say the press
* Have an innovative formula, say the marketing people
* Be aspirational and 'must-have', say the PRs
* Be sold to us at £1.50 so we can sell them at a fiver, say the retailers

It's not easy to find silk-like organic ingredients for £1.50 a bottle cost price, including packaging of course. 'What we want is the Jo Malone of the hair world,' they chorus. 'At £1.50?' I dare to venture. After all, shampoo is only a mild form of detergent, whichever way you look at it. But we're all, women in particular, a sucker for those air-brushed adverts showing glossy manes swishing around in a wind machine. We all want to buy into the dream that lustrous locks can be ours. Mrs Housewife would like to believe she's a client of famous Hairdresser X, even if she can't afford to go to a good local salon, let alone his – if she could use his products, then it's nearly the same, isn't it? I suppose it's akin to buying a Prada purse and shopping for clothes at Primark. If you get it right there's a lot of money to be made out of products, but only if you can establish a serious following. And making a brand established means sales of over £4 million per year.

The reason this is appealing to so many celeb hairdressers is that it's a key strategy for their exit plan. There's no need to snip away behind a chair after the age of forty-five if you've just flogged your brand for tens of millions and can afford to spend half your life touring the Greek islands on your yacht, with the odd personal appearance being the most taxing part of your working year. Many of the household-name hairdressers have had little input into their product ingredients or researched their development, preferring to leave all that to the marketeers. But, there is much more profit in a successful range than in a normal salon.

Salons are dependant on good staff, and you only get good staff if you invest a hell of a lot of time and energy into building a dream team, whereas products are just reliant on being 'on message' (correctly targetting) to your potential consumer. That's a hell of a lot easier than relying on, motivating and nurturing a gaggle of mad hairdressers. Either that, or you go the franchise route and make your name so mega that every newly qualified stylist will be gagging to give you 10 per cent of their turnover just to have a little piece of your profile to impress their own customers. It's no hassle for you – you don't have to look after a team of artistic, temperamental, mercurial and slightly unreliable people – your franchisee does. You just take your cut, pardon the pun.

Hairdressing is all about brand awareness these days. The retailers are keenly aware that designer hair care is a saturated market, and that's why they make their deals so tough.

Buy One Get One Free – otherwise known by the very apt acronym BOGOF – will cost you, they say, for it's the poor manufacturer who picks up the tab, not your local chemist or supermarket. No wonder they can afford to be so generous.

Gondola End – the end-of-shelf special promotion that catches your eye as you whizz up and down the aisles at your local supermarket – can cost £20k for twenty stores and you have to provide them with all the marketing tools – they're just selling you the space.

3 for 2 – the brand manufacturer gives you the free product, not your friendly high-street store. And don't forget, it's fast becoming retail ethics that you pay for your 'get-in' listing in the first place, and that isn't going to be cheap – we're talking tens of thousands. And if you're selling through catalogues, all that page space won't come for free, either – thousands are spent securing a prominent place in Christmas editions.

As a manufacturer, you are contractually obliged to agree to all of these items. What if there isn't enough profit margin? Or you don't want to give away half your turnover? Tough shit, you'll be delisted and they'll find somebody who will – and there's plenty of us queuing up.

Far from being fair, it's all about who has the most money to spend. Everybody wants a slice of the action, and with the hair-care market worth over £1 billion, who can blame them? Competition between brands isn't so much hot as scorching, with designer hair care being a notoriously difficult market. Consumers' choice, research tells us, is largely down to what packaging a woman thinks will look nice in her bathroom, not what's in the bottle. So unless you turn into Laurence Llewelyn-Bowen and understand what's becoming trendy in interior design, your expensive design concepts can be as successful as a pork chop at a Jewish wedding.

* * * *

*B*ack to Binty.

Shit, I just know I'm going to fuck up and call her Bounty – I start thinking about 'The Taste of Paradise' slogan, begging it to get the fuck out of my head before I talk to Meredith. Meredith is always telling me off. She expects me to be a style guru, a hairdressing legend and happening socialite when sometimes I just feel like an extremely knackered, normal bloke who would love to crawl into bed at 8 p.m. and watch the footie on Sky Sports with a bar of Galaxy and a copy of *Loaded*. We've long since stopped arguing about it – I think she'd prefer it if I were single and out on the town every night. Then she'd be able to fix me up with one of her upper-crust 'gels' or an ex-*Big Brother* contestant so I became gossip-column fodder. As it is she has to live with me as I am. She knows, however, that I know how to play the game, and will turn on the charm and pizzazz, transforming Binty's hair with a little of my hair wizardry magic.

You're probably wondering why I need a PR in the first place. Good question, and one I ask myself frequently as I sign off their princely sum of a retainer every month. When I first started my own salon, the focus was on getting it busy and paying the rent. Once I'd worked on that, and established a support network of my secretary and salon manager to attend to the detail, the next job was to get some decent celebrity clients, so that I could convincingly answer the media when they asked whose hair I did. PR is the way to do that, so I went to the best. The hardest, most ruthless, but the best, of that there is no doubt. Together we have formulated my grand

plan. She has steered my career with a grim and steely deter-
mination and developed me into the 'snipper' to the stars.
Meredith's strongest point is her ability to think outside the
box and see an opportunity in everything I do, seizing it, ruth-
lessly, and hopefully before my rivals do.

I have a love/hate relationship with Meredith. In fact, our
conversations remind me of those mid-seventies video tennis
games you played on your telly – black screens with a bat and
ball. If her flunkies fuck up and miss me out of an important
hair article, where all my peers are mentioned and I am very
obviously absent, I go mad. Then she has a go at me for not
being seen out and about at the right launch or opening party,
or not going to enough of the catwalk shows. It is, as they say,
blame culture. I respect her enormously, but I never kid myself
about whose side she's really on – hers. When she knows our
relationship is going through a rocky patch, she'll pull something amazing out of the bag just at the right time. It's like a
wife putting on a little negligée after a week of fearful PMT.

She did just this the other night, when she invited me to a
magazine launch. It was the Thursday of London Fashion
Week – the night of all nights, as Thursday is the big going out
night in London and LFW happens only twice a year. There
were invites flying around all over the place – two magazine
launches; one socialite's twenty-first birthday, which was the
hottest ticket in town, plus all the designers seemed to be having their after-show parties on the same night. Meredith insisted I join her VIP table at one of the magazine launches, and
her entourage was impressive. A household-name interior
designer, two BAFTA-award-winning actresses, the head of
one of the best model agencies in town – and me.

I have long since ceased to be too impressed by events like
these. The room was full of stick-thin women dressed in the
sort of designer clothing that everybody says looks fabulous,
yet to my male eye just looks a bloody mess. They call it vintage, but to me it looks more 'pulled it out of the back of the
wardrobe because it's come back into fashion'. True vintage is

defined by being over ten years old, apparently, and is often purchased from chic boutiques which are really glorified charity shops. No amount of luxurious perfume can get rid of the stale odour, though, the smell gives it away every time.

There's an arty set of fashionistas who seemingly deem themselves too iconic and serious to bother with female grooming, believing that true chic is entirely determined by what label is worn and is nothing to do with whether you've got any make-up on or if your eyebrows look like a ferret has crawled across your face and come to rest on your forehead. These women are the type to walk around with white, unshaved legs and a moustache that would do Freddie Mercury proud, all in the name of being a true fashion guru, claiming to be so much more serious about fashion than the latest crop of super-groomed footballers' wives who are gracing the media. Their conversation is peppered with references to how they 'knew Julien when he was just a boy from the valleys', or how 'Stella's new collection is just such a departure from her days at St Martins'. I often wonder, as I scan the room, whether they realise how ridiculous they look? Far better to get a nice flattering outfit from Top Shop and spend the rest on getting your scrawny arses down to the salon for some urgent electrolysis or much-needed waxing, if you ask me. And try prettying up your ugly feet by painting your toenails if you're going to walk about in Tarty Trotters.

As usual, the room was full of people trying to be more important than each other. I am known to skulk in the corner at events like these, fascinated by the in-crowd and indulging in a serious spot of people-watching.

One getting-on-a-bit model had a superbly public bust-up with a beautiful young It-girl about town which resulted in near fisticuffs. I chuckled away in a very un-PC fashion throughout. A mutual friend had introduced the two feline sex kittens, not realising there was 'history' between them. They'd fallen out over a modelling assignment for an expensive advertising campaign, by all accounts; the younger of the two winning the prestigious contract, much to the more experienced model's chagrin. So when the coked-out fading star reminded the feisty young girl about town about her unscrupulous 'poaching', feathers flew.

'You . . . are an ugly old witch . . . a washed-up old coke-head of a has-been who should get her fucking knitting out and start drawing her fucking pension,' she screamed, as loudly as she could in front of everybody.

Not known for being able to control her emotions that well, the shocked recipient went for a swipe at the glam young thing and missed terribly before being dragged away by one of her entourage and hushed in a corner. Hilarious and well worth being dragged out on a weekday night for. Can't say the old pro didn't have it coming, and ever since the young model's

Top Tips

On styling your hair

* Invest in a professional dryer – professional salon dryers are from 2800–3200 watt AC dryers (most consumer ones are only 1800 watt). You will be able to blow-dry your hair literally in half the time. Although they are heavier, you'll soon get used to the weight.
* Always use a nozzle to direct heat downwards – this will help keep the cuticles flat, reflecting light and encouraging hair to shine.
* Towel dry hair to 70 per cent dry before using a dryer to prevent heat damage– unless your hair is naturally frizzy, when you will get a better and longer lasting result by blow-drying from wet.
* Warm styling products through hands before distributing evenly throughout hair – they will work better and more efficiently.
* Always comb from ends to roots, starting at the bottom ends and working your way up towards the roots, not roots towards ends. Hair will untangle more easily, and there will be less pressure and potential breakage to the hair.

fees have rocketed, so in demand is she since striking a blow for every poor journalist who's ever been subjected to the elder model's appalling behaviour.

Other than enjoying the unexpected entertainment, I don't really enjoy these events to their full force, as I can't help wondering which ditzy PR company had organised such a shambolic bash. I, along with everybody else, was happy to enjoy the lashings of free baby-sized Dom Perignon drunk straight from the bottle with a straw – *UK salons have 80 million visits per year.* guaranteed to get you hammered in double time – and the hopelessly trendy mini Yorkshire pudding and horseradished roast beef canapés. Not that anybody but me seemed to be eating them. Food is the enemy to be conquered for lots of these women, which is great for me as I'm always starving when I finish work, so am the sole nibbler at many a celebrity gathering. Champagne is always de rigueur at these events, owing to its immediate effect and lack of calories. If you want to stay a size 6, it's not just the nibbles you have to avoid, spirits are out, too. It always makes me smile when the media attend press breakfasts or product launches in the morning, as nobody ever seems to eat a bloody thing, totally ignoring all the delicious pastries and croissants being offered around. The food always remains untouched by the women, and some of the men, come to think of it. Even I have learned to watch my waistline at such events, though I feel so ashamed of the waste that it seems only polite to wolf down a few pain au chocolats.

Unusually for these sorts of occasions, there was no mention of why we were all there. No magazine posters adorning the walls, no speech, no presentation, not even copies of the magazine. 'We've had a nightmare with the printers – they're not ready in time for this evening' said the hapless editor. Somebody had spent all that money and hadn't even bothered to try and get their message across, or worse, they'd left it to some inexperienced PR team, who had forgotten to set themselves a crucial objective before planning the party – the actual reason for it. Ask any one of those people in the morning why they were there and I doubt they could tell you. £100k wasted on getting fashion's movers and shakers bladdered and they didn't even have to suffer a speech to remind them why they were there! The round of endless partying merge into one another for the regular crew on the social scene – one restaurant opening looks just the same as somebody else's new fragrance launch after a while.

I need to get some background info on Binty.

'What's the story?' I ask Meredith, knowing my last chance to converse is over – you can never get a word in with her: she's a one-woman bout of verbal diarrhoea.

'*Dazzle* is writing a guide to the world of celebrity hairdressing – whose salons are the best, most cutting edge and who's doing who,' she barks. 'Binty has been everywhere; you're the last salon she's reviewing. Do you know she's going out with the lead singer of Dogstar? She's just been invited to stay at Highgrove, too. She really is the hippest chick and a complete darling.'

I don't dare tell Meredith I have no idea who Dogstar are – I'll ask one of the juniors or look in *Heat* – and that I couldn't really give a toss whether she's a mate of Wills or Harry. I'll bullshit my way through the interview, like I normally do, and Meredith will have her faith restored, never really knowing how wary I am. Journalists still make me incredibly nervous as they have the power to make or break a career. I'm always so worried that some terrible indiscretion will spill forth like an unwelcome bout of Tourette's and my career as trusted confidante and stylist to the stars will be over as quickly as it began.

Of course, Binty is late, and for one horrible moment I think she is going to cancel and reschedule yet again. Annoying, to say the least, when I have a list of paying clients ready to fill her slot four times over.

You might be wondering whether journalists like her pay

for their hair. Not a chance. In fact, I don't suppose they ever have to pay for anything much. Even the junior beauty ones get given basketfuls of skin products, hair care and perfume, while the more influential senior beauty editors, whose sanction and praise is so crucial it can establish or ruin a brand or salon, are used to a fabulous life of perks and privilege. They often get flown all over the world, stay at the most luxurious hotels and are ferried around London in taxis to attend the launch of every big product from the wealthy, established brands, who are, ironically, the biggest advertisers in the magazines. Funny, that. If you don't believe me, just check out who gets mentioned in the sought-after editorial pages compared to who's buying the most advertising space. Inevitably, they end up giving away their mountains of goodies to their more junior assistants, much to the PRs' dismay. Even the fashionistas rarely have to pay for skin or hair care, let alone visits to the salon. As a celebrity hairdresser, it does no harm to get the key editors on your side, whether they're fashion or hair orientated, to ensure they are networking you with the right people. In fact, a Condé Nast business card can virtually guarantee you a passport to freedom.

At last Binty arrives, a quite respectable twenty minutes late, and I try and find my junior, who is frequently being pinched by the other stylists to shampoo while I prepare to do her consultation. Other stylists would rarely pinch each other's juniors, but somehow nobody thinks twice about nicking mine. Because I'm the boss, I suppose, and they know I can't say no as the smooth-running of the salon should always be my priority. And if they can't get their client shampooed on time, smooth running it ain't. I need her though. The one thing I cannot risk is a bad backwash experience – wet collar, loss of water pressure, crap shampoo technique, non-existent head massage, tangled hair – not really the image I want to portray to any client, let alone a journalist. At least now I don't have side-washes – where the junior stood to the side of the basin to shampoo – so I don't have to worry about the body-odour issues. Everyone who's ever had a haircut must have had a smelly, sweaty armpit over their face while supposedly enjoying a relaxing cleanse and condition at one time or another, and if it happens with one of my staff, I have to call them into the office and break the news gently. That's why we still keep a can of deodorant in the loo, just to be safe.

Tangled long hair from a bad shampoo is very easily done. Once, when I first opened my salon, an untrained junior attempted to wash a young teenage client's waist-length hair. After twenty minutes there was still no sign so, panic rising, I headed off to the backwash to find out the reason for the delay. The sight that greeted me made my chest rise in panic. There, looking like a rasta was the young girl, with hair so badly tangled that the combs and conditioners the frantic junior was trying to tug through became lost in a clump of mats. The mistake?

1. Not brushing it through before she started.
2. Massaging it by piling it all on top of the crown and getting it matted and tangled.
3. Not pulling it smooth and flattening the cuticle – the overlapping outside layer of the hair, like fish scales – as she went along.

You see, if you have long hair, you need only ever shampoo the roots, the lather and water will work their way through the rest of the hair which should be enough to cleanse the midlengths and ends. You should certainly never pile it all up on top of your head and wash it, mangling it up like a tangled ball of wool.

There was no solution for this poor girl. Even with gallons of fabric softener – the idiot-proof way to untangle the worst-case hair scenario – and three of us combing it, an hour later the clumps still weren't shifting. In fact, they were getting worse. Her whole head resembled a doormat. She was in tears, the junior was in tears and, to be honest, I felt like welling up too. She ended up with a neat, tidy and very free bob. A lesson learned – now shampoo training is the most vital part of our salon education. I want Binty to experience the best.

Binty is exactly what I expected her to be: all couture creamy blonde buttery highlights and expensively manicured nails, dressed head to toe in Balenciaga and Marc Jacobs, with a Chloé Paddington swinging from her arm – my secretary informs me on the bag bit; she always has a little peek at my VIPs to give me some insider info. Don't let the upper-class giggles fool you, 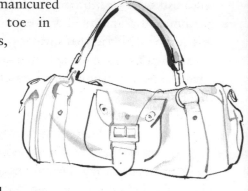 she whispers in my ear as she heads back to the office, she's already checking out the salon with her beady, deadly critical eye, ready to write her hairdressing hit list. A one-woman, Jimmy-Choo'ed firing squad.

After having had a guided tour from Meredith's flunky, Seraphina, who's been dispatched to the salon to ensure Binty's visit is hitch-free – and to shove a couple of my most recent press releases into her already over-stuffed Paddington – we get down to our interview. I shoot a 'don't you dare try to interrupt or finish off any of my bloody sentences' look at the inexperienced PR girl, and she swallows nervously.

Binty asks me the age-old questions:

'Who do you do?' I tell her some names.

'Give us some gossip,' she says. I try and think of some that won't upset my clients, yet will be juicy enough to appease her journalistic curiosity.

Which celeb haircut is my most requested at the moment? I have to be truthful, if a little un-original, and admit it's Posh Spice's Pob, with Reese Witherspoon coming a close second, yet again.

What are you going to do with my hair? I analyse it, not bad in texture – fine but lots of it. Natural wave, easy. I know I can win her over. I give her some suggestions and, flicking through a style book, we agree on a new look for her – well, as new as she's prepared to let me go. Relaxing at last, I ensure she's escorted to the backwash for what I hope will be the shampoo of a lifetime. I dash over to the kitchen, not trusting any junior with the chef's order.

'She wants a carrot and mango smoothie, and for fuck's sake make her cappuccino perfect – and put it in the posh logoed china!'

'The bill?' he asks, gingerly.

'Yeah, no bill,' I sigh. I'm paying.

I do actually love cutting hair, even on the journalists who make me feel so edgy. There's something immensely satisfying about the feel and precision of the blade on the wet hair, and the lovely, thick, slicing noise it makes. It is a comforting, beautiful sound. Isn't that what they call intrinsic work satisfaction? I never tire of taking a clean section, and preparing to slice through it with my sharp, decisive blades, so precisely tuned that one drop on the hard, limestone floor of the salon will result in them going off to the scissor man to be rebalanced.

Now he's a character, the scissor man. He makes Del Boy look like Bill Gates. He drives around in a brand new Porsche, as blingy as hell, with a collection of watches that are growing at the same rate as his annual turnover, clearly. He plays a clever game with me, though, never forgetting to add the odd,

'Cor, Shaun, you must be doing all right mate – like the wrist candy.' I am, after all, his client, and this makes a nice change, seeing as it's not often that the tables are turned. He presumably gets away with staying under the VAT registration limit by the constant, endless changing of his company names. One minute he's Sunshine Scissors Ltd the next Sunny Scissors & Co, and he's an expert in faux-bewilderment. 'No idea whatcha mean, mate. I've been Sunny Scissors for months . . .' Next time my blades need a sharpen, he will have morphed into some other take on the original company name. These East End barrow boys, you've got to watch 'em.

Binty notices that my fingers are plastered – I'm getting used to my new 'blades' – and is intrigued as I show her my latest Japanese scissors, another purchase from the scissor man, marvelling at the £500 price tag. Journalists tend to marvel a lot at prices, presumably because they never have to pay for anything. If only the editors would teach them to tip, I think. When they're doing a write-up on the salon, it's absolutely fine for them not to feel obliged. However, if they're getting a very hefty discount and frequenting the salon for a multitude of treatments all the time, not tipping is a cardinal sin.

Q: What's a brunette's mating call?
A: Has the blonde left yet?

I wouldn't want you to think I begrudge journalists their role in my success; I have a lot to thank them for, as the beauty press play a huge part in making our industry credible. I just wish some of them would be a little more grateful for the freebies and look after my staff better than they do. Hairdressers rely on their tips, and it's the ultimate insult not to slip a note in your hairdresser's pocket to say how much you love your new look. It's even worse not to tip the junior and is guaranteed to piss off the stylist or colourist, who often feel they have to compensate their helper's wages if a client is on the squeaky side. Seeing as the salon owner has to make up for any freebies commission-wise to the staff, the least I would hope is that any 'comps' show a little gratuitous thanks to my team.

Back in my apprentice days, a boy I trained with used to get his revenge on tight-fisted clients as he shampooed them at the

backwash. When their eyes were closed in restful abandon-
ment, he would gob silently into the lathery mix, much to the
amusement of the less brave amongst us. The client would rise
from the chair: 'Wonderful shampoo. Thank you, Steven,' she
would say, blissfully unaware of what had gone on.

I was always worried they'd open their eyes and see
him, but at the first stirring of eyeball activity, he had a
unique knack of sucking the spit straight back up, like a
salival bungee jump.

He was a complete charmer, and very well-spoken too, but
in the staff room he'd shout, 'Tight Bitch!' as he desperately
scraped enough coins together to purchase a bite of lunch, half
a Fosters in the pub and his obligatory ten Rothmans – the
sustenance required to get through a busy, perm-neutralising,
hand-chafing afternoon. He had a worse trick, reserved only
for the meanest clients in the salon. He would go and make
them a nice frothy coffee – this was long before the days of the
cappuccino – and you can imagine what went into that. The
foam wasn't whipped milk, I can assure you. A word of advice:
best not get a reputation for being a tight tipper. Generosity
never goes unnoticed, whatever your profession.

The very first salon I worked in was not, it has to be said, at
the upper echelons of artistic hairdressing. It was a local gaff –
a Maison Flo – and I chose it not for its hairdressing expertise,
but because it had some great-looking local girls training there.
This was, of course, before I followed my mother's advice and
realised that in order to be taken seriously and fulfil my dream,
the city was the only place to be; I would never get to that level
if I trained locally. My success as a hairdresser would depend
on who my mentor was and how good the salon's staff were.
And how do you know what's good when you're straight from
school and don't know what you're looking for? I knew as
much about what made a good hairdresser as the average
punter, and seeing as my mum had always cut my hair, I didn't
really know how to tell a good salon from a bad one. Most
salons prefer to 'grow their own', so realising this, and the fact

that nobody could be bothered to teach me anything, I didn't stay long in suburban hairdressing hell.

The final straw came when I was dossing at the salon reception one wet Saturday afternoon. While all my mates were hanging around the local funfair chatting up the birds, I was hiding behind the desk in an attempt to avoid neutralising yet another perm, when a very old lady with a mop of curls staggered slowly to the desk to check in. I was amazed that she'd even managed to push open the heavy door, let alone make it in to get her hair done. She leaned on the desk, breathing heavily for what seemed like an eternity, oxygen slowly filling back into her lungs, then finally, she gasped, 'I've got an appointment.'

'Fine,' I said, offering to take her coat, when she added, 'And so has my mother.' Round the corner came an even more unsteady, elderly lady, her perm curled tightly around her even more wrinkly face.

Later, once they'd been shampooed and set, I sat them under the bank of hood dryers. People shout under the hood dryer, forgetting the whole salon can hear them as they can hear nothing but the whoosh of warm air. In fact, I was prone to mouthing silently to the deaf old ladies who would anxiously shriek, 'Pardon? I can't hear you boy!' repeatedly until I boomed, 'DO YOU WANT A COFFEE?' once they'd turned their whistling hearing aids up. Harmless fun and it was guaranteed to give the other trainees a good laugh.

Once the pair were sitting safely under the dryer, their faces going more puce as the heat gathered pace, I heard them say, 'What do you think of it here, Mother?'

'Not much, dear, but it's cheap.'

They tipped me 5p each, and I was tempted to shout after them, 'Have it back, you obviously need it more than I do,' before worrying that my mum would say I was being unkind.

I later found out that the mother passed away peacefully under that very same dryer just a few months later, much to the salon's guilty amusement. Apparently, a new junior spent five minutes trying to wake her before running to get

Mr Christopher, the salon owner, to raise the alarm and call for an ambulance. The daughter dozed peacefully under her dryer while the whole episode took place.

'No point in getting her out until she's dry,' said Mr Christopher.

Mother was stretchered out with her rollers in, the staff frantically trying to remove them as Pre-menstrual Pattie, Mother's stylist, was notoriously territorial about her rollers. 'Not my yellows, please. Grab 'em quick,' she barked at the poor, terrified assistant. All rollers are colour coded, with some being more popular than others, and their ownership – salon or stylist? – was as hotly contested as Gibraltar or the Falklands. There's a lot of nicking that goes on where salon equipment is concerned, and that's why all brushes and dryers have initials carefully painted on them in the manicurist's most stand-out shades of nail varnish. It looks particularly fetching when it gets old and starts chipping away.

10.8 million women now colour their hair; 7.1 million straighten it and only 2.2 perm it.

That was my revelation, my cathartic moment – the realisation that this was not the élite of the hairdressing world. Well, that and the fact they diluted the cheap shampoo we used at the backwash, hung out the perm papers to dry, re-using them when they were supposed to be disposable, and never laundered their stinky gowns. It was hardly top-class stuff. If I wanted to make some half-decent money out of a career in hairdressing, it wasn't going to be there.

Realising I needed to be where the action was, I hot-footed it to London once I'd left school and applied for six or seven apprenticeships before I was finally accepted by a leading salon. In those days the élite salons were really over-subscribed; the days of parents paying for their children to have an apprenticeship were not long over, so getting a place in any of the top salons was considered very lucky, but Lady Luck was on my side.

The salon where I did my apprenticeship was in a particularly trendy London enclave, and to say it was an eye-opener is to understate its significance to a poor, naïve suburban boy like me. It was a different world. It was also my first experience of gay culture. My first encounter with screaming, mincing, stereotypical queens, and they were great, though it has to be said, not my cup of tea. They were really funny – gay humour really is the wittiest. It was like working with twenty different versions of Boy George and Pete Burns. They were shocking, explicit and hilarious. Some of them were ageing Quentin Crisp types, and some were young and trendy. They all teased me remorselessly. And not just me, because there were three of us straight boys who started our training that year.

HAIR FACTS

Temporary colour sits in between the cuticle layers, while permanent colour goes into the cortex. The peroxide is the oxidising agent that is mixed with tint or bleach to make it active. Permanent colour molecules enter through the cuticle and into the cortex, where they swell and remain. Although most 'tints' or permanent colours stop working after the development time has elapsed, bleach carries on being active until the oxidisation is complete – hence hair can 'over-cook' and massive damage can be done if it's 'over-processed'.

One of those apprentices was 'Surfer' Leo. He was a blonde, Californian long-haired pretty boy. They never stopped going after him, both in their teasingly sexual way and by taking the piss out of him. One of the very campest ones, Pascale, used to say to him, 'Darling Leo, just you come on over and sit on my face so your balls hang over my nose like a pair of castanets,' to which the whole staff room would erupt into laughter. I don't know how we put up with it, actually. Another of Pascale's party pieces was to lie on the staff-room couch, legs akimbo, making groany, sexual noises as he tickled his balls through the tight, seam-splitting denim of his jeans; all the while looking across the room at the three of us, who were desperately trying to ignore his gaze and concentrate on munching our ham and cheese toasties. His grunts and groans were often audible, much to our embarrassment, on the salon floor. It would never be allowed to happen in this politically correct age, but back then hairdressing was changing – there was a new generation of heterosexual men getting into it as a career, and we were paving the path for the future. Ironically, I was never offended by any of this overt sexual harassment; as long as they kept their hands to themselves, which they always did where I was concerned. They knew they'd get what for if they'd tried any funny business. I just thought they were side-splittingly funny. I still love a bit of toilet humour, and this lot were downright filthy.

The first person I assisted was Adrian. Adrian liked to dress – for some unfathomable reason – as a samurai. His full regalia included a sword and bright-red costume, which he would wear whenever the mood took him, delighting in the shock and bemusement of the clients and staff. It had to be seen to be believed. He would stick real twigs and foliage to his costume and was sometimes unable to get through the salon door without turning sideways. How he managed to do any hairdressing was beyond me as he could barely lift up his arms, such was the weight of the adornments. 'Here comes the bloody New Forest,' the gay brigade used to tease as he struggled to get in, branches snapping off in the doorway as he moved. The Sharons and Traceys of the salon I'd left behind would never have been able to comprehend this different hairdressing world.

Adrian also sometimes liked to dress like Marcel Marceau, minus the black and white make-up. This was at the time when punk was dying and the New Romantics were beginning – I suppose you would have stood out if you didn't explore your sexuality with a streak of eyeliner and some mind-altering clothes, let alone drugs. Apparently Adrian was straight, or at least he never tried it on with me, he just liked to express himself. Sometimes he would come to work as a pirate, other days he would come with a clean, freshly scrubbed face, devoid of make-up. He once came to work as a geisha. To comment on any of Adrian's outfits was considered suburban. To be cool, you had to look like you'd seen it all before and that nothing fazed you. Not that he cared, as most of the time he was snoozing in the staff room between clients.

There was a peculiar mixed bag of stylists, all of whom taught me more about hairdressing in a few short years than I would have learned in a lifetime at a provincial salon. The range of skills was awesome, and watching those masters at work was a breathtaking lesson in hairdressing skill. This was hairdressing at its purest – an exquisite art form. Most of the stylists in London at that time had come from one of the two main salon family trees, Vidal Sassoon or Leonard. Sassoon's trademark was precision cutting, whereas Leonard's look was much softer, concentrating on the finish as much as the cut. Both revolutionised hairdressing in their own unique ways. From these two royal lines, most modern celebrity hairdressers are spawned. And I was working with those who had worked and trained under the originals. A training of this calibre was priceless and I never forgot it, even if it was a little sporadic and disorganised. I even consider it my duty to pass on the knowledge I was given to my own trainees, such as the techniques I learned from one master, Renee.

Although Renee was renowned for his hot Mediterranean temper, it also didn't take me long to find out what else he was famous for. Renee, it transpired, was partial to the booze, and had a stash of little miniatures hidden safely in his roller trolley, discreetly out of sight of the boss and his clients. I soon realised how he managed to swig the contents so tactfully; he had a little trick of hiding them in the palm of his hand and tossing them into the bottom of the bin once he'd finished. He was last seen sitting on a park bench outside Victoria Station, jollying along the other winos.

In his heyday his backcombing genius was something to behold. He could get hair up and perfect, precise and beautiful, the likes of which you wouldn't see in this modern age. Each hair was perfectly sculpted into place – something similar now would require a serious amount of airbrushing. His *pièce de résistance* was using a toothbrush spritzed in Elnett to catch the straggly hairs around the hairline, a trick I use in most of my photographic work even now. He also taught me the amazing knack of covering up tell-tale face-lift scars with some fancy brushwork.

> I'm not offended by all the dumb blonde jokes because I know I'm not dumb. I also know I'm not blonde.
> Dolly Parton

Ever wondered why every hairdresser is an expert on who's had plastic surgery? Face lifts normally result in the old nip/tuck scar being discreetly hidden in the hairline, so you get to know the signs long before the gossip mags cotton on, either by washing hair at the backwash or by combing through wet hair before cutting and blow-drying. Some clients can be on their third or fourth set of scars. The ones who overdo it the most have skin so tightly drawn it resembles a weathered old drum you might find in a Moroccan souk. They come with faces wetly smothered in Vaseline or Elizabeth Arden Eight Hour Cream to enable them to display emotion or move without cracking. Try air-kissing them and you'd be glued to their tight, wet cheeks.

One client who I used to do every week but mysteriously stopped coming – I still wonder where she went – was so lifted that her eyes – if you could call them that, slits would be a more appropriate term – permanently watered. It has to be said, she looked like a pug dog in a hurricane. She would dab at her tiny eyes constantly, filling tissue after tissue with sticky, gloopy liquid. Worse, the rims of her eyes turned outward, so talking to her was like looking at two fried eggs in a bucket of blood. With the money she had, there was no excuse for not going to a top surgeon, or at least one who was prepared to tell her when to stop – for that, they say, is the true professional: the one who turns down your money. Nowadays, it's Botox and fillers that my younger clients aspire to. One woman I do was incensed and astounded to find her City boyfriend was prone to a spot of cross-dressing. However, her angry display was ruined, she said, from overindulging in botulism, which left her as expressionless as one of the blow-up dolls he was also partial to.

All this reminiscing, when I should be concentrating on Binty.

'And of course he's flying over from New York any time now, so I'll only have a trim because, well, I really have to have a cut with him for a piece I'm doing, and it's been so long since he cut my hair…' I knew it, the bloody hair guru was making his annual visit. Great, we'll be rectifying all his mistakes for the next three months and having to swallow all that undeserved praise and adulation.

I press on, determined to make my mark on her look, with a signature cut. Wearable chic, I call it. After a jooshy blow-dry, I show her through the back mirror and hope for a positive reaction. Her hair looks great – the cut is soft and feminine and I can tell she loves it, thank God.

'I think your salon's fab, Shaun. Love it. And my hair is to die for. By the way, did you know that the reason he's coming back is that he's looking to open a London flagship salon? After all, his New York waiting list is twelve weeks now. Can you believe it?'

Wait till I tell my PR that one, I think wearily, as Binty jumps out of the chair, knowing that we'll have a ferocious battle of wits about who knew first.

This bollocks about waiting lists is no more than a publicity dream, guaranteed to get my blood boiling. Even a Z-list celebrity hairdresser would have a waiting list if he was only doing three bloody clients a week, and spending most of his time in the gym or with his bit of skirt – or trouser, depending on his preference. Don't the press ever learn not to believe the hype? I myself have a very respectable and honest six-week waiting list, and seeing as I'm snipping away behind my chair for at least three and a half full days out of five with the rest of my time spent on photographic shoots or filming, I'm very proud of my demand levels.

'Great interview, and divine coffee, too,' she giggles excitedly, checking out the familiar soap actress who's just arrived for her waxing appointment.

Journalists, I decide, just don't do eye contact. Their heads swivel, desperate not to miss something or, more to the point, someone, like something out of the Exorcist. Binty, hair bouncy and shining, skips off back to the fantasy world of *Dazzle* magazine, leaving her press releases, stained from her coffee cup and covered in hair, on the table next to my styling section. Like so many journalists who are writing about the salon or me, it's vital they get the credits right. It's no good if they publish the wrong salon phone number, which has happened to me, or print the wrong picture of me, ditto, or forget to mention me all together. No wonder the PRs are so desperate to make sure the visits go smoothly. It has been known for me to do a photo shoot and get no credit at all, which defeats the whole object of doing it.

I call Meredith for a debrief and tell her the news.

'Oh, I knew about that ages ago,' she lies. Meredith *hates* to be the last person to find out about anything. 'American *Vogue* have already started calling him a hair icon, you know, and listed him as one of the top twenty most influential fashion people of the decade.'

Well, there's no accounting for taste.

I decide to get my own back.

'By the way, Binty left her press releases here – didn't Seraphina pick up on that?' One-nil to me, then, I think as I hear Meredith screeching for her flunky, ready to bollock her senseless and annoyed that I've made her look foolish.

I head to reception to pay for Binty's coffees – and bloody Seraphina's, I find out; that can come off Meredith's bill – as I don't want my poor chef to be out of pocket. I sub-let the space to him and his Brazilian cronies, knowing that his never-ending family are relying on his weekly takings back in the slums of Rio.

'By the way,' I ask the desk. 'Did she tip?'

Not a fucking sausage, they chorus.

I put my hand in my pocket, fishing for some change and sigh.

This is the second, and no doubt not the last, time that day that I'll be coughing up, I think as I skulk off to look for my junior so I can replenish her tip box and make sure she's ready for our next, most challenging appointment of the day.

How to cut your own fringe

1. Shampoo and condition your hair.
2. Get a semi-professional pair of very sharp scissors, suitable for haircutting (Boots sell these). DO NOT use kitchen, toenail or bush-trimming scissors.
3. Section from eyebrow to eyebrow only — NEVER go over the outside edge of each eyebrow.
4. Take a section two centimetres wide only. Don't cut more than this or you'll be cutting too far back.
5. Comb with the narrowest teeth of a cutting comb and pull taut.
6. DO NOT LOOK UP — or your fringe will be two inches shorter than you want it.
7. Split the hair into three sections — central, left and right.
8. Cut the central section first. Cut just one centimetre off, very slowly. If you need to cut more off you can, but you can't stick it back on so be sparing!
9. Next, marry the left and right sections with the central one as your guideline.
10. As a rule, work out where you want the fringe to sit when dry and cut a good two centimetres below this length — i.e. cut below the eyebrow height if you want the finished result to be above the eyebrows.
11. Once finished, blow-dry to see how the hair is sitting before you go back and trim more off.
12. If you cock up, don't try and rectify it. Get down to a good salon fast.

Chapter 5

1.30 p.m. —
Celebrity photo shoot

I don't need to be buzzed and told that my next client is in. It is obvious from the whirlwind that surrounds her every visit and the way our normal clients are turning round in their chairs to catch a glimpse of her. The salon buzzes; there are teams of people running after her as she struts through to find me, her shearling coat trailing along the salon floor. Her frantic secretary is whispering into a mobile, which is permanently tucked behind her ear, while simultaneously trying to fan out the dead animal like an over-anxious bridesmaid. If the stiletto boot goes through that, she'll be wishing she'd taken a duvet day today. To the astonishment of my staff, Ms A walks straight into our office, plonking herself down on my desk, and immediately asks me to give her a Marlboro Light, seemingly oblivious to our strict no-smoking policy.

'I'm here, Shaun,' she purrs.

'So I see.' I smile.

Lord knows I hope she's in a good mood today. The photographer has been here for an hour already, faffing around with the boiling hot lights which have already fucked up the air-conditioning.

A nervous fashion stylist, clipboard clenched under an increasingly sweat-stained armpit, taps bird-like on the door.

'Hello, so nice to meet you,' she quivers, gingerly holding a timid, sweaty hand out to my famous client.

The complete lack of interest and deafening lack of response leads me to try and rescue the poor girl.

'Hi, I'm Shaun. Thanks for coming today. What outfits do you have? It would be great if I had some sort of story, so I know what to do hair-wise.'

The nervous girl fiddles anxiously with the zipper on her wheelie suitcase and finally produces four or five stunning size 8 dresses from her fashionistas box of tricks.

'I thought she'd look amazing in purple velvet, so I brought a Julien MacDonald,' she offers, voice rising in that annoyingly Antipodean style at the end of each sentence, as if asking a question.

'I hate bloody purple,' growls my A-lister. 'It makes my skin look like shit. I want to be pretty and girly, like the Snow Queen, and wear white. Haven't you got any Alice Temperley?'

Snow Queen – now there's a slip of the tongue, I think knowingly. Ms A doesn't buy her jeans from Gap Kids for no reason, you know, she has a penchant for the models' drug of choice, their favourite slimming aid, and one that certainly isn't part of the WeightWatchers Points system. The old Charlie, the devil's dandruff, commonly known as cocaine. I've not been an angel in the past, but the unbelievable rise in the everyday use of the deadly stuff is alarming, even to me. But as long as it's cheaper than a Starbucks latte, with fewer calories, I can't see its spiralling consumption doing anything other than accelerate, unfortunately, as it sure doesn't help the naughtier, more party-prone members of my team to get their act together after a heavy weekend.

> 50 per cent of people will have 50 per cent white hair by the time they are 50 years old.

The nervous stylist is already making trembling calls from her mobile, desperate to pull in the said-garment and pacify Ms A, a modern-day (sometimes) loveable brat if ever I saw one. Still, she hasn't done me any harm. Being able to say she comes in is how I get people like Binty to write about me in the first place, so I act like Willy Wonka to her Veruca Salt.

'Shaun, I have to look wonderful. I'm off to LA tomorrow to go after a fabulous new movie role. I want you to make me look fabulously Hollywood. I need to appeal to those casting agents. I want them to love me. I need to be taken seriously. I need to prove myself as a person, not just a bloody actress.'

Yeah, and earn some more money, I think, trying not to be cynical. And the PR will get a nice cut of the contract.

'If bloody Kelly Brook can do it, so can I,' she states firmly, sparking up her fag and nearly burning the purple frock that sits, discarded, on her lap. The nervous assistant is now ashen-faced. Two thousand pounds' worth of dress may be about to be ruined, and she alone will bear the brunt of the designer's PR's fury.

Before I can tell her what creative genius I am about to perform on her hair, her attention span has run its notoriously short course and she swivels round to start rummaging through the anxious girl's case of beautiful clothes and shoes for herself.

'I love it!' she says, grabbing a pretty Issa dress and starting to peel off her jeans to try it on, much to the now pink-necked, shaking stylist's relief. She doesn't know where to look as the scrawny, braless – and titless, she's so thin – body wriggles into the outfit, so she starts checking herself out in the glass office door's reflection.

Embarrassed? Not a bit of it. She knows that I, and most other people come to think of it, have seen it all before, and as for the stylist, she is so insignificant that Ms A has probably already forgotten she's even there. Thank God, her jeans look cleaner today than last time I saw her.

That time, when I did her hair for a major photographic shoot, she peeled off her jeans – worn knickerless – and kicked them towards her ever-present, clipboard-clenching assistant, gusset exposed wrong side up for everyone to see. My assistant stylist prodded my arm, motioning with a twitch of his head for me to gaze at the dreaded garment. Ms A-lister, despite promoting a line in luxury bath products, seemed not such an expert in the art of her own personal hygiene.

A couple of days later, my stand-in arrived to style her hair in my absence for a chat show appearance, and was disgusted to find the same jeans and gusset, still awaiting a little refreshment in the form of a much-needed trip though the washing machine, left out for all to view on the dressing-room floor. This time, he was appalled to see the knickerless jeans in an even worse state and texted me the gross news. Look closely at her in pictures, and you can see her looking, shall we say, a little rough around the edges? Thank God for airbrushing. All the make-up artists, hairdressers and fashion stylists in the world can't make up for a good scrub in the bath. A spot of perfume wouldn't go amiss, either.

Today, it is the toenails that give the game away. They are black, and her feet even blacker. The stylist clocks this. My eyes catch hers, as shocked, her mouth opens and closes in bewilderment as she reaches for a pair of closed-in stilettos. Despite all this, Ms A is another one destined to reach every best-dressed list; they obviously never look very closely. 'All fur coat and no knickers' my Grandmother would say.

There are two questions every celebrity hairdresser dreads.

One is, 'What would you do with my hair?' and the other is, 'Do those celebrities pay like everyone else?'

'What would you do with my hair?' is fine when you have a paying client, one who is on her pilgrimage and has seen you on a TV makeover show and waited six weeks for a booking, desperate to have her life transformed. The trouble is, that's never where it ends. It's a question I get asked in my local coffee shop on a Sunday morning. I get asked it at the school gates, when I'm picking up the children. I get asked it at the pub, when I am innocently ordering a pint. Worse, I get asked at dinner parties. The starter is being served, the men are all talking about their serious careers as bankers or lawyers, and one of the women asks the dreaded question, deciding that my funny, frivolous career is a topic warranting such great mirth that the room is automatically silenced. What are the husbands thinking? Probably, Bloody arsehole. Who does he think he is, acting the superstar? This is just guaranteed to embarrass me and make me look a twat. I feebly answer, your hair is fine. Then, guilty that I have made the woman feel stupid, I feel like I have to pay her some lip service and ask, 'Where do you go?' which then looks to the husbands like I am touting for business. I can't win.

Would an accountant get asked, 'What do you think of my fiscals?' Never. Would an office manager ever get asked, 'Tell me about the Excel spreadsheets you did today?' No. Everybody knows that *nobody* wants to talk about work in their spare time. Yet hairdressing somehow isn't classed as 'work' and people are endlessly fascinated with my style guidance. My honest opinion? Come for a haircut and I'll be delighted to tell you then.

Q: What do you call a good-looking man with a mousey-haired woman?
A: A hostage.

The spin-off to this is that I often get told, head down to avoid eye contact and in a frantic scream of embarrassment, 'Don't look at my hair! I'd have done it if I'd known I was going to see *you*!' I've had this from nurses at the maternity hospital when my wife was giving birth. I've had it at parent/teacher evenings, when they meet me for the first time. I've even had it when visiting my sick father at his hospital bedside.

The truth? I hadn't even noticed their bloody hair. Unless it's during work hours, it has to be something pretty exceptional for me to even look at anyone's hair, and then it's usually because I think they might be a client. When I'm not in work mode, I switch off.

As for celebrities paying, I would love to tell you that they do, but I'd be lying – and I don't have any secrets from you.

This, rightly or wrongly, is how it works.

There is a sliding scale in the celebrity ranks. The true A-listers normally pay, but I'm talking Hollywood royalty A-listers, the ones about whom you say, 'They just don't make 'em like that any more'. The ones that when you ring up and tell your mates, they say, 'Wow! You did *him?*' They wouldn't dream of taking something for nothing, and would probably be quite offended if you even suggested such a scummy, low-life arrangement.

Then you have your modern-day level A-lister. Most automatically presume that they'll get everything for nothing, but they know how the game works and will be sure to tip well and make sure they earn their keep by mentioning you in relevant articles and even doing a spot of networking for you if the mood takes them. They were created and conceived in the celebrity age, the you-scratch-my-back era.

Sadly, it can all go downhill from here. The further down the ranks you go, the more troublesome and dreadful they can become. The C-listers and below are sometimes so desperate to prove they're A-listers that they feel that if they act all demanding and divalike, you may believe they're more

important than they are. They tend to get very above their station, and become quite cut-throat and mercenary about their visit, wanting discount cards for their mums, friends and aunties and talking very loudly to their agents on their mobiles, peppering their conversations with all sorts of pretentious rubbish like 'Of course, next year when I do my own series for UK Minor Celebs Style TV . . .' (viewing figures 35) in a vain attempt to impress you into giving them the world and treating them like they are Marilyn Monroe. Iconic is not a word that springs to mind, more moronic.

It's like the banks who only lend money to those who can prove they don't need it. The ones who can afford it more than anybody else never have to cough up, although the true class acts would never take advantage. The modern day genre of the celebrity incarnate doesn't pay for anything much, neither hairdressing nor beauty appointments, clothes, perfume, skin care products, theatre tickets, holidays or even food, in some cases. They'll borrow £3K's worth of expensive designer dresses to wear to film premieres, and then forget to return them. Who's going to ring them up and ask for them back when some appreciative designer has seen the glorious celeb photographed in their new frock in every newspaper in the Western hemisphere? Sales will rocket. They'll become hot. Remember what Liz Hurley did for Versace? Couture houses, being extortionately expensive, have an élite niche of seriously wealthy paying clients, but the people who can afford to wear their clothes aren't necessarily the ones who are going to make them mainstream. They need to be in the public eye, and being mainstream is where the big money is. Diffusion lines and perfumes all hinge on celebrity endorsement. And it doesn't end there.

Like journalists, a celebrity only has to shower their praise on the latest restaurant or jar of face cream and a brand can make millions. People even favour certain schools because of the famous offspring who go there. Hype? You'd better believe it. Endorsed by a world-famous, Oscar-winning actress and the waiting list at Harrods is like a queue for sustenance in a third-world country.

Opening a new hotel? Simply invite a carefully chosen selection of networking A-listers down for a complimentary weekend of hospitality, and bingo, guaranteed press, perfect for encouraging hordes of paying townies to part with their hard-earned cash and make you some great profit.

We're all to blame for this, of course, because of our endless fascination with the cult of celebrity. Will we ever tire of it? There are celebrity chefs, celebrity florists, celebrity health gurus, celebrity authors and now even celebrity hairdressers – thank God.

And no, I don't get anything for free – yet – apart from the odd complimentary tickets to the premiere of some film nobody's heard of, which the PR's pack of wolves chuck my way if nobody further up the pecking order can go. But I'm looking forward to the day when I do get a few – free holidays, cars, watches, jewellery. For now, I can dream.

My PR is the expert at this. She's got it sussed, and her methods have shaped my career as celebrity endorsement have definitely helped catapult my career to stardom. My success isn't just down to having a good celeb list, though, as I had a very successful business before anyone famous walked through the door. But by gaining a celebrity client following, I've been able to take my career to the next level, and for that I'll always be grateful to the celebrities who walk through my door, many of whom I have called upon to help me out with PR opportunities over the years.

A good PR has an élite cluster of celebs on her books, all different so there is no conflict of interest. Take Meredith; she has a hairdresser (me), a jewellery designer, a florist and a fashion house. Doing a shoot? If Meredith's got anything to do with it, her celebs will only wear clothes from her fashion-designer client, jewellery from her jeweller client, the flowers will be done by her florist and the hair by me, etc. One shoot keeps us all happy, and we all rely on each other to network and create new opportunities.

The new breed of celeb, and their PRs, know how it works and expect a favour to be called in now and again. A celebrity magazine might tempt me with the offer of a double-page makeover spread, if I can find the celebrity to do it. There is the carrot: they leave it to me to arrange, get a couple of pages filled and all at no cost or hassle to them. That's how it works, and that's when I go calling at the doors of my celebs, the ones who have enjoyed all the freebies, because it's pay-back time.

Of course, the top magazines will only give you precious editorial coverage of a makeover if it's newsworthy. Think Gwen Stefani going back to her natural brunette, and you get the picture. And to hook in the weekly gossip and lifestyle mags, it would have to be Gwen Stefani goes brunette in her luxury Malibu villa, wearing her beautiful new couture collection available from Selfridges. It's the way of the journalistic world.

Research suggests that women who have their hair coloured experience a rollercoaster of emotions that peak when hair is freshly coloured and trough before they next colour their hair again.

Added to this, there is an even newer kid on the block, the reality celeb. Two weeks ago they were nobody, and now not only do they have an agent, they have scorching appeal, even if there's only a relatively short window for them to cash in on it. For when they get out of the *Big Brother* house, as bizarre as it sounds, they are hotter than any A-lister; so much so that I'd rather get them in the salon during that short time-frame than a Hollywood starlet. However, their fame is short-lived, so you have to strike while the iron is hot. These new-found stars can create a paparazzi feeding frenzy unlike anything I've witnessed, and if you get one of them in, the column inches are guaranteed and the staff and clients just love it.

I particularly dread Tuesdays, when most of the celebrity

magazines come out. It is little short of torture to see the girl-of-the-moment sporting a new cut, which the media are raving about, particularly when you have the rival snipper's name thrust in your face by every appointment sitting in your chair that day as they tell you how wonderful they think it is. Worse is the client asking why they didn't come to you to have it cut. The flip-side of this of course, is when disaster strikes and a celebrity has a haircut the media hates, and then you think smugly, Thank Fuck it's not got my name on it.

Then comes the worry of whether your hard-earned reputation as 'snipper to the stars' is about to be snatched away from you by some up-and-coming new boy in town. Even worse is waking up on a Sunday morning to find a profile in one of the tabloids on one of your competitors, not only is it guaranteed to ruin your weekend, but your cherished Sunday morning shag too. This means you're straight on the phone to your – now useless – PR on Monday morning to find out why you weren't asked instead, having wailed and complained to your poor partner all weekend, who gently reminds you that a mere fortnight ago you enjoyed a double-page spread in a rival Sunday supplement. This, however, goes some small way to making you feel a little bit better, but doesn't appease for long, because that's now yesterday's fish and chip paper, you tell yourself.

Q: What do brunettes miss most about a party?
A: The invitation.

Ms A is ready to be washed, happy with the dress and shoes, thank God. My junior pulls a face from the backwash as I walk past to check on her progress – her hair is obviously mega-stinky and hasn't seen a bottle of shampoo since God was a lad. Great, that means I'll be running even later if she has to wash it three times. She could do with washing her face, too, while she's at it – there are tell-tale tidemarks around her chin. Her legs are crossed and her feet are up on our expensive leather chairs, the heels of her boots nearly ripping the fabric. I'll fucking kill her if she makes a hole in those – the last time I got them reupholstered they cost £400 each and I had to wait six months to get the bloody fabric from Japan. Do I tell her? I decide not to, but hover around, watching intently until she finally plants her stiletto heels on terra firma. No point pissing her off, or the next hour will be hell. My junior is now subtly peering into her ears, while she's enjoying a spectacular head massage. 'You could grow potatoes in those' she mouths to me cheekily, pushing the boundary a bit too far. Still, I can't help smiling, mainly because she's taken her heels off my upholstery at last.

I have another client, a TV presenter, who insists on putting her feet up on the tables in front of my mirrors. Oblivious to the worried looks of the entire salon, who are mortified at the thought of two thousand pounds' worth of chunky antique mirror crashing down on her as she chats into her mobile earpiece. Not because of her health and safety, you understand. It's the bloody cost and hassle of replacing the mirror, meaning some poor bugger won't have a section to work in and will have to 'float', using the free sections when other stylists are on their day off – every hairdresser's nightmare. Having a lockable section out of working order is a license to get all your precious equipment, carefully collated over the years swiped. Pinched by your light-fingered colleagues, never to return, nail-polished initials scratched away and miraculously replaced with the new owner's monogram.

Don't get me wrong, some of our celebrities are delightful – no trouble at all, don't expect anything much, mention me or the salon as often as they can and are wonderful clients to have. Some have the more typical dual personality, that delightful celebrity double act of ignorance and arrogance. This particular brand of personality disorder isn't assigned to mania or depression, more boredom and self-obsession. It simply hasn't occurred to Ms Feet on the Mirror that somebody has had to work hard to make the money to pay for her foot furniture – the lack of respect breathtaking. I can't blame her, when everyone around her, including me, in my own laid-back kind of way, is bowing and scraping.

She's a moody bugger, too. She really is hard work. And very intense. Conversations with her are really deep and psychological: 'Shaun, I really feel that your music should reflect more about who you are and what you want to say about yourself as a person.' Oh, piss off, I think, you're not talking to one of your reality-TV victims now, nodding sagely at her profound wisdom as if I'm discovering the meaning of life, the elixir of eternal youth and unlocking the secrets of the universe from the Dalai Lama.

Their chemical addictions are often replaced by a more dangerous one altogether, an addiction to their own image. I suppose it is inevitable that they'll start to believe that they're famous because they're really something special. And from the highest A-lister to the lowest C-lister, this tends to be the mindset, for they're all equally tricky at times. Interesting as I find all this, it's often refreshing to come back down to earth and deal with normal women whose problems revolve around satisfying their husbands and juggling careers, childcare and their own sense of self. Their visits to me are important for them. Sitting in my chair and being revitalised is often the only 'me time' in their busy schedules. Normal women don't suffer the insecurities of being in the public eye, and they're much surer of themselves than the beautiful ones tend to be; they also seem to have higher self-esteem.

The flip-side of all this adoration, from the celebrities' point of view, is that they're rarely left alone by the public, who all want them to be genuine, sincere and chatty and will be very put out if they get given the cold shoulder or catch them on an off day. One lovely daytime star I do confided that she always has the same driver to pick her up and take her to the studio.

Not, she insists, for any diva-like reasons, but because she's known him for so long she doesn't have to go through the obligatory chat and banter but can just relax in his presence, affording precious down-time and comfortable silence. This is something I hear often from celebs, and it's partly why they stay loyal to their stable of service providers. She even goes ten miles out of her way to get her car serviced, just because they know her and she doesn't have to do the celebrity patter. Stick with who you know and you're bound to feel more comfortable. I hope it's true of us snippers, too. I used to think that sort of attitude was a bit pompous and self-indulgent, but I've since come round to their way of thinking: if you surround yourself with people you know, your life will become easier and more manageable, enabling you to feel like you're not on show the whole time.

Another B-lister who has married well and fashioned herself as a regular style guru in the glossies has suspended her alcohol and drug problem long enough to deliver a son and heir to her rather fusty, serious older husband. She's been trumpeted by the press for regaining her skeletal figure faster than you can say 'lactate', when really the coke-fuelled partying sessions, the 37-week gestation and the combined caesarean tummy-tuck op are responsible. You could practically see the poor thing's skull through her non-existent bump, so it's hardly surprising she was still wearing her pre-pregnancy jeans when she was full term, and happy to pass the credit on to her personal trainer. Quite obscene really. This girl was brought (or should I say dragged) up on some gritty, Irish council estate, and now she's rather above her station, dropping her accent faster than you can open an account at Harvey Nics and trading in her rough-around-the-edges mates for Chelsea's finest. Her networking skills are second to none. Still, she has to live with herself, not me.

The last time she came in, baby in tow, my cheery receptionist, herself a new mum, leaned over the desk to coo at him, attempting to hold his chubby little hand, and was scolded by the Norland nanny: '*Don't* touch the baby! Please, she'll murder me. Nobody is allowed to *touch* the baby.'

'Didn't want to touch the bloody ugly-looking thing anyway,' my poor offended employee told me afterwards. 'Just attempting a bit of Shaun Lockes customer service, you know, being nice to the punters. Where the bloody hell does she think I'm from – the sodding leper colony?' she huffed.

'Just remember, she started on children's TV, with her hand up a fucking glove puppet's arse all day. She's just a complete media tart,' I retort sharply in an attempt to soothe her ruffled feathers.

She is as well, a lot of them are. After all, they've got the pick of the bunch. Ask any celebrity hairdresser who they do, and there are a couple of names who will appear on their list, guaranteed. Hers is bound to be one of them. 'Who does her hair?' More like, 'Who doesn't do her hair?' She makes the most ridiculous demands, like asking for a blow-dry at one hour's notice on a Sunday morning then, when you fail to oblige, she stomps off like a diva to the next poor sod until she drives him to distraction. She makes Ms A look like a pussycat. Still, everybody gets their comeuppance. I saw her at a launch party recently, and the girl on the door asked her what her name was. She replied, giving just her Christian name, through gritted, determined and very angry teeth, much to my amusement.

The professional hair-colouring market is worth nearly £515 million per annum.

It had little effect, as the girl, who clearly didn't know who she was, just said, 'Yes, but what's your surname?' Lovely stuff – I do believe in karma. Ironically, she doesn't come any more. She remains one of the few celebrities to whom I could honestly say good riddance. Whoever she's gone to – this week, for they are destined not to be flavour of the month for long – they're welcome to her.

Ms A's lunch, destined to be untouched, has arrived at my section, much to the make-up girl's despair. Doing her hair is like shooting at a moving duck on a fairground stall at the best of times. She hasn't got a hope in hell of getting her to sit still long enough to have liquid eyeliner painstakingly painted on, and we're up against the clock. I'm amazed she got here on time at all, until I find out that the only reason she did was that the magazine featuring the piece ordered a car to not only collect her, but wake her up an hour before, so scared were they that she'd ruin their very expensive shoot through her night-before antics, tales of which she is recounting to several of my stylists.

The staff like her, especially now they know her little foibles, and it's hard not to. Staff always love working in a salon where there are lots of celeb clients, although inevitably their commission suffers a bit. It's great to go home to mum and say, 'Guess who came in today.' When I was training, seeing a famous face was the highlight of my day and always made me feel I was working in the right place. Sometimes I pinch myself that this is happening in my own salon, and find myself rushing home to impress Mrs Locks with who's been in that day. It's something I never thought would come my way, that's for sure.

As she picks over her salad, I ponder over how many clients come in for their lunch. Some people are surprised to hear that catering is such big business in salons like mine; but it always has been. These days it's just more sophisticated.

When I was training, we had Winnie and Buzz. Buzz, for some unknown reason, liked to wear a yellow and black stripy jumper – I think he modelled himself on an early version of Sting – and would, if he felt adventurous, couple this with some rather fetching black tights. He was close to 6 foot tall, and spoke with a thick Tyneside accent. Winnie, his business partner, was a short, fat Scottish woman, and as distant and terse as he was close, sweaty and in your face. Winnie was a no-nonsense sort of a person. She looked and sounded like a cross between the woman in the Flash adverts and Jimmy Cranky. She didn't take any shit from anyone.

Once, she served a client a prawn salad, only to be called back two minutes later to find the ashen-faced client holding the half-eaten remains of a bright blue, blood-soaked catering plaster.

'Oh! I wondered where that had gone,' she said, grabbing it and scuttling back to the kitchen.

The stylist left his horrified client, chasing after her.

'Aren't you going to make her another one, Winnie?'

'Wassa point?' she asked, in her thick Rab C Nesbitt accent. 'She's anorexic that one, she's only going to chuck it up anyway.'

She was absolutely right, of course, we have lots of anorexic and bulimic clients. One American lady in her late fifties who comes every six weeks has a penchant for barphing down the sink and not the bloody loo, causing me to spend a fortune – more than the value of her bookings, come to think of it – on Dyno-Rod – I think that's what they call a loss leader. And you thought it was all glamour? Not a bit of it, get your sleeves rolled up and your arm down the U-Bend, if you want to make it as a star crimper.

My Brazilian lads have better customer service skills than Winnie, thank God, and more hygiene prowess than my A-lister, even though I can scarcely tell them apart. They all just keep on coming – uncles, cousins, brothers – I'll have the whole of Copacabana Beach in the kitchen soon if I'm not careful.

It's not uncommon for a salon to employ staff from all over

the globe, particularly as there's a large shortage of apprentices from this country. Most prefer to train at college, presumably because some out-of-date careers advisor is looking to get their quota of government funding, even though it's by far the worst way to learn. I would very rarely employ a college-trained hairdresser. In fact, I tend only to employ the staff I train myself. I need to know they can hack not only the pace and the clients' demands, but the standard of work. Good salons will send their apprentices off to local colleges on day release to gain their NVQ qualifications, although the standards of teaching are often appalling, while the experience of working on a salon floor and learning hands-on through an apprenticeship can never be replicated.

We employed a Spanish boy to train as an apprentice a few years ago, even though his English was dire – he made Manuel from *Fawlty Towers* sound like Stephen Fry. He was so eager to learn, he was like an over-enthusiastic Andrex puppy.

On his second week, my regular junior was on holiday and I reluctantly agreed that he could help me for the morning.

'Go and get some Velcro rollers, Antonio,' I instructed slowly.

'Green ones, you understand?'

He nodded silently, beaming nervously at me, while remaining rooted to the spot.

I told him again and finally, he scuttled off purposefully – in the wrong direction.

He was gone for an eternity. 'Where the hell did he go?' I asked another stylist. The rollers were only by the window; hairdressers are notoriously lazy, ordering our minions to do the slightest of tasks. Many will get a junior to hold hair for them if there are enough staff in, instead of using sectioning clips. Dreadful, I know, but guilty as charged, my Lord.

Two seconds later, I could see him scurrying towards me like a rat out of an aqueduct, desperate to please, proudly presenting me with a bottle of Highland Spring fizzy water on a tray.

'You', I told him, 'are a waste of space.' I was tempted to rap his forehead with my comb, Basil style, as he gazed intently into my eyes, worried that he'd got it wrong again. He did – frequently. Heated rollers? I got a cappuccino. A mug of tea? Curling tongs. In fact, it wasn't until he grudgingly admitted he couldn't understand a word I said that we started to get along. Ironically, his English is much better now and he's still with me. He's good, too.

In fact, he's my stand in for Ms A, who has now, finally, got clean hair and is sitting in my chair, ready to be beautified.

My internal line buzzes. It is my salon manager, and he sounds as if his feathers are ruffled, which is rare for him.

He whispers some very, very bad news down the line to me.

Ms A's rival is just about to walk in for a beauty appointment. Shit. This happens a lot. My salon manager is like the maître d' of a good restaurant, he keeps the peace and ensures most of our valued clients are oblivious to the behind-the-scene shenanigans going on. Ms A fell out with Mrs B when she nicked Ms A's boyfriend, and worse, went off and married him. As if that weren't enough, they are now both up for the same movie role, and they abhor one another. Even he's going to have to work some magic to keep these two apart. The sparks will fly and they'll kick off, the shoot will fuck up, and worse, both of them will call me and tell me that they 'won't be able to carry on coming, which is such a shame, because I love your salon, Shaun, but how could you do this to me? *You know* how I feel about her . . . and I thought you valued me way above her.' It will be celebrity kindergarten, and if I'm not bloody careful I'll lose both of them.

'Don't worry, Shaun, I'll walk her through the other side,

just turn you chair round, and whatever you do, don't let her face the mirror.' We've been through this routine before many times. Usually it's because of some secretary bumping into the wife, or worse, the ex-wife coming face to face with her younger, slimmer, prettier replacement. We are expert at manoeuvring them around like dodgems at a fairground, and usually they never know what's going on. It's a little harder when you've got some newly discovered celeb coming in for five hours' worth of hair extensions, as happened recently, especially when their new boyfriend is sitting there for the duration like a love-sick puppy and his ex comes in for a lengthy colour appointment. The keep-them-apart game gets a little frantic then, and the hordes of paparazzi outside don't help.

HAIR FACTS

On average we have between 100,000 and 150,000 hairs on our heads. It is normal to lose between 70 and 100 per day. People with naturally blonde hair have an average of 140,000 hairs on their heads; brunettes have 100,000 and redheads have 80-90,000.

Worse is keeping the journos away from the A-listers who are so A-list they're really *not* in it for the publicity, like girl-friends of the young aristos. If some newshound spots them in the salon and puts a call through to one of the dailies, I am left reassuring an anxious mother that I'm not snitching on her daughter's custom in order to increase my profile, and am often left praying that she believes me, for they are clients I'd never want to piss off, with their social connections.

The worst one used to occur regularly. The whole love triangle were my clients – I did the secretary, the husband *and* the wife. All insisted on coming to me, and even though it was one of the rare occasions when I wholeheartedly recommended they go somewhere else, they never would. It was like juggling hot coals. The wife would come in, questioning me about whether her husband ever gave anything away or let anything slip, as she seemed to sense what was going on, and while she was in the cloakroom putting her gown back, the secretary would arrive, sneaking past her, with the husband waiting in the café across the road, peering though the windows until the coast was clear to come in for his cut. Quite why they all seemed to come on the same day bewildered me. He must have got thoroughly turned on by the whole thing. Although the wife came for a blow-dry at least three times a week, the adulterous duo never actually had the nerve to ask our manager when she was booked, trying to make out that nothing was going on. This left him in the awkward position of not being able to be honest with them and explain that she was going to be there when they called to schedule.

What is it with men and secretaries? The worst example of this game of salon musical chairs was the woman who came to me regularly, and used to confide in me about her husband's suspected infidelity with his beautiful, young, glamorous PA. At the same time, across the salon, she spotted the young thing, who was busy showing off the latest gift – a very nice piece of jewellery that was sure to have bolstered his company expense account. She was busy boasting to her stylist what a good boss he was, and what a tender, thoughtful lover he made. The ensuing cat fight was not a pretty sight, I can assure you, with the girlfriend being escorted by her stylist through the staff entrance in floods of tears, while the wife was comforted by me with a complimentary glass of house champagne.

Ms A hasn't noticed her ex-friend, so I'm in the clear for now. Mrs B is going into the treatment rooms for some waxing and a pedicure, so I can breathe again. I won't mention it to the fashion stylist, or her nervous, angry red rash will get so bad she'll start coming out in hives. Her neck is now puce, as she worries about the dress which is now splattered with mayonnaise from the club sandwich that was pushed to one side after a bird-like peck at its contents. Our star client, of course, is oblivious – grease-stained silk just isn't her problem. Even at home, it would be just another item on her secretary's to-do list. But a dress borrowed for a shoot? She wouldn't even give it a second thought.

I tell the crew I'm on a deadline, desperate for them not to miss the only time I have free in my carefully manoeuvred column. Can't we just bloody get on with it? Camera men, make-up artists, fashion stylists – rarely do they work on paying clients. They have yet to grasp the concept of the word 'appointment' and that, as a hairdresser working a column, time is my commodity. Their slot with me is now almost over, and they are still standing about drinking Diet Coke and texting on their mobiles, as if they have all the time in the world, which, being their only gig of the week, they probably do. Still, it could have been worse. Sometimes on a studio shoot they'd be ordered to arrive at 9 a.m., actually turning up at 10, then commence a long leisurely breakfast – the studios always provide top-notch catering facilities, and some other poor sod picks up the tab – before finally getting round to starting work at 1 p.m.; just as lunch is delivered. It's 3 p.m. by the time anything is in the can, and then it's a frantic rush to get it all done, and everybody is still there at 10 p.m. It drives me, crazy. I just can't bear wasting time like that – time, for me, is money.

Because they mostly do freelance, and this is bound to be one of the only bookings they've got all week, coupled with the fact that they're all getting paid by the hour, it's inevitable that they'll drag it out as long as possible. In fact, I'm probably the only one who isn't getting paid here. As they're using the salon as a location, they don't feel they need to cough up for me as I'm getting valuable publicity out of the whole exercise. Ms A probably won't be getting any dosh either – as her next career move is going to be based solely on what exposure she's been getting, she's no doubt waived her normal fee to ensure she gets the next gig she's so desperate for. Next time you look at all those beautifully shot articles in the Sunday supplements, you'll now realise it's all the publicity machines working in motion to produce the final result.

Inevitably, I get bossy and take control of shoots like these, conscious of the fact that if I run late my day is fucked and I won't eat until tonight, which is no good for my digestion or my yet-to-be-diagnosed ulcer/irritable bowel syndrome. I grab my Velcro rollers and set to work. It's crucial to see her in make-up and dress to figure out a look that will work with the rest of her styling. Many successful hairdressers go on to be photographers, and it doesn't surprise me, although it's not something that particularly interests me as there's too much buggering about. I might be artistic, or autistic as my wife jokes, but I like to see some viable commercial success. The thought of hanging around all day waiting for everyone to get their shit together fills me with dread. I'm far too anxious and impatient.

At least I'm not having to do catwalk hair – my biggest nightmare. Fashion shows are notorious for being disorganised and stressful for the hairdressers involved. Not only does the brief for the hair change at the designer's whim – e.g. we've packed all the necessary tools for floaty, dreamy natural hair and suddenly it has to be funky and androgynous at two minutes' notice – but the emaciated models are too busy munching on a lettuce-leaf lunch, puffing on never-ending cigarettes and drinking copious cans of Red Bull to keep their energy levels up that backstage tempers are seriously frayed before us lowly hairdressers are allowed to get anywhere near them. Even when the credits are checked four times in the show programme, we're bound to be missed off; our hair genius demoted and praise heaped on the designer as they take their customary end-of-runway bow.

Luckily, that's a dim and distant memory today as Ms A's hair goes like a dream. When it's clean, it's a delight to work with, just as she is when she's happy. She wants volume, so we joosh her up with some scrunching and backcombing to give her a sexy, girl-next-door look. Tousled and pouting, no wonder she looks like a screen goddess when she glistens out at you from magazine covers. I think of the filthy pants and realise that things aren't always what they seem.

There is a touching vulnerability to Ms A, for all her bravado. She's actually quite insecure and tells me she's desperate to be in a steady relationship, of which she has little hope, because normal men like me tend to run a mile from women like her. Do I fancy her? No, not a bit. Needy just doesn't do it for me. I steer well clear of emotional entanglement with on-the-edge women; in my single days I had enough girlfriends like that to last me a lifetime. Nowadays, for all my flirty patter and banter, I'm all mouth and no trousers.

Teenagers and young men in their twenties are most likely to dye their hair blonde.

Not that Ms A would ever try it on with me. There are very few clients I meet that I fancy any more, and if I do it's strictly on a shop-window basis. Ms A is a nice girl at heart, and I do hope she meets her Prince Charming one day, although I can't see her finding anyone who'd be able to put up with her demanding ways.

Some privileged women tend to be like that; I see it often with my wealthy or famous clients. They also tend to have no sense of waste. I suppose if somebody has never been poor or had to work hard, they wouldn't. I don't think it's her fault, she's lived a life of wealth and luxury and then become famous and been fawned over as a celebrity. We cater to some very rich women. They have the sort of wealth that means they leave Chanel watches in the loo without even realising. Other things that have been left in our cloakroom include a Joseph Sheepskin coat, a Hermès scarf, a pair of diamond earrings, a Gucci belt and some D&G sunglasses. Don't they notice that something is missing? That they've left something behind? Still, it's great for an end-of-year share-out amongst the management team.

Such extravagance is other-worldly to me. In half term, when the children are off school, the yummy mummies bring their little darlings in, ordering them sandwiches and fresh milkshakes while their hair is being trimmed, only for them to leave half the contents on the styling section. My Mum would have made me eat up everything she'd paid for, and I suppose therein the difference lies.

Shoot over, Ms A gets back into her jeans. She finally decides to talk to the poor, emotionally drained girl she's been ignoring all day. I realise that she's only doing this to pre-empt the call her assistant will make the following day to the dress designer's agent, by making sure she leaves some heavy hints about how much she just adored the dress in the hope it will find its way into her wardrobe as a permanent fixture. Knowing her, it will. I check my watch, which hasn't gone unnoticed by my clients – I've had lots of admiring glances. Mrs B is now halfway through a Rose Oil Body Massage, so there's no chance they'll meet up. They'll be ships that pass in the night. I breathe a huge sigh of relief, remembering the worst collision course I ever had to deal with.

Once, the fiancé of a world-famous entrepreneur introduced him to her married friend at a dinner party, only for the two of them to run off together, much to the disgrace of London society at the time. The beautiful fiancé was left bewildered and shattered, but not so shattered that she gave back her ice diamond – stunned that her betrothed had done such an obvious U-turn. He married her newly divorced friend, who controversially left her children to go and live

with him in a different country. The two remained apart for
years – every social function was carefully engineered to keep
the warring women at bay – only for them to meet, finally, at
my bloody salon.

Worse, they had consecutive appointments with the same
stylist, who inevitably lost the clientele of both.

'How the hell did that happen?' I barked at the new, inexperienced receptionist, a lovely Essex girl who'd made the
booking, clearly oblivious to the finite intricacies of élite
London society.

'I didn't bloody know she nicked her boyfriend, did I? They
ain't on the telly or nothing, are they?' She told me, dropping
her aitches in a way she never would on telephone duty.

'Oh and you may as well find out now, get all the shit over
and done with like, the bloody *Daily Mail* phoned up and
asked me about it, too. Don't worry, I didn't say nothing
much. Just told 'em the truth of what happened, that she
called her a money-grabbing bitch and the other one told 'er
at least she got a ring on her finger. We all saw it, so
I thought it best to be honest.'

Great. No, I've had quite enough of all that.

Ms A leaves the salon with a wave, paparazzi
waiting as ever. She's happy to be papped today,
make-up fresh and hair beautifully styled from
the shoot, but she can't show it. She postures the
'Leave me alone, I'm only human' stance, coat
clasped across her chest and head down, Dior
sunglasses wrapped firmly around her eyes. Phew!
The worst bit of my day is over.

I am just settling down with my salad lunch –
still trying to keep the near-forties paunch at bay
– when my line buzzes.

'Shaun, Ms A on line one for you.' This can't be
good. Why on earth is she calling when I've only
just said goodbye to her?

She's put through.

'Shaun, I can't believe you're so mean to me. That hideous little man that sells the *Big Issue* has told me that Mrs B was in at the same time as me. How could you? I just don't think I'll be able to come in again, you know how I feel about that *bitch*!'

Oh, shit. The bloody *Big Issue* guy.

Serves me right for not dealing with him months ago. Now, the remainder of my snatched lunch break will be spent soothing her fragile ego and trying to get myself out of the shit . . .

Countdown to the top 20 crap salon names

20. Beyond the Fringe
19. Hairport
18. Hairloom
17. Razor's Edge
16. Snippers
15. Hair Necessity
14. Hair Affair
13. Hair's Looking at You...
12. Head Masters
11. Burke & Hair
10. Barber Blacksheep
9. Barber'ellas
8. Hair We Go
7. A Cut Above
6. Have it off!
5. Headquarters
4. Shortcuts
3. Cutting Edge
2. Curl Up and Dye
1. Scissors Palace

Chapter 6

3 p.m. —
Downtime: the editor

There have been some pretty scuzzy types in the hairdressing industry, and with the distinct lack of business brains shown by most of the creative types I meet, I realised I needed financial expertise behind me to allow me to concentrate on being the front man. That's where my salon manager and secretary come in. They actually run the business for me, leaving me free to pursue my dizzy quest for fame. We've been a working trio for over ten years now, and our personalities fit together like a pyramid puzzle. Each one's strength is another's weakness. I'm very lucky to have such a loyal team. They may crunch the numbers, but I never make the mistake of not knowing exactly what those numbers are, even if learning the business side has been difficult for me.

While my salon manager deals with the clients and staff if I'm not around, he also keeps more than a passing eye on reception to ensure calls are answered swiftly and that customer service is as good as it should be. People tend to use him as the first line of defence for any problems they have, with only serious concerns or decisions reaching my ears. My secretary, on the other hand, deals with all the admin. And there's shit loads of it, with the number of staff I have: stock orders, appraisals, interviews, holiday rotas, you name it, it falls on her. Most hairdressers I know have a morbid fear of paperwork and hyperventilate if they have to deal with any kind of admin, so having an office manager is essential. In fact, pen and paper have been known to bring me out in a rash.

I do get involved with the day-to-day running of the salon, and like to be aware of any issues that need to be addressed, so we try and fit some downtime into my column every day to run through what's happening in the business. Normally, it's non-crucial issues like Lady F is nicking the loo rolls and paper hand towels again – 'They are simply *marvellous* for dusting! Mrs Collins the housekeeper likes me to keep her stocked up' – she says as she stuffs another £20 worth into her Hermès Birkin.

Or Ms S-C is trying to pay by cheque again. She refuses to pay any other way, the bank having taken back all her debit cards, and this leads to a massive amount of paper-chasing – 'I can assure you they *never* ask me for my cheque guarantee card in Fortnum's; they know me there!' Despite her assurances, it will probably bounce and cost us bank charges.

Or Mrs P is trying to say she didn't have extra lights and a toner, and even though she's going through a messy divorce and is fighting for every penny, she has actually had it all done. 'Your prices really don't seem to keep in line with inflation, do they?' she says, or, 'I only had a trim, not a cut!' This is a real bugbear for us hairdressers, as it takes as long to trim as it does to cut – the amount of hair you cut off is irrelevant, as you still have to do the same amount of sectioning, etc.

Thankfully, it's usually about trivial matters such as staff lateness, booking problems, customer comments or admin problems like bounced cheques. (One of the restaurants I frequent doesn't take credit cards, but has a unique way of protecting itself against the retailer's bane, bounced cheques: they name and shame them by papering their cloakroom area and loos with the offending cheques, all marked 'refer to drawer'.)

Most women who colour their hair opt for permanent colour (40 per cent) followed by highlights (17 per cent).

A lot of our wealthy clients leave their credit card details on file with us so their trust-fund offspring can come in for a regular haircut. We had one client who was furious with us for giving her twenty-five-year-old son the details of the card – he asked; how were we to know. He went on a mammoth spending spree, not only with us, which was fantastic business as he treated all his top totty or anyone he'd pulled in Chinawhite to our top-to-toe days and the full Monty – colour, manicure, pedicure, lunch, highlights – but unfortunately he racked up some mega hotel bills, not to mention some gastronomic feasts at most of London's top restaurants. She was incredibly angry with us, but hardly bothered to mention it to her son. This same client is probably our wealthiest – and our nicest, unless we fuck up over her bookings – her fingers are literally laden with diamonds the size of ice cubes, and she's very generous with the tips, especially at Christmas.

In the Christmases of old, when people really did splash out on their regular stylists, we used to get some amazing presents. Christmas week in the late eighties would result in the juniors notching up a good £100 in tips, and that wasn't including the presents, for we got all sorts of goodies, Armani wallets, cashmere socks, fantastic aftershave, the lot. But that was nothing in comparison to what the stylists used to take home, literally by the taxi load, day after day over the Christmas working period. Now I am no longer deemed tippable, I'm lucky if I get the odd bottle of champers, and very welcome it is too, I'll have you know. In fact, Christmas costs me dear. First, there's the staff party to arrange – always in January as December is just too busy – then there are all the presents for the staff themselves – everybody gets champagne and the managers and juniors get a bonus – and this is before we've even got around to splashing out on the journalists. They get

Less hair to cut, but more face to wash . . .
Unknown — on going bald

treated to a tasteful monogrammed little something, all discreetly designed to remind them of what it's all about.

There's usually never anything really business-threatening
to ponder in our meetings. Today we discuss, again, another
notorious client of ours who, even though she books a standing appointment weekly and spends a fortune at the salon, is
a tad light-fingered. She, of course, thinks we don't know this.
She is also a doctor, a title she uses with alarming frequency –
no doubt she thinks it gives her extra credibility. The juniors
come and tell me that she has pinched various items every time
she comes in – salon-sized backwash treatments, travel-sized
hairsprays, and worse, testers off the make-up stand. She nicks
more testers off that stand than we get given by the product
company. Every week she takes a lipstick over to the window
to see what it looks like in the daylight only for it to never be
seen again, distracting the beautician with a request for a particular magazine while she sneaks it into her handbag. I think
she's harmless and refuse to do anything about it, even though
her Artful Dodger stealing skills are constantly debated at our
meetings. She spends a fortune with us, and no doubt she con-
siders it her little privilege. As long as she's spending the
money, I'm willing to turn a blind eye. I find it all faintly
amusing and we have an unspoken agreement, via lengthy eye
contact. She knows I know and we leave it at that. I think she
may have a psychological need to steal, like some Hollywood
celebrities. She should know, she's the doctor.

We also chat about the behaviour of one of our famous
clients, who is getting a tad erratic. One of my senior stylists
was sent to her house the other day for a home visit. It is customary to charge a multiple of the salon price for any private
visits during salon hours, plus travelling time and expenses. It
is therefore a privilege normally only reserved for the exceed-
ingly wealthy or those who aren't picking up the tab, but
billing either their production company or the TV station.

On this particular occasion, she wanted something different
on her normal chestnut mane, waving a picture off the catwalk

under the nose of the stylist and demanding he replicate a particular curly look. This he did, painstakingly inserting roller by roller and expertly whooshing it with some styling spritz and a shot from the dryer, section by section. Ninety minutes into coiffing his creation, his glamorous client got up and, without saying a word, dunked her hair under the bathroom shower attachment, soaking his creation into an unrecognisable mess. Seething, she screamed, 'I hate it, I hate it, I HATE IT!' before calmly taking her place back on the stool, hair now damp and ready to start again. 'It's so *last year*!' she hissed through gritted teeth, before picking up her copy of *Vogue* and demanding he start again, coiffing her straight this time. We agree she's becoming a bit of a liability, and wonder whether a bad bout of PMT got the better of her or she was just using the poor crimper as an emotional punch-bag. Funnily, she has never again mentioned the incident, her bizarre antics eradicated from her memory. Not from ours, though.

God knows what might happen next time she wants a colour change. We all agree not to do anything radical should her flighty whims leave us with a problem that's not as easy to erase as a few rollers.

Next, it's our weekly rundown of miscellaneous items.

'Can we have a model night on head lice, Shaun?' I'm asked.

Model night is our weekly training evening for our juniors – my hairdressers of tomorrow.

'Why, what this time?' I sigh.

'One of the technicians had a woman in for a root tint the other day, and as they were running behind they got their junior to start off. By the time they got over to the client the junior was halfway through, and her scalp was fucking crawling with the bastards. They had no bloody option but to carry on until it was finished. The poor woman was in floods after she'd been rinsed off and told she couldn't stay for the cut and blow-dry.'

We've had this before. The little critters aren't easy to spot. The whitish yellowy eggs stick to the hair and look like a bad bout of dandruff, until you realise they won't come off the hair shaft. They're so bloody contagious we have to incinerate the gown used, and destroy the towels and banish anyone who

has them from the salon instantly. Even the most refined of society ladies with school-age children are prone to a 'little visit' as we call it, now and then. And the nanny is always the one who's bound to get it in the neck for putting madam in that situation in the first place. If you have more than one hairdresser peering into your scalp for longer than a minute, you can normally guarantee what's coming. Either that, or you've got some weird sort of alopecia that you hadn't spotted. Either way, you can pretty much start to panic.

This leads me to the next hairdressing enigma, sterilising the equipment. Brushes, combs and all the tools used on you by your hairdresser should technically be washed in unpleasant-smelling disinfectant after every client. I can tell you now, this is rarely the case in any salon I've ever been in. Brushes are lucky to be washed weekly, and the disinfectant bottle sits on the shelf, gathering dust, its presence only required for the odd health and safety checks from the local council. I'd love to know the sales figures for Barbicide, they'd make very interesting reading. You're lucky if the average hairdresser gets rid of yesterday's hair in the brush before it finds its way into your beautifully cleansed mane, let alone get it washed in disinfectant. As for combs, they very rarely see a trip to the sterilising fluid. Rollers? Forget it. I can't remember the last time they were washed. Curling tongs? Have you ever looked at all the brown muck burned onto the inside of the barrel? This is heated-on product remains, not burnt hair, by the way. Same goes for heated rollers. We try to make sure we meet acceptable standards for hygiene, although I'm sure most salons are far from what you'd call squeaky clean. In fact, speaking from experience, the more of a reputation the salon has for being fabulous, the less likely its staff are to be concerned about hygiene, although things are bound to get litigious sooner or later. At the rate all these regulations are moving, I can see the day when red tape and legislation is going to call for disposable brushes and equipment.

There's also the fact that some clients are plain dirty. Once I did a woman whose hair literally made me gag. Her scalp was so encrusted with dermatitis I was unable to comb it. As I tried to section it, the comb got stuck in yellow layers of skin. If I tugged, great flakes of scalp landed in my lap, like huge layers of flaky pastry. It was terrible. It must be the worst cut I've ever done, as all I was able to do was trim up the length without combing it so it was perfectly smooth and straight. That was one time I did head for the Barbicide bottle, pronto.

This universal disregard for hygiene, of course, goes largely unnoticed by the great British public. The same cannot always be said for some of our clients . . .

Poor Ethel, our cloakroom lady, has never let me forget one experience. A young Italian guy came in to book a walk-in haircut. Although the majority of our business is pre-booked, the odd walk-in client is great as we can normally find somebody to fit them in, even if the salon is full. This guy checked in, then immediately asked where the toilets were. We found one of our Italian stylists to cut his hair, as the guy didn't speak very good English, who stood at reception with a gown, waiting for him to come out so he could start. After five minutes there was still no sign of life from the loo, but lots of straining noises were audible through the walls. Ethel was listening out for him as the stylist, fed up of waiting, retired to the staff room for a coffee, telling reception to call him if he ever emerged.

I was working away on one of my regulars when Ethel

came up. I knew this meant trouble as Ethel rarely leaves the cloakroom, even having her lunch in there sometimes as she doesn't want to miss a tip. In fact, I'm convinced Ethel earns more than me. She's very canny and has a trick of taking any silver out of her tip dish, leaving only a handful of pound coins. This is very carefully planned, and she never lets it fill up or get lower than this. The reason she does so is to embarrass people into feeling that if everybody else has left a pound, they must too. She's no fool. I call her my Thoroughbred, as she's often to be found peering out of her stable-style cloakroom door like a horse.

'Mr Lockes,' she says. 'I think you'd better come with me.'

I excuse myself from my client, dreading what I'm going to find.

Ethel is babbling on . . . 'And you see he just walked in for a trim. Well, we weren't to know what he was up to, were we? He's been in there a bleeding lifetime, and I didn't like to knock, cos it's rude innit. Course he buggered off when we wasn't looking, otherwise I'd 'ave given him a piece of me mind.'

The sight that greeted me was one I will never forget. Watery shit was smeared all over the walls, ceiling and floor. There was literally tons of it and the smell was so vile, I can still remember it today. It took poor old Ethel and me hours to clear it up. I didn't feel I could ask anyone else to do it, and Ethel felt so bad, as if she was in some way responsible, that she insisted on helping me. No matter how much disinfectant we used, the smell lingered for weeks. All that, and he hadn't even bloody paid for a haircut. I still wonder what on earth he could have eaten to produce so much shit. Amazing.

See what we're up against? And still we smile.

When I was training, my stylist used to say to me, 'Whenever you have a really difficult, awkward client, always imagine her sitting on the loo, having a shit. It'll work every time.' And it does. I offer the little pearl of wisdom to my reception team regularly, especially when the notorious Mrs X is about.

Back to our meeting. There's another problem, says my sec-retary – the new Thai manicurist, cruelly christened Ting Tong (I suppose I am her Mr Dudley). Somebody has been winding her up, and I bet I know who – my sadistic artistic director has a wicked sense of humour. The poor girl speaks hardly any English and is related to our original Thai manicurist, who has shipped in various cousins, nieces, etc. from Bangkok. I had heard via a reliable source that he was in the staff room telling her what to say when people say good morning to her.

My secretary continues, 'Well, somebody has been teaching her to say "Bruddy fucking awful, Madam," with a beaming smile and a bow. She said it to Baroness Mountcroft the other day, who came and complained to me. I asked the poor girl why on earth she was speaking to clients like that, and she burst into tears and said she'd been told it was the correct grammatical reply.'

He's such a bugger. It's his ultimate party trick, teaching awful English sayings to the new foreign members of staff. It does make me laugh.

Our downtime invariably descends into a good old gossip about our competitors – whose salon is in the shit financially, whose is busy, whose is quiet, whose is about to undergo mass walk-out, whose star player is planning to open up yards down the road, completely unbeknown to his boss. It's like the wife being the last one to find out about the affair. As all of this talk gives me an attack of the collywobbles, worrying whether it will happen to me one day, I decide to change the subject and talk about something more fun.

There is a famous client whose wife has a notoriously bad boob job. One of Meredith's PR girls actually told me about this, and at a recent dinner party I got the chance to see it for myself.

She told me that as a teenager she used to go on holiday with the couple, who were friendly with her parents, and the woman's left tit used to twitch furiously. The implant must have got stuck behind a nerve or something, as it used to sit there, ticking away like some cartoon bomb.

This lady is famously fond of wearing dangerously low-cut evening dresses, so at this recent event, I was able to see the twitching mammary gland in all its finery. It did, indeed, spend the entire evening attempting to twitch free from the restraints of the dress, blinking at me like a belisha beacon. This vital business information is imparted to my key staff – and to several of my mates in the hairdressing fraternity, for I am, it has to be said, a dreadful gossip – to howls of delight.

I have had to temper my overwhelming desire to suppress the good old gossip gene, and have trained myself to keep a secret. I still don't find it easy and tend to spill the beans a little too often, so I've learned the knack of never using real names in a bid to control my freedom of speech. If I get caught ever being openly indiscreet, my credibility will be shot to pieces.

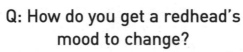

Q: How do you get a redhead's mood to change?
A: Wait ten seconds.

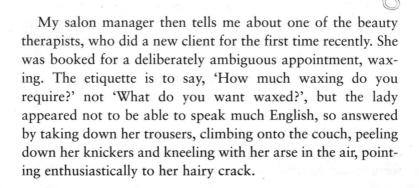

My salon manager then tells me about one of the beauty therapists, who did a new client for the first time recently. She was booked for a deliberately ambiguous appointment, waxing. The etiquette is to say, 'How much waxing do you require?' not 'What do you want waxed?', but the lady appeared not to be able to speak much English, so answered by taking down her trousers, climbing onto the couch, peeling down her knickers and kneeling with her arse in the air, pointing enthusiastically to her hairy crack.

'What did she say?' I ask him, collapsing with giggles.

'We're not licensed for the chocolate starfish, Madam,' he joked. At least, I hope he joked.

The poor therapists really do get a bum deal. Not only do they have to attend to the less than savoury contents of client's anuses, they have to deal with the most unbelievable staff medical problems, too. One of our stylists was in a treatment room the other day having a rather nasty testicular boil lanced. The poor therapist was so fed up of hearing the constant barrage of winging over the offending intruder that she offered to hold a tablespoon over a boiling kettle and try to get the horrible thing to explode. Talk about beyond the call of duty.

Cultivating team spirit in a salon is vital, and our meetings are a great team-building exercise. When I was training, my big bosses still didn't know my name by the time I was in the second year of my apprenticeship. They would swan in late and chuck the keys to their latest Porsche at the most senior junior, telling them to go and feed their meters all day. We were the scummy minions, only essential for our shampooing prowess and to fetch and carry for them. Sometimes, you got tricks played on you, like being sent out to buy some tartan or stripy paint. Still, better than being sent out for a tube of KY Jelly for your gay stylist, which one of the straight, innocent and totally unaware apprentices was sent on an errand for.

As long as we were there to shampoo, nobody seemed to give a shit about our training, except perhaps the stylist we were assigned to. They often volunteered to stay behind and teach us, and you could learn a lot just by watching them work; it was a like a full-on training session every day. There was no structure or plan to running their business, though, and that's where I wanted to be different. Right from the start I wanted to do everything right, to reward people and motivate them, to run a slick operation. However, I've learned a cautionary lesson – only invest in them once they've earned their stripes and your respect, as most juniors leave quite quickly after starting, simply because they can't hack the tiring, full-on hairdressing day.

I wouldn't say my climb – it was more like a slow, laborious ascent – to the top has been ruthless, but it has been a struggle having my own business. I remember going to see a clairvoyant and she told me that I would be starting with a huge business. At the time I wondered what she meant, but in my early twenties everything became clear. My hazardous path to the top had begun. My warring bosses had finally 'divorced' and after a series of very dodgy changes of hands, the receivers asked if I wanted to buy it. Hence I bought out a bankrupt salon; the one I had trained in. It had been bled dry and needed massive re-investment and turning around, and so, nerve-wrackingly, I started big, as some of the original team were still there and were willing to give me a chance. Fate, or Lady Luck, had turned in my favour.

Of course, not knowing anything about finances, I had to buy in that particular area of expertise, but I soon spotted where to find it. The cerebral help that was to prove so vital was working alongside me. My secretary was one of the salon receptionists, and I'd always thought her financial skills and organisational talent were wasted making bookings. Of course, this had all been totally overlooked by the previous salon owners. Had they utilised and developed her skills, they probably never would have gone bust in the first place.

I soon found out that 'starting big' involved getting the salon to run at a profit, and that meant dispensing with life's little luxuries, like having a salon cleaner. For the first five years, I got in an hour early to mop the floor myself. The salon I'd worked in had swung from making profit to loss in a matter of months. And they didn't have any of the scams going that the more unscrupulous subsequent salon owners of old did, like crossing out whole days of bookings to make the tax-man think they hadn't worked that day and so they could pocket the cash themselves. They'd merely lost a few key players, the bosses had fallen out and bingo, the free-for-all vibe swept through the place like wildfire.

All of a sudden, stock was disappearing left, right and centre, which meant there was none for the clients. There is a magnitude of hair colours, with most salons stocking at least four different ranges, each containing about sixty colours. It's not much fun going to the dispensary (mixing room) to find there's nothing there. It then becomes a mass-panic to get out, staff and clients alike, and this is what I'd bought into: a business that had the remnants of some decent staff to build upon but was losing money hand over fist, as well as gaining a reputation with product suppliers for never being able to pay its bills. It would be a good five years before I treated myself to Jimmy, my cleaner. In the meantime, it was all about 'cutting my cloth' as my accountant said. Gone were the hired towels – at £3,000 a month in the early nineties you can see the problem. As lovely as it was to have all the salon's towels delivered at 8 a.m. and collected at 7 p.m., it was an extortionate amount of money to pay. Much cheaper to get down to Comet and buy two washing machines and dryers, then buy your own towels.

* * * *

'*I*'ve had a phone call from Lucas's head receptionist.' My secretary brings me back to the here and now of our meeting.

'There's a 'nut-nut' on the loose – she's told me to watch out.' Blimey, here we go again.

Nut-nut is the official expression we use in the salon for somebody who has no intention of paying, whatever happens. We've had them in various guises, and this one sounded like a corker.

'Apparently she's a young Eastern European woman, who

pretends not to be able to speak any English. She spent a whole day at Lucas's spa, having over £400 worth of stuff done, and when it came to the bill, she pretended she didn't have the right cards with her. He let her go to the cashpoint, leaving her handbag as security, only to find, when she didn't return after a couple of hours, that it was stuffed with a brick and various brochures for the top salons in the country, one of which was ours.'

Poor Lucas, for once in my life I can sympathise with him.

Just then, my internal line rings. It's reception, and from the background noise it sounds like chaos.

'Shaun, you'd better come down, right now.'

The meeting is abruptly closed and I get my salon manager to come with me.

A woman is sobbing and shaking, and it looks like she's hyperventilating, with the whole of my front-of-house team scowling at her.

'Don't let that fool you, Shaun,' barks one of my receptionists, unsympathetically. I shoot her a murderous look for such shoddy standards of client care, just about to comfort the poor woman and find out what was wrong.

'And don't worry, she doesn't speak any English, well, according to her anyway,' she continues, haughtily.

'What the bloody hell is going on – somebody explain!!!' I growl, about to famously lose it, as I am prone to do at times of stress.

We hardly ever get complaints and on the rare occasion we do, I expect a little bit more in the customer relations department than this!

'She's been here all day – had every sodding treatment under the sun, and now she's pretending she doesn't understand English, and that she only has Amex and needs to go to the bank and get some money out.'

'So, what are you being so hard on her for?!' I shout.

'See for yourself!' She passes me a very cheap, plastic, fake leather handbag, and smugly informs me to peer inside.

There, I find the delightful sight of a run-of-the-mill house brick.

'My friend Sandra works at Lucas's and she told me about their little incident when we were out for a drink the other night, so when she gave me her acted-out sob story I got suspicious and checked out the bag for evidence. Don't worry, Shaun, the rozzers are coming. I wish I'd have trusted my intuition – I didn't like the look of her when she came in. I knew she was trouble,' she said.

'Well done, girls,' I grudgingly mutter, although what I'm praising them for, I don't know. I'll never get my bloody money back on the bitch. 'What's the damage?'

'You won't like it, Shaun. Don't ask – she's been drinking champagne since 9 a.m. and she's had the whole bloody lot done, and we've fitted her in for extras, too. Leave it to us, don't get involved. Go out and have a fag to calm down. The police said she's been doing it all over London, and that's not all – she's done all the health farms too. They say this is the first time anyone's actually caught her, let alone detained her, so she's going down,' she states proudly.

As Churchill famously said, 'Keep buggering on.' I contemplate the treat of drawing in a deep lug of deliciously forbidden Marlboro as I watch the police arrive to escort the howling woman for a night in the Met's finest accommodation.

As I'm pushing open the heavy swing doors to get out into the London gloom, Binty jumps out of a cab.

'Shaun, I left my sunglasses.'

Shame, about four of the staff had their eye on those, I think.

'Oh *crapola*, I'm so late. My editor-in-chief kept me at the office for simply ages – I'm so glad you're here still, I'm on my way to the Louboutin Boutique launch; I need to speak to you. Does my hair still look OK? Thanks so much, by the way, lots of compliments from the gals back at the mag.'

Binty waffles on, like something out of an Enid Blyton novel, all lashings of ginger-beer and gung-ho jolly hockey sticks.

She continues, stuffing the sunglasses into her Dior trench pocket.

'Anyway, you're just the man I need. The Ed's in tears, that rotten bloody man has ruined her hair, and he's supposed to be the hair guru! He'd only just flown in, too, maybe he was jet-lagged. Still, it looks dreadful – I mean, even I can see it's not straight. Look, if you've got any nouce whatsoever, you'll get your arse over there right now and sort her out. She's livid and it's not a pretty sight, and her regular hairdresser Lucas is busy, his receptionist tells us, meeting with a product company or something, so I said I'd be sure you'd go over and help.'

Quietly trying to contain my excitement, I realise that sometimes the freebies really do pay off. Binty has come up with the proverbial cookies and I'm getting a golden opportunity to nick the adulation of one of Stamford Street's finest; and all right under the nose of my nearest and dearest rival. There is a God, after all. Sod my hour-long review of the salon's finances, this is an opportunity not to be missed.

Kissing Binty on both cheeks, and thanking her again, deciding it must be fate, I weave my way through the traffic, scissors in pocket as always, just in case of an eventuality like this. If I can make her happy, who knows what will come of it? A weekly column in one of her titles? A regular makeover feature in one of her monthlies? My mind is racing. The possibilities, as they say, are endless. Shit, I'd better be on top form, I can't afford to blow this one.

And for once, my PR won't be able to take the credit. Although knowing her she'll try to, no doubt reminding me that it was she who'd got Binty in for an appointment in the first place, I think, as I dial her number to tell her the good news.

The golden rules of hairdressing

* Never talk about politics, religion or sex.
* What you don't see with your eyes, don't witness with your mouth.
* Listen for the clues the client gives you during the consultation and you should be able to keep them happy.
* A client will vote with their feet if you don't listen; they'll go off and find a hairdresser who does.
* Remember a client is always a client, never your friend. If either of you cross the boundary, you could end up losing your client.
* There is no such thing as a bad haircut or colour if you visit a reputable salon — just a bad consultation and a lack of communication.
* All clients are a walking advertisement for your salon.
* A client's haircut or colour carries your own designer label — she is walking around with your name advertised on her head.
* Hairdressing is a service industry — we're a labour-intensive business and salons are only as good as their staff.
* Time is the salon's commodity, so if a client cancels, it is fair and just to charge cancellation fees like any other profession. A booking is charged for by the amount of time you spend on the client and the amount of product the salon has to use.

* Do a thorough consultation to work out whether a client wants to 'whisper, shout or scream' her colour or cut and stick to those guidelines.
* Always remember that it's the 'bread and butter' clients who pay your wages.
* The client is the most important person in the salon.
* Hair is the only accessory you wear 24 hours a day.
* Sex sells hairdressing!

Chapter 7

4 p.m. —
Meeting with
a manufacturer

s I walk back into the salon, smugly satisfied that Ms Editor's hair is now gratefully restored to an elegant, decently cut bob – fuck, that was a truly *awful* haircut, I smile to myself – I think of the little teasers and promises she's left me with. 'I'm going to tell Kate all about you,' and, 'Erin is bound to want to come and see you; she's heard all about you, too,' she firmly stated, admiring her new look in the floor-to-ceiling glass of her office window, relieved that her hair has been salvaged in time for a very important Fashion Week party.

'It looked great after he blow-dried it. I just don't understand . . .' she had told me.

'It's all in the finish,' I explain. 'He's great at finishing – the styling part – and it's not until you look at the cut that you can see where his talents *don't* lie.' I can't deny I'm enjoying the fact that he's been 'outed', but I have learned not to be too optimistic about the chances of taking his crown, of being the next big thing.

It's very easy to get carried away with the excitement of the next project, but the reality is that most of these bright ideas don't materialise into anything of any substance. I've lost count of the numerous TV show pilots I've done with the possible participants all geared up ready to get a contract when all they end up receiving is the 'no' phone call. Or the number of producers who've been in for a complimentary haircut and promised me that their project really will become something credible, only to tell me later that 'the new head of daytime is moving away from the makeover genre'. And even though I'm thrilled that I've made an important new contact who could well practise what she preaches, I am fully aware

179

that the reality of the here and now is what's important. The people who tell you they can shit miracles don't always live up to their promises. What is real is the loyal clients that come into the salon every week – they are my focus because they are my bread and butter. And anyway, the real reason I don't want to get too excited is in case I'm disappointed, which more often than not is the case. In my early career I would call my friends and family at the merest sniff of a new programme or venture. Now I only tell them about something the day before I do it; just in case. Hearing the disappointment in their voices when things don't pan out is worse than facing it myself.

Meredith calls my mobile, her chunky jewellery jingling away in the background as she talks animatedly. I can visualise her hands frantically running through her mop as we speak.

'Shaun, couldn't wait to tell you, dear heart. Our little friend at IPC magazines has just been on the phone – she's thrilled with her hair, and you. Well done, darling one, you've really pulled it out of the bag. I've told her she should get you writing a regular column, and she's thinking about it. She'd love to feature you doing a complete restyle on one of your celebs, preferably a guy, as they're sick of C-listers. They want someone fabulous. Have a ponder and get back to me. I told her I can offer her that hot new stage actor, but she wants someone far more elusive. We can't miss this one, Shaun, so get thinking. And just think, none of this would have happened if Binty hadn't come in to see you . . . Ciao.'

Aah, I was waiting for that one – I knew she'd take the credit somewhere along the line. Another thing for me to stress about, I think, half pleased and half pissed off at the worry and sleepless nights my new mission will undoubtedly cause.

Before I even contemplate that, though, I have a new client to worry about. And in some ways, as unstarry as he is, he's just as important.

There are about four or five major professional salon product manufacturers, who make all the colouring, perming and styling products we use on, and retail to, the clients. None of them are available on the high street, although they all make diffusion lines with supposedly inferior technology and ingredients. Some are French, some Swiss and some German. None of them, unfortunately, are British. That always bothers me; although British hairdressing is the best in the world, we have never had a representative product company that's been able to compete with the biggies.

Most salons are firmly ensconced in either the French or German camp of suppliers. It's a very peculiar loyalty that's provoked and is akin to deciding whether you're a bath or shower type person, a boxer or Y-fronts wearer or, according to Mrs Lockes, whether you wear a bra to bed or not. If you are pro one particular brand, you'll never, whatever happens, want to switch to the other. And the product companies look after you very well, depending on how much you spend with them and how good your media profile is. If you don't have your own product range, you're perfect press fodder for them, endorsing their ranges with a peppering of media quotes and trend predictions with references to 'Get Ms A's celebrity look by using X shampoo and Y styling product'.

That's another matter, bloody trend predictions: trying to keep up with the fashion journalists and predict whose hair is going to be hot for either spring/summer or autumn/winter, and what colours are going to be in demand. Thank God it's only twice a year. I dread it – get it wrong and everybody will remember how far off the mark you were; get it right and no bugger will, with all the journalists taking the glory for being hairy Mystic Megs, because it was their column rather than your input that is such a crucial barometer of style. And they want to get all the credit from their editors whose jobs they desperately aspire to.

Of course, if a celebrity hairdresser does switch product houses, there are all sorts of whispers as to why. Is he in the shit financially? What is the 'house' planning to do with him? Make him their international style spokesman or creative director and pay him a massive retainer? What little sweetener has he had? Should I meet with the other side and find out what they are willing to offer me? If they do defect, the gossip in the trade press will be delicious. Is the other product house folding? How bad are things? And what made him change? Inevitably, lots of rumours fly around. 'Product X has paid for the whole of Y's new salon, you know. It's not even owned by him any more – the staff are even getting pay slips from the product house,' and other bullshit abound, but, as they say, there's no smoke without fire. Product companies have been known to discreetly back businesses in return for grabbing a 'star client', whom they hope will encourage other salon owners to swap, or merely just to get a long-term return on their short-term investment.

Of course, it's a bugger of an upheaval to switch over. All the stock has to be uplifted – the new product house buys the old one's remnants and sells them on to a salon wholesaler so you don't suffer financially – if you're clever enough to broker it into your deal in the first place – and all the colourists have to be retrained, as there are massive technical differences between all the houses, which inevitably leads to massive amounts of time not on the salon floor, so takings suffer.

You may also even risk losing staff – 'I just can't work with it, sorry, mate. I'm off to X's salon; they'll never change over' – or worse, clients – 'I can't put my finger on what's changed about my colour, Shaun. It just isn't the same and it took *so* long to get it just perfect'. Then comes training the whole staff, including receptionists, on the new retail product range, let alone switching the clients over to it, by criticising what you were selling before in order to promote your new miracle home care. What if retail sales drop? At a healthy 10 per cent of turnover that could mean all your profit gets arseholed in one fell swoop. In short, it's so much hassle it had better bloody be worth it. And it's up to them to make sure it is. The dangled carrot has to be pretty massive to swap.

It pays to put all your eggs in one hairy basket. It is true, stay loyal to one brand and there's no question that you rack up points similar to owning – and remembering to use – your Nectar card. Brand loyalty, they call it. Every little press mention and product endorsement can't do your discount any harm, can it? There are a number of ways to get your jollies off them, either straight discount on your spend or retrospective discount in the form of a nice fat cheque every quarter, which rarely finds its way out of the salon owner's pocket. Or if that doesn't turn you on, try some international work – all arranged and paid for by them – fancy doing a show in Tokyo? Off you go then, my son, if that's what lights your fire. Go and get paid a fortune at our expense, and it gives you some nice newsy meat for the trade press at the same time.

Then there are the all-expenses-paid hairdressing congresses – now there's a term with a loose definition. Two hundred pissed-up hairdressers all letting their hair down in some dog-and-pony-show of a five-star hotel, and all in the name of work. The conference itself consists of about three hours out of the thirty-six, and can hardly be described as a slog. There are a few presentations about some new products and some video footage of the various events the company has held during the year, and that's about as taxing as it gets, but still half the hairdressers fail to make their way out of the bar to attend. If it's not the bar, it's a shocker of a coke fest, but hard-drug use doesn't even compare with the booze bill that's notched up.

On one skiing jolly I went on, the bar bill alone at the plush hotel – I am reliably informed, because they would never do anything so crass as disclose this info – was a whopping £10k for fifteen people for three days. The expenses for the whole trip racked in at over £45k, and that doesn't include the bill for damages. One person got so hammered he pissed on the hotel lobby carpet, and it cost the product company well over £5k to replace it. The MD at the time didn't seem to give a toss, ordering the most expensive champagne from breakfast till, well, breakfast again, so I – not normally one to take the piss out of other people's generosity – decided, if you can't beat them, you may as well join them. For me, going on one of these trips is a real treat – for once, I am the client, and that doesn't often happen. We like a bit of customer service ourselves now and again, us star snippers, and we're more than prone to a few toddler-tantrums if they screw up.

Today, I'm meeting the new MD of my existing product house, who's coming in for a haircut, and worse, he's a foreigner, so conversation is going to be stilted. Worse still, he's French, which makes it even harder. And if he is very French, it will be an excruciating forty minutes because he'll have no conversation skills at all, so I'll have to do all the work, and nervously keep the conversation going in that typically English way. Shit. I could do without this today. I think I feel a migraine coming on. I don't have anything against the French, but they do tend to be difficult.

One of our worst clients is French, Mrs L. Her dog Truffles is a pain in the arse. It's a greasy little Schitzu, which she carries around in a basket, and it has a terrible habit of chasing rollers around the salon and chewing them to pieces. It costs me a bloody fortune, as even *I'd* draw the line at allowing the rollers to be reused once they're covered in dog saliva. We always know she's coming because Truffles leaps out of the basket and comes in first, walking through the salon as cocky as anything and fully aware that it can do what it bloody well likes due to its demanding, infatuated owner. Mrs Fontaine is bloody hard work, and if I don't stroke the pooch, she comes up to me with a harsh, 'Oh come on, Shaun, don't be such a

booolly. 'Ow could anyone not luv my leetle Truffles?' God
only knows what she'd think if she saw me putting the toe of
my designer trainers firmly up its little Parisian arse and boot-
ing it firmly away, its claws screeching across the slippery
salon floor like Bambi on ice. I save that for when she's snoozing with the Carmen rollers in.

I've never been an animal lover, but Truffles takes the bis-
cuit, chewing the handles of some very expensive designer
handbags left lying at the backwash while their unsuspecting
owners are having a blissfully relaxing head massage. Thank
God I've never had to cough up for a new Lariat. Luckily, Mrs
Fontaine still hasn't figured out why Truffles growls fiercely
every time I go near her.

* * * *

I snap back into reality. Suddenly, my mind is working
overtime preparing for the VIP visit. I buzz through
to my head colourist to make sure he's hidden any
evidence of my Frenchman's competition. There are always
some tubes lurking about as some manufacturers are better at
things than others. High-lift blonde tints? Go to the Germans,
the French just can't cut it, to my mind. Bleach? Only the
French get it right for me, the German version doesn't have the
clarity. Semi-permanents? The French again, I'm afraid, the
others just don't get the coverage on grey. Perms? We like the
Swiss, who somehow manage to have more bounce and condition. So however loyal you try to be to one brand, you're
bound to have a few skeletons in your stock cupboard. What
it should be about, after all, is offering the clients the best that
hairdressing has to offer.

Of course, for the product manufacturers, more lucrative
and prestigious than even landing a big salon like mine is to
land a chain, whether it's company-owned or not. All that regular ordering is fantastic – a secure turnover that's bound to
impress the boardroom.

It's rumoured that one big salon chain, which used a particular product supplier with whom they enjoyed a mutually beneficial relationship over the years, were poached by a rival manufacturer. The story goes that on the way back to the airport, after the product company had completed their two days of negotiations, proposals and presentations, not to mention some fabulous wining and dining, their limo pulled over onto the hard shoulder and they were asked by the MD, James Bond-style, to go and take a look in the boot. Inside, they found a bag stuffed full of used notes. 'A little present for you to take home to England,' he informed them. A month later, a shocked trade press announced the change of brands, to much fanfare, gossip and bewilderment.

So you can see how important it is to get Mr Frenchy's hair right. I am in his 'star stable' and our relationship is going to be crucial. I need to keep him happy in order to remain one of his major players, which can only benefit my profile, and he needs to keep me happy, because if he loses me to a rival, it won't look very good on his CV or with the powers that be. We're hardly going to have a life-long friendship: the average shelf-life of an MD is about three years as they

According to a recent survey by a psychologist, your hair is your most identifiable feature. A doctor staged mock criminal line-ups, and found that small changes to hairstyle made volunteers more than 40 per cent less likely to pick the right villain.

move around a lot, from country to country and even continent to continent, so none of the funny handshake stuff can escalate too badly. Having been with my current supplier for most of my time as a major salon owner, I have lots of English mates in the company, many of whom are used to being passed over in this endless game of directorial continental chess. Most of them have stayed in the same position for years, watching various executives come and go like ships in a harbour. If they don't like a new arrival they don't sweat about it – keep your powder dry and wait for him to move on. They always do eventually.

I am buzzed and told he's in. Having briefed my salon manager, I know that at this precise moment he's being schmoozed and offered the world. I decide it's time to stop putting it off and come out to meet him.

'Antoine, nice to meet you,' I shake his hand.

'Ah, so 'ere is zee Shaun Lockes, at last,' he says, 'I've 'erd a lot about you.'

'Me, too,' I lie.

In fact, I haven't heard anything much. It was a beauty editor friend of mine who'd called up and told me about the change, and she's relying on me to do the fact-finding and report back, especially as she gets taken on a few jollies by them, too, so any change is good gossip fodder. I am to call her as soon as he's gone. Always on the lookout for a replacement for her useless boyfriend, she's hoping Mr Frog is a dish, and single too, as the next jolly is to Dubai, and she's absolutely determined to look the best of the journalistic bunch in her bikini. All the magazine editors are flown out together, so have to pretend they all get on and are able to be professional about things. Seeing as this is one of the bitchiest industries in the world, that's a tall order. Already, Miss Beauty Editor has informed me of her opposite at a rival magazine's spell in the Priory: 'That poor girl, it's rumoured the stress was so bad she'd even resorted to (hushed voice) a touch of the old rocks. Not that I'm one to gossip, Shaun, so don't let that notoriously huge gob of yours let that slip or she'll know it's come from me . . .'

I find out how he wants his hair, and then finish my patter with the obligatory, 'Come through and we'll get started.'

I take him through to the backwash, where I'm horrified to catch a glimpse of a competitor's bottle of technical cleanser at the basin. Hopefully my optical sign language, subtle head-nodding and frantic pupil dilation will not go unnoticed by one of my colourists, who's just about to perform a toner on some poor lady. He catches my eye and I mouth the product-company name which, thankfully he picks up on, carefully placing a towel over the logo. Phew.

I never like to see colourists 'doing a toner'. To me, what it really spells out is, 'colour fuck up – emergency 999!' Mental note to self: to find out what went wrong with that colour today. I must remember to ask my head colourist to fish about. If there's time, he can catch the client on the way out with a subtle, 'Everything OK today for you?' I know I can rely on him to ask the right searching questions. We can't afford to screw up. Training and re-training, that's the key. Constantly trying to improve and iron out the colouring wrinkles.

Antoine has informed me that he wants to lunch – 'Just a sondvich, if zats OK?' – as he sits down in the comfy leather chair.

Yes, of course, I say welcomingly, thinking, Shit, the chef better bloody well have whatever he wants in.

'Chicken salad on granary, pleaze' he says, after briefly glimpsing through the menu. Well, at least he's been Anglicised enough to remember his Ps and Qs.

As my junior takes him into shampoo heaven, I rush back to the kitchen, placing the order with precise and detailed instructions, followed by the usual, 'And don't fuck up, Paco, or your arse will be winging its way back to Sugar Loaf Mountain quicker than you can say . . .' He smiles. We love a little banter.

Antoine is now sitting at my section. Thank God I got my regular junior to shampoo. Once, I made the mistake of getting his predecessor washed by a work-experience girl – there was nobody else, it was one of those days – and she'd sat him down with a very fetching Carmen Miranda-style turban, neatly swirled and tucked around his head. God, he looked a prat. Luckily, he was possessed with a sense of humour and thought the whole episode entirely amusing.

I notice that Antoine is discreetly looking around the salon, taking it all in. He is watching one of my stylists cutting in the mirror, and having a good old look around at the salon equipment and furniture. Can't say I blame him – they did shell out for some of it, in the form of a nice little 'refurbishment contribution'. He's looking to see whether its money well spent.

I get started on his hair. He has a very old-fashioned, Hugh Grant-style haircut, all foppish public schoolboy. I've tried to talk him into something more befitting his new role in Premier Hair Division – he's rumoured to have come from some other part of the French empire, and it shows – but he's not having any of it. Well, I've got three years to try, and I won't give up. It's better if he has a trendy look, as every salon owner is bound to be asking their sales rep where the new MD gets his hair cut and from now on he'll be  wearing my designer label on his head. He chose me because it's the politically correct thing to do, and I think he's better off sitting in my chair than some of the other arsehole celeb hairdressers. Forgive my immaturity – we cannot help but have a child-like jealously of each other, which is normally dependent on who's currently the most talked about in town.

They come in several variations, my breed. There are the 'old school' – the ones who've been at it for years and are very well thought of. Some are very kind and nice – generous, encouraging and supportive – while others are the exact opposite, jealous of your up-and-coming celebrity because their own star is waning and they can't help trying to put you down, unwilling to recognise that their shelf life is coming to its natural conclusion, and as truculent as a two-year-old about making way for somebody else.

There is the 'middle ground' – the current stable of media luvvies. Not old enough to be considered establishment, but young enough to be living in the limelight – this is me –

respectful of those who have gone before them – well some of them – and, I like to think, encouraging and supportive of new talent coming up – unless they open up round the corner and nick my staff and clients, or steal my thunder in the media, which they inevitably will one day.

Then there's the 'hip and happening' brigade – normally the worst kind. Pretending to flout convention and mock the hairdressing world, they are anti-establishment; they try to be renegade, but just look desperate to shock. These bad-boy, self-styled anarchists turn up to industry events worse for wear on the old devil's dandruff, dressed in a totally unacceptable trendy manner, deliberately not befitting the seriousness of the occasion, and they don't have a nice word to say about anybody, least of all other hairdressers. They swear when they make speeches, and worse, they treat their young, girly, groupie fanbase like shit and are wholly misogynistic – says Mrs Lockes. This is because she heard one of them on the phone to one of his many girlfriends, ordering her to sneak out of her parents' house at 3 a.m. and 'get her fifteen-year-old arse' over to his flat to 'warm his bed', all while putting his hand up some other bit of skirt's skirt. 'How can these girls let themselves be treated like that?' Mrs Lockes lectures. 'Don't they have *any* respect for themselves?'.

Antoine isn't too bad, and before long we're chatting away about various people we know, and his sideways move into the mad, bad world of hairdressing from the comparative tranquillity of the fragrance division. He's hard work, but no more so than I thought he was going to be. His sandwich arrives, together with his fresh juice. Thank God Paco hasn't let me down and it looks great.

He takes a large bite and I ask him subtly about the next product price increase. These companies are very smart, and my switched-on secretary, who does all the admin and ordering, has noticed that in addition to their annual price hike, which is way above inflation, their products are repackaged and reformulated with increasing regularity, all with the excuse that they're streamlining for the European market, when in reality the change of name and pack size results in a sneaky little increase, dressed up as rebranding.

He is just about to reply when he stops, mid-mouthful.

Shit, I swallow hard, realising something must be wrong. Everything seems to go in slow-motion as he stops chewing and pulls out a long, seemingly never-ending, black hair from his mouthful of sandwich, the remains of which is now being carefully placed back on my logoed plate as he does so. My Adam's apple feels the size of a rugby ball. Silently, he hands me the hair, and nodding wordlessly, like an astronaut in a world without gravity, I take it, hardly daring to breath, and examine it for what seems like an eternity.

We both sit, silent and motionless, staring at the intruder.

'Excuse me, Antoine' I state calmly, walking slowly and purposefully, John Wayne-style, towards the kitchen.

'You twat!' I scream at Paco, his long hair escaping wildly from the constraints of his chef's hat, as he haphazardly and swiftly tucks it pitifully inside the starchy fabric.

'Do you *know* who that is, you useless tool? How could you do this to me?' I implode.

'Eet not mine, Boss, I donna know how it got in there,' Paco has a dreadful habit of not accepting what I say, but trying to wriggle out of the bleeding obvious fuck-ups he makes from time to time by murmuring a variety of crap excuses in broken English.

'Not yours? Not fucking yours? It's a great fucking thick, black Brazilian mother . . . who the fuck else's is it? I'll deal with you later.'

I worry I'm turning into Basil Fawlty. The similarities are all too obvious, Mrs Lockes keeps telling me. I take some deep breaths, desperate for a nicotine injection, but there's no time, and walk calmly back toward Antoine.

'I'm sorry about that, Antoine.' I soothe. 'Can I get you anything else?'

'No, do not worry, Shaun, I am not 'ungry any more.' He smiles faintly. I can't say I blame him. Hardly French bloody gastronomy is it?

Still, things can't get any worse, can they?

I carry on snipping, Antoine is now telling me about the company's latest research into the hair-colouring market and I try to sound interested.

'And did you know, Shaun, that 40 per cent of British women have coloured hair but only 28 per cent have their hair coloured in a salon? 8 per cent have it coloured at home, and 24 per cent have either a mix of home or salon . . . and in the winter women colour their hair twice, on average.'

'Really? How fascinating,' I reply, my mind busy on other matters, still quietly seething and plotting revenge on Paco. Perhaps I'll ban him from having his radio on for the next Man U match. Hmm. Or even from playing his Black Sabbath CD. Now, that's guaranteed to get to him.

'And the average frequency of visits to the hairdresser is between five and seven weeks. Twenty million women pay to have their hair done at least once a year.'

Snap out of it, I think, make some effort.

'I read an interesting survey on hair recently,' I lie. For Mrs Lockes does that sort of thing and often tells me stuff she thinks I may find interesting for small talk with my clients. She read it in *Grazia*.

'Women, on average, spend twenty-four minutes a day on their hair, thirty minutes, no, hang on, let me get this right, yes, that's it, thirty minutes on their face, and twenty-six minutes choosing clothes and getting dressed.' So busy am I trying to get my statistics right, I don't notice that as I'm cutting round his ear hairline, my razor-sharp new blades have just taken a chunk out of his left earlobe.

Oh, fuck, fuck, fuck.

'Zat ees very interesting, Shaun. I luv zat. I will mention it at our next zales reps conference.' He hasn't noticed, but I have.

You see, for some bizarre medical reason, if you cut someone's ear, and I don't know why, maybe it's because it's made up of tissue and not muscle, or perhaps all bloody eight pints are stored there, it never, ever seems to stop bleeding. It's as if it's the one part of the body that doesn't contain clotting agent. I studied it when I did my Science of the Hair and Scalp theory. Oh, but the ear is cruel, for it doesn't bleed straight away. It lulls you into a false sense of security, so you think you've got away with it, even if the sound of the skin being nicked and the evidence sitting in your blades tells you otherwise. You think, by some miracle, this human ear is going to be different. Until the first, tell-tale signs appear. Then you know you're right, royally fucked, as they say.

Antoine has stopped mid-flow, as he sees me ask my junior to run and get a tissue – tissue? Who am I kidding? You need a bloody Andrex factory to deal with a cut ear. I dab at the cut, our conversation a series of stilted remarks, talking over the top of each other, as if we're doing an interview via satellite and there's a time delay.

'It's just a little.'

'Iz zere a problem?'

'. . . nick to the ear . . . don't worry, it will stop in a minute . . .'

'Ees OK, Shaun. . .'

'. . . Just cover your . . . pull the gown around and . . . your shirt . . .' Until, finally defeated, I declare, 'I'll just run and grab a plaster.'

My mind is racing as I dash over to the plaster cupboard. I haven't done this since I trained, for fuck's sake, what's the matter with me. And to *him* of all people. Bollocks. Bollocks. Bollocks.

But if I'd thought I was in trouble before, the sight that

greets me on the way back to my section is heart-stopping. For there is Antoine, visibly grey from shock, with both his hands cupped under his left ear, smiling weakly as he collects the droplets that are dripping from the gash with increasing regularity, before his man-made cup overfloweth, as they say, with his own blood. It is like Lady Macbeth, I decide.

Bloody scissor man. Sunny Scissors, my arse. That bloody git is going to get it if he ever sets foot in here again. The ultimate advance in technology, Japanese blades – Kamikaze more like. £600 to be humiliated and ridiculed by the tool of my trade – my French copy book forever blotted, as badly as Antoine's pristine white YSL shirt was.

And there Antoine sits, nervously watching me finish his haircut, gently cradling his wound. Every so often my assistant rushes over with a new batch of wadding to mop up the blood. Plasters? Forget it, we both decide, now showing some camaraderie for our togetherness in the situation, for Antoine can no longer be kept in the dark over the severity of the accident. After four soaked plasters, we agree to use tissues, and plenty of them. What a bloody day, literally. I have caused the most important, most influential man in the whole sodding industry to require a blood transfusion on the first day of his new directorship. And worse, he's still starving, not just due to loss-of-blood-induced fatigue, but because I have a useless chef who won't get his stupid, head-banging hair cut, even though he works in a sodding hair salon.

I think of my mates at the product company, and how their new boss will ask them why there's so much fuss about Shaun Lockes. I will have the piss ripped out of me mercilessly. I wonder how long it will be before I get a call? Still, they can talk, because they've all been shitting themselves since his arrival, desperate to impress. They even secured all the billboard advertising hoarding from the route from Heathrow to their offices, just to ensure that he and the international division were impressed with what the British team have been

doing. They've even been known to fabricate the odd incentive, promotion or advert. Cheaper and quicker to mock something up with the printer and make out it happened, telling
him, 'And this was the in-salon promotion we ran last July . . .'
than to risk his displeasure. Not that they need worry; their
careers will long outlive his short shelf life. Most of those guys
have been with the Company so long they are practically
unsackable.

Now I've maimed their new boss for life. Not only have I
physically scarred him, but emotionally too: he'd never want
to visit a hairdressers again. Great, he's probably going to
need therapy to get through the next three years now.

Visibly relieved that his ordeal is over, I escort him out of
my torture chamber onto the relative safety of London's
streets. He waves at me, and then quickly remembers to cup
his hand back under his ear, just in case he loses the wadding.

* * * *

'Ear, Ear, you're brave, Shorn, I'll give you that.'
I turn round to find one of my colourists, chuckling
with one of the other stylists.

'Don't worry, mate, Antoine hasn't turned into Van Gogh
quite yet. He's more the John Paul Getty type. His surgeon
says that he can save some of the main tissue . . . The stitches
are quite neat, actually,' he says, laughing so ferociously I
think he's never going to stop.

'All right, you buggers, get it over with. Blimey, news travels fast.'

I walk back into the salon and nobody seems to be able to
resist the odd shout of, 'Shaun, we're over *ear*,' or humming a
line from Rod Stewart's 'The First Cut is the Deepest' as they
walk by. Bastards.

Why on earth did I ever decide to become a bloody hairdresser I wonder, catching some fresh air on the nearest park
bench. I reach for a Marlboro Light and ponder. Shit, I've

smoked a lot today, never mind, I can always go back to the Allen Carr clinic. I'm now on my fourth visit and I think they're beginning to regret their 'No smoking after one session – or your money back' pledge – I'm going to bankrupt them, for sure. Worrying about my smoking problem takes my mind off Antoine at least. I mustn't let a little thing like an earlobe get me down, even if it is attached to one of the most important men in hairdressing.

I check the time and realise I'd better get back to the salon and resume my day. On the way, I check the topiary – it needs a prune to get those box balls perfect. I remove the fag ends from the planters, while I'm at it. The sodding bastards come out here for a quick lug and are too lazy to shove their butts down the nearest drain like I do. No time, they'll tell me. Lead by example, I think of my father's words, and try to remember to write it on my list of bollockings for the staff meeting tomorrow. Jimmy needs to change that bulb on the sign, I think my name ought to be in lights after all. Must make a mental note, I think, already forgetting what the last one was.

Booking etiquette

* Avoid first thing in the morning appointments if you want a re-style. Your hairdresser could be either half asleep or recovering from the excesses of the night before.

* Never book anything serious — like a major style or colour change — if you are being 'fitted in'. Best to pick a quiet time to be sure you'll get plenty of attention. If they are 'fitting you in' in the first place it could be you're doing something on a whim — think it through first.

* Try not to book on a Monday for an image overhaul — as you shouldn't eat fish on a Monday in a restaurant — your hairdresser may still be a little 'out of it' from the excesses of the weekend.

* Avoid Saturdays — why come on the busiest day if you don't have to? You won't get as much attention as on a quieter weekday slot.

* Don't book a colour change after 3 p.m. — everybody knows it takes hours and your colourist will be more engrossed in thinking about whether she'll get home in time for EastEnders than wondering 'What did you mean by mocha, exactly?'

* Don't book anything radical if you are in a hurry; the hairdresser will sense you are rushing them along. Allow time for a thorough consultation.

* Try to arrive on time for your appointment to allow time for a consultation. Never accept being shampooed by a junior before

the hairdresser has seen your hair in its natural state.
It speaks volumes about the stylist's professionalism.
* Best not to book a gay stylist or colourist during Gay
  Pride week — they will not be concentrating on you,
  guaranteed.

The ideal appointment time?

11 am or 2 pm — before/after lunch/elevenses.
Not yet tired, still 'into' the day, peak creativity.

Chapter 8

5 p.m. Pop star —
restyle and colour

efore I can even contemplate my growing to-do list, which now includes Meredith's task of finding somebody for the article, I want to think about the stylist Frankie told me is on the market. My mind is working overtime. I know what the salon he comes from is like, and the type of staff they have. It's renowned for being bitchy – it comes from the top, so it's hardly surprising – so what is this guy going to be like? Moreover, do I trade test him? Do I break the unwritten rule about getting somebody 'fabulous' to prove their skill by doing a model for my scrutiny? If I ask him and he refuses, where do I go from there? Will I risk losing him if I persist? If I don't, how do I know how good he is? He's bound to be on big money and want a guarantee for the first few months. What if he's crap, I can't feed him any new business and none of his clients follow? And as there's a group of them, what if they turn into a little unionist gang, upsetting my carefully cultivated apple cart?

My head is pounding. I need to ask around in the staff room. One of my seniors used to work at the salon, so he may be able to give me some background info before I call. I buzz down to the desk to find out where he is, and am pissed off to find out he's incommunicado – he's on a shoot for one of our A-listers, who's on a magazine cover and is playing the PR game by insisting we do her hair. Perhaps I'll have to take a chance on him. One thing's for sure, before I call him, I have to sort out the rest of my afternoon and get back on schedule.

As wonderful and unexpected as events may have turned out today, I can't help but be relieved that for the remainder of the day I am home, amongst the salon's familiar, safe walls, and the real-life busy-ness of the only hairdressing world that really matters: the salon floor. It's comforting to see one of my favourite old clients as I head through the backwash area where she is waiting to turn her tangled mop into something more chi-chi.

She has long been able to afford to come to me, but favours my cheaper, yet still very good, graduate stylists.

I last bumped into her at Stop Smoking Forever clinic.

'Fancy a fag, Shaun?' She grins sheepishly at me, and we go and take our familiar places on the bench outside the salon.

She's just come from her weekly London lunch – she comes up to town to see her friends and get her hair done. Since she moved to the country a while ago, one of the biggest frustrations of leaving city life behind is, according to her, that 'they just can't get my hair right'. I'm glad to hear it.

Her other half is playing up again, and over the years I've heard it all. I've been a good shoulder to cry on, and there even used to be a bit of chemistry between us years ago; it just never went anywhere. Being a whole ladder up the social scale, she would never have taken someone like me seriously, but I think at times she flirted with the idea. She, too, has ended up being far from my type – much too much of a loose cannon – but we're firm friends, and right now she is spilling some pretty unpleasant beans.

Her useless buffoon of a husband is an Italian count, who uses his title to make a career in professional networking for some very unsavoury Russian billionaires and Arabs, while being paid enormous sums of money to get them connections and network them into the upper echelons of respectable British society. But this time, he's gone too far. He's been caught *in flagrante* with a prostitute.

This, the latest in a series of indiscretions, has been discovered by his poor wife when she called his temporary secretary. Told that he was at the very hotel she'd excitedly hoped he'd booked for their wedding anniversary – sentimental to her, as it was where they'd spent their honeymoon night – she envisaged that he was making preparations or booking a suite for a forthcoming romantic evening. Although the warning bells started ringing when she called reception and asked to be put through to his room, she thought there was no way even he would sink so low as to desecrate such a special memory. Her illusions were shattered when a breathless woman picked up the phone while clearly being given a good rogering.

'Why don't you just leave him?' I venture, stubbing out my fag guiltily. 'After all, you hardly had a good word to say about him after the latest shenanigans, so what hope is there now?'

'What, and have no money? Sod that. I'm not cut out to be a single mother. The only hope left for us was to move to the country, away from all this craziness. I still need some space and time to sort my head out.'

A small proportion of my clients are seriously fucked up. With her spiralling drug habit, their confusing love-life, odd going's-on in the financial department and his penchant for all manner of kinky things, their kids are bound to be in rehab before their eighteenth birthdays, I think sadly.

It helps to use one of our new foreign juniors when listening to shocking secrets like these. Having a junior who can't speak good English is very valuable on such occasions, and many 'most-wanted' hairdressers employ at least one for that very reason. Poor Katia, one of my Portuguese assistants, is irreplaceable at times like these. Gazing at my lightning-quick fingers, she is completely and perfectly oblivious to the content of whatever sordid conversation is going on.

Salt water
Perfect for the beach hair look – stylists use saline solutions to give hair the just-stepped-out-of-the-ocean effortless glamour look.

It's sad that so many women seem to be saddled with the same problem, and that so few of them have people they can confide in. One client recently told me how she'd been taken in by a con-man. The lonely divorcee, noted for her large financial settlement, was thrilled to meet her knight in shining armour and sported a whopper of a diamond engagement ring during one of her visits to the salon, which she was desperate to show off, confiding that she'd never been so happy.

Unfortunately, her flashy ring turned out to be not so precious when she found out it was from the Argos catalogue: all too obvious evidence that was now backed up by her now depleted bank account. I doubt she'll ever trust another man again. She's still mortified that she spent a year flashing around a piece of jewellery worth less than her weekly trip to Waitrose.

And she's not alone in the shame stakes. Take Anna, for example.

Anna has a secret that only I know.

She's a very attractive American girl who started coming to me a few months ago. Despite being tall, leggy, blonde and beautiful, her conversation is littered with examples of her overwhelming insecurity. In fact, it took her enormous courage to even believe she was good enough to become a Shaun Lockes client and walk through the salon doors, she often tells me. She constantly puts herself down and it's very sad – there are only so many times you can reassure somebody that they have worth, value and beauty. Anna seems to have an invisible barrier around and doesn't let anybody through, so convinced is she that she's a 'useless, stupid, irrelevant' person. After a while, it gets plain tedious – the praise I heap on her just falls on deaf ears.

'Why *are* you so bloody insecure?' I asked her one day, getting impatient with the way she constantly plays the martyr and never listens to the endless motivational, encouraging compliments I pay her.

'Something must have happened to you to make you like this. Is it something to do with your husband?' Her 'husband', although they're not actually married, they just pretend to be in order for her to confirm with the other mums at the school gates, is a Russian millionaire, and their weird relationship doesn't seem to help matters. He shags around endlessly, barely bothering to cover his tracks, which must make her feel even worse about herself.

'Oh not really. He thinks I'm blonde and stupid, and he's right, isn't he?' she asks, her doe eyes misting over, looking for reassurance again, having already decided that whatever my reply, it won't make any difference. She's destined to be a victim; her mind is very firmly made up that she's worthless.

'You're only as stupid as you keep telling everyone you are,' I say, trying not to lose my patience again.

'Well, the trouble is, he knows me for who I really am,' she says, voice hushed to a whisper.

'And who is that exactly?' I ask, intrigued and partially convinced she's going to shockingly confess to being some tranny or having had a sex change.

'I was a hooker,' she says slowly, and at last everything is clear.

'*Was* a hooker? Or *am* a hooker?' I ask tentatively.

'Was. I got in with the wrong sort. I was an au pair, newly arrived in London, and before I knew where I was my new Greek boyfriend was organising some pretty heavy threesomes. I was young, naïve and didn't really know what was going on. Then he started to drop out and money started to change hands, and I realised he was acting as my pimp. It didn't really dawn on me that I was a prostitute, it just sort of happened. That's when I met my husband, he was one of my clients . . .' she sobs quietly.

I've been shocked in my career before, but this has to be up there with finding out the ending in the film *The Sixth Sense*. I have never forgiven Mrs Lockes for that. Even before the titles had started to roll, she told me loudly – spoiling it for a good four rows in front and behind – 'Well, it's so bloody obvious, we might as well go home. Bruce Willis is dead. He's a ghost!'

Poor Anna. I can't help but look at her in a different light, now, even though I try and make myself forget her revelation.

It seems that I am one of the only people she has told, but you don't need to be a shrink to work out that the secret is a burden on her personality and mannerisms, and by acting in such a way, she subconsciously seems desperate to reveal her secret to anyone who will listen.

Being a hairdresser for many years, you become a bit of an amateur psychiatrist. In fact, I think I'm a better one than some of the people I know who are psychoanalysts. One woman shrink I do changed her name to something very off-the-wall, creating a whole new mother earth persona with it. She reinvented herself with some pretty heavy-duty plastic surgery, too. Not only that, her brood of adopted, and therefore fatherless, children would do Mia Farrow proud. And she plans to adopt another four, Angelina Jolie style, from even more distant shores, only content when she has a playroom resembling the United Nations.

Due to my meeting so many interesting people, it's quite rare that I get shocked, but Anna's managed it. I did have another revelation recently, though which, as broad-minded as I am, brought out the Mary Whitehouse in me.

One of my newish regular clients came in for her six-weekly cut a few months ago. Late forties, a pillar of society, a picture of respectability and part of the Mayfair set. All Prada and Chanel No 5; the Fenwick's of Bond Street type. I'd spent an hour coiffing and bouffing her, preening her to perfection, when I showed her the back in the mirror. There were tears in her eyes. God, I must have really worked some magic today, I thought.

'Can I talk to you, Shaun?' she asked. 'Of course,' I said, 'you can tell me anything, you know that.'

'I'm gay,' she said, 'and I can't tell anyone about it. I'm having an affair with my husband's sister, and we're madly, passionately in love – we have been for years. We think we should be together. Life is so short, Shaun, one has to be happy, doesn't one? Oh, it's so fabulous to come out. I've been wanting to tell someone for *ever*. I knew I was different as a gal, but it was only when I married my husband and was introduced to his family that it clicked with his sister. She's such a wonderful lover.'

There she was, this middle-aged, married woman, with two blonde, angelic curly-haired children boarding in the Chilterns, and a boring lawyer husband, who would no doubt fantasise about his staid wife having a little girl-on-girl action, though, granted, probably not if it involved his sister. I would imagine that most men – even me – would draw the line at that incestuous little triangle. And imagine explaining it to the children . . .

Why had she chosen to tell me, her hairdresser? Not her best friend, not her own family, not her poor, misguided husband, but somebody who'd only cut her hair three times. What on earth was she going to tell me once I'd been doing her hair for years? I thought, wondering how on earth to respond. Hairdressers seem to have an in-built unshockable gene, and if their flabber is well and truly gasted, they tend to have a very good way of hiding it. In this particular case, I had to advise my lady to stay well and truly inside her closet. I mean, incest in Belgravia? Good heavens!

Life is an endless struggle full of frustrations and challenges, but eventually you find a hair stylist you like.
Unknown

Of course, the benefit of this cathartic revelation syndrome is that the client leaves her appointment with me feeling fabulous. Not just because of her hair, but because she's off-loaded some horrendous little secret she's been carrying around and it's literally a weight off her shoulders. They say a problem shared . . .

Back to Anna. For this isn't the only tawdry little confessions she makes, she has another, far more sinister one: she has blonde obsession. And she's not the only one. For a lot of women, being blonde is an all-encompassing passion. There have been countless psychological studies on the subject, and it never ceases to fascinate many intellectuals, from Freud to Woody Allen – and Arthur Miller come to think of it. Theories abound on the subject, but I've always found it amazingly simple. Being blonde is iconic. Immortalised by the ultimate blonde Marilyn Monroe, women never seem to want to stop emulating the sex appeal she oozed. Some clients just want to be blonde at any cost, to give themselves a touch of that magical sexy glamour. They don't just want to *look* blonde, they want to *feel* blonde. They want to buy into the blondes-have-more-fun theory. I've seen women beg colourists to leave the bleach on longer just to get it that little bit lighter, regardless of the fact that we've warned them they may be taking their hair home with them in a carrier bag if we do. Being blonde is so vital to them because many see it as the ultimate way to make a statement about their looks. Some women admit that once they get blonde obsession they're hooked for ever, chained to the peroxide bottle like an alcoholic to the single malt.

Surveys suggest that women between the ages of 18 and 24 change their hairstyles 20 times on average, and 4 times between the ages of 50 and 80.

Blonde obsession is an unbelievably common addiction. There should be hairdressing rehab clinics; just picture it, the Hair Priory. Women can sit around in group therapy and discuss their peroxide habit. Why do women crave being blonde? And do blondes really have more fun? It's a question I've had to answer in a million interviews, and I'm still not sure. All I know is that once you've succumbed to your inner blonde and trodden those platinum-coated stairs to bombshell heaven, nothing else will ever be good enough and you'll never be able to go back. And it spirals, like a heroin habit, sometimes becoming an all-consuming quest or colouring Holy Grail. Highlights? Forget it, after a couple of years that's like giving a wino alcohol-free lager. It has to be full-on, in your face, blockbuster Hollywood blonde. Look at Madonna; she started off with some subtle highlights in her 'Like A Virgin' era, only to pump up the tint levels with her Blonde Ambition tour. Can she give it up? No, she goes through dark phases, but she always comes back to blonde, and looks as bewitched as ever, even though it's far from the natural colour God intended for her. Check out the eyebrows if you don't believe me, although they have long since been tinted a matching honey-toned hue.

Blonde obsession isn't just fiction, it's fact.

When I was new to hairdressing, I worked with a senior colourist who had to take some leave to have a minor operation. All his clients were passed on to another senior, whose trademark was to give everyone a 'little sparkle'. What this involved was adding a tiny bit of bleach to all their colour formulas, making them all just half a shade lighter, but with the same colour tones.

'I can't put my finger on what he does differently,' they'd tell me. 'I just look a little brighter somehow, more sun-kissed. But he followed the same formula, I don't understand. He just makes me look a little more *sparkly*!'

When the other poor colourist returned to his somewhat depleted client list, he was bewildered by the level of defection. He'd lost the majority of the clientele it had taken him so long to build up, and all because they'd got addicted to going lighter, without even knowing it.

As for Anna? Her husband doesn't know she isn't natural in the blonde department, and she's incredibly careful and cunning to cover her tracks. Sure, she's fair, but she's far from the Scandinavian ash platinum he thinks she is. And with a Brazilian bikini wax and eyebrows tinted a matching colour, her secret is safe, as long as she coughs up regularly enough to keep her landing strip regrowth in check and her roots at bay. No wonder she's emotionally screwed up.

I wander back into reception, confused by all this thinking, becoming more so as I study the computer printout of my column in bewilderment.

'What's going on, girls? I thought I had a bridal trial. What's happened to her? Can we call her and check she's not going to be a no-show? Did we take a credit-card deposit?'

I am just about to get angry that another precious hour of my day has gone tits up, when my secretary emerges from her office to explain.

'I cancelled her, Shorn. I know you hate brides, and she's gone to someone else, so don't worry.'

'What did you do that for?' I ask, baffled.

'Mr Pop has called!' She shrieks, barely able to contain her excitement.

'He's just off on the European leg of his tour and wants an image revamp before he goes. He's upstairs being coloured now,' she says starrily. It's not often the whole salon goes into raptures, but when Mr Pop Star's around even the yummy mummies run up to him for an autograph.

'He was so sweet when he came in,' they chorus from reception. 'He said, "I've come for an appointment. My name is . . ." and we all just wanted to yell, we *know* who you are!' they cry, giggling like schoolgirls.

Mr Pop, as we call him, is very pleasant, it has to be said. No bother, nice to everybody, very unassuming, shy and undemanding, I sometimes wonder whether the flurry he causes at the salon will put him off coming back; but it doesn't seem to. He's upstairs as we speak, quietly setting a hundred women's hearts aflutter and behaving like the gentleman he is. Great, I think, glad that I haven't had time to go and give the *Big Issue* guy a piece of my mind, for he's sure to have been papped on the way in; and he's the sort of celeb who'll be on the front of all the dailies, not just at the back of *Heat* magazine.

No time to ring and tell Meredith, I think, bounding through the salon to find out what he wants me to do with his hair. I am guiltily pleased to not have to endure a bridal trial, as well. Brides can be a pain in the arse. First, you have to do the trial – the dry-run – and this is only after hours and hours of consultation with a usually very highly stressed bride-to-be, whose big day you become responsible for making or break-ing. It's a massive undertaking.

Once the trial is out of the way, and you've discussed the head-dress, the veil, the tiara, the jewellery, the make-up and the styling, you have to make sure the bride is happy with her test look. There are numerous phone calls to determine how well it stayed and to discuss what to change and do differ-ently on the big day itself. It's all very time-consuming. Some-times, you might have three separate trials before you finally please the neurotic young wife-to-be. Then comes the worst bit, you have to negotiate the price. Not only of the trials, but, and this brings me out in hives, of the day itself.

I would rather not mix business with pleasure. It's very hard with brides, as clients often start with a tell-tale, 'Shaun, I would love you and your wife to come to my wedding,' when what they really mean is, 'I will give you the honour of com-ing to the whole day – and we've got major family fall-outs for places, so an honour it bloody well is – and you can do my hair. Not only will you do my hair, but you'll be on call for the whole day, and all for the price of a wedding breakfast. Well, you didn't expect anything else, did you? Don't you know how much this is all costing? *Poor* daddy, and we're going halves, you know . . .'

Hence the dilemma. Of course, if it was one of our real friends, this is normally the deal – the hair *is* the wedding present – but, for one of my clients . . . ?

It's not just brides that bring on this dilemma, it happens with clients throw-ing sensational parties, too, although I'm far more up for an evening of social pleasure, even if

I have to swallow my fee, than the pressure of a wedding.

Mrs Lockes goes mad, of course. 'Bloody well tell them what you'd charge if they were a new client. Get the conversation round to the money, Shaun; don't sell yourself short. You're such a softy,' she says, cross that I have got myself into a mess.

The day itself? That's when the headaches really start, especially if the whole glorious occasion is being covered by a celeb magazine and the event has to be *On average, women colour their hair twice during the winter months.* shrouded in secrecy and photographed from beginning to end. Added stress for the poor crimper who has to cover the blushing bride from the attentions of any pappers hiding in the bushes while his expert styling is squashed by a blanket and an umbrella. Blushing bride, I hear you ask? With that fat cheque stashed in the bank? Not exactly what the sanctity of marriage is meant to be about, is it? Still, I'd probably have done it if somebody had been fool enough to pay for my nuptials.

Celebrity wedding or not, time, on a wedding day, doesn't stand still. One minute you look at your watch and its 9 a.m., and you're enjoying a leisurely glass of Buck's Fizz to settle your anxious client's nerves, then two minutes later, it's noon and the panic commences.

Not only does the mother normally interfere – usually she hasn't seen the wedding-trial look and gently enquires, 'I didn't know you were wearing it like *that*, darling,' causing a sudden departure from your practised-to-a-fine-art style – she is bound to find you a million other people to coiff, just to be sure she's getting her (or her daughter's) money's worth.

Suddenly the bridesmaids come pouring out of the woodwork, as do nieces, grandmothers, aunties and matrons-of-honour.

'Shorn, be a darling. Just give little Matilda's hair a tidy-up will you?' and the whole day descends into one of your worst salon nightmares, all for the price of a meal that you are too tired to eat and a crap hotel. And all at the expense of three costly days off the salon floor.

You are totally unable to relax for the whole day. Ever fearful that your work may unravel, you watch as the now much relieved bride goes on to party like mad, confident that her hair will remain in place, and that your expert, beady eye will never allow her to look anything other than completely gorgeous. Pressure, pressure, pressure. Never again, I tell myself after every wedding. Never. So you can see why I'm glad to have got off the hook today.

I find Mr Pop sitting quietly with my head colourist, telling him how he wants to look. He's been voted 'Best Male Haircut' by the press for the last two years running, so having a change could be crucial for his career and mine. There are too many examples of celebrities cocking up their patiently cultivated look by a rash decision at the hairdressers, and it's not just his carefully tended appearance I'm conscious of preserving. Even if he requests something diverse, his cut will have my name written all over it, and if it's slated it's bound to be my fault. On the other hand, if it becomes a revolutionary trend, his agent will no doubt take all the credit.

'Hey, how are you, Shaun?' he says, shaking my hand.

'Great, and thanks for those concert tickets. Mrs Lockes loved it and so did I. What are we going to do? I hear you want a new look.'

We discuss his face shape, possible colour tones and how radical he wants to go. He's quite up for something major and suggests a full head crop, but I talk him into keeping the length and vamping it up with some creamy vanilla-toned streaks instead. He's thinking of doing something to wow the audience, but I'm more concerned about how he's going to look under the stage lights, and from experience I don't want him to look too washed out. Agreed, I let my colour man work the magic and wait until I'm buzzed and told that he is ready. Wistfully, I realise that I could ask him to do the article for Ms Editor, not that he needs the publicity . . .

I've never wanted to do colour, although I find it fascinating. In the top London salons you normally have to choose between being a stylist or colourist. Increasingly throughout Britain, I am told, hairdressers are also starting to specialise in one particular field. We've always done this in London, having to decide right from our apprentice days which one we were more interested in, so that we could start practising on the relevant models on training night. It's always been considered that the two fields are so different and so specialised, it's impossible to be an expert in both. Years ago colourists were thought to be the poor relation, and some salons used to reflect that in their commission structure, with the colourists giving a percentage of their earnings to the stylists for feeding them the client. We stopped that in our salon when we dared to venture that sometimes the client was more loyal to their colourist than their stylist. That seems to be the general cultural shift in salons, and now, with colour figures booming, I wonder whether the situation isn't reversing, with the stylists playing second fiddle to the colourists.

While I wait, I check my emails in the way only a technophobe like me can – with the help of my secretary. There is a message from one of my celebrity TV presenters asking me to call her. I dial her mobile and she sounds panicky. The last time I saw her, I told her I was going to do her ex-colleague. Should I say hello from you? I asked innocently. 'Yes, why not,' she had said. Now, it looks like she's had second thoughts on the matter.

'Shaun, I've been thinking. For your own sake, don't tell her you do me – she won't like it. She likes to think she discovers everybody, and she won't come back if you tell her you've been doing me for years. She simply has to be the one to find people. It's not worth pissing her off – let her think she's the first and only. She'll earn her massive discount and champion you, but not if she knows I got there first.' Sweet of her to tell me. I don't doubt for a minute that it's true either; but for such an established and cultured celebrity, it strikes me that she's just as 'kindergarten' as some of the makeover-show women, or some of us celebrity hairdressers.

Mr Pop is now ready and sitting in my section.

We chat away, and I notice embarrassingly that I suddenly have six female assistants, all with a very star-struck look on their face. Now here's a dilemma: if I tell them to bugger off in front of him I'll embarrass him, but if they don't leave us alone they're going to make him feel uncomfortable. He's already been papped through the window, and word must have got out because all of a sudden the salon seems to be full of clients, sales reps, staff and even the sodding window cleaner, walking past my section and gawping. You could argue that this is why we need a VIP room, but judging from the reaction of the clients, I'm sure they're glad we don't squirrel away our most famous customers, as they seem to be as intrigued as ever with the presence of Mr Pop.

I shoot all of my new-found helpers one of my venomous looks, gritting my teeth angrily so they get the message, while Mr Pop has his head down and I'm cutting the nape; miraculously they scatter, finally realising I mean business, and leave us in peace. It's stressful enough doing somebody so unbelievably famous, half a dozen on-lookers staring at your every move is just what you don't need. And what you certainly don't need is a distraction from the very person who's supposed to be helping you.

Once I had a nightmare assistant, who put me off having a male junior ever again. Looking back, I think he had a personality disorder. I would constantly catch him hovering around, shiftily peeking into my brush bag, or waiting outside the office. I would ask him what he was doing and he'd say, 'Just checking, just checking, just checking, just . . .' and he'd rabbit on and on, repeating the same sentence and shuffling around uncomfortably, sometimes going around in circles with his head down. The muttering would carry on until I broke the monotony and gave him a proper job to get on with. So concerned was I that I called his parents, gently enquiring how he behaved at home and hoping they would be able to shed some light on the situation by giving me some sort of explanation for his weird behaviour. No, they told me, as far as they were concerned he was a normal teenage boy. Feeling sorry for him and wanting to give him the benefit of the doubt, I made a pact with myself that I would keep him with me for a fortnight and see if things improved.

The worst thing about him was his wind. Wind is a problem in a lot of salons. When I was training, Rene (or Rennie as we called him) would often guff loudly and have a fit of the giggles, wafting it along the line of sections, past each of the hairdressers in turn, with a whoosh of his hairdryer. Nobody could help but laugh, although the clients were oblivious to our little home-made wind tunnel. However, you don't expect this from a seen-but-not-heard junior. This boy would stand there, passing me rollers, while the most horrendous smell came from his direction. One look at his embarrassed little face and he'd start with the rain man routine: 'Wasn't me, wasn't me, wasn't me, wasn't . . .' and off he'd go, spinning

HAIR FACTS

Thick and fine hair is determined by the size of the hair follicle. The follicles of straight hair grow straight out of the scalp, curly hairs grow at an angle, resulting in the hair bending into an 's' shape and therefore producing curls.

around and shuffling from left to right. I honestly thought he was autistic, so I called his parents again, this time mentioning the delicate matter. No, as far as we're concerned he's just a normal boy, they said. Although how normal they were, and how much of a gauge they could be to his normality, I was beginning to question.

He also had unbelievably sweaty hands. It's impossible to be a hairdresser if you have sweaty hands – forget it. It's like being a colourist if you're colour blind; it's a non-starter. On model nights, he'd be blow-drying some poor student's freshly washed hair and the sweat from his hands would keep it in a permanently damp state. It was like painting the Forth Bridge, watching him go back over the same sections as soon as he'd touched them.

I persevered with him, trying to be the caring, undiscriminating boss, even though by now the whole salon had christened him Raymond Babbitt (the Dustin Hoffman character in *Rain Man*). However, my patience ran out the day I was called to do the hair of one of England's top models – at her Chelsea townhouse. I had lusted after this gorgeous woman for years, and doing her hair for the first time, I wanted everything to be perfect. Until I realised that the only junior free to go with me was little Raymond Babbitt. I briefed him in the taxi.

'Now, don't say a bloody word. Not a thing, right?'

He nodded.

'And don't, whatever you do, FART. We are going to her house, right? It's not the salon now. Hold your gas inside your trousers. Take some sodding Imodium or something.'

He nodded again, venturing a 'It wasn't me, it wasn't me, it . . .' Until he saw my furious glare and lapsed into silence.

Nervous about coming face to face with the nation's top totty, I took a shot of my trusted Rescue Remedy and steeled myself for the next hour. However, when I finally got shown into the messy boudoir – knickers, nighties, high heels, etc., thrown carelessly all over the floor and bed: very sexy as was her reputation – I couldn't help getting a little hot under the collar when I saw her sitting at her dressing table, clad only in a vest and G-string. What would *Loaded* have paid to get a shot like that? I wondered.

We got on well, and it turned out that she wanted a cut, too. I was just trimming her trademark glorious mane when Raymond did a corker.

'Fuck me, what is that pong?' she said, staring at me.

Here I was, trying to keep my cool while facing my number-one pin-up's erect nipples in a see-through vest, and she thinks I've farted. Unbelievable.

I shot him a glimpse, mentally begging him not to start his routine, but to no avail. 'T'wasn't me, t'wasn't me, t'wasn't me. . .'

Great. So he was either blaming his boss or accusing one of Britain's top models of chuffing.

'Go and get some rollers out of the session bag,' I barked, desperate to stop the uncontrollable flow that was coming fast and frequently from his mouth and arse.

She turned to stare at me, bemused, with a half smile on her face.

'Is your assistant for real?' she asked, one of her famously arched eyebrows raised in bewilderment.

I tried to explain his little nuances to her. Luckily, she was vaguely amused, and I carried on cutting until he returned, cheeks puce with embarrassment.

Then, just as I was about to cut a graduated layer into the back, combing the section smooth, ready for cutting, he did it again. But this time she wasn't smiling, because we'd both heard the ripping sound of cut hair.

Let me explain – every hairdresser's nightmare is to forget to close their blades in between sections while combing. We hold our scissors and comb in the same hand, so if they are even ever so slightly open while you're between snips and combing the next bit of hair you run the risk of cutting something off that you shouldn't. We all do it from time to time; it's actually quite harmless and it's not unlike how we do a strand test pre-colour or perm in the salon, although that's just a few strands. It's easily done. This horrendous, horrific embarrassment is bad enough if you have a client with a two-inch crop, let alone my model's trademark mane. There was no getting away from it, she'd heard it – we all had, even Raymond. In the noise, hustle and bustle of the salon, I may have got away with it, but in the silence of her bedroom, it was as deafening as Krakatoa erupting. This hideous lapse in concentration was due to my useless junior's overactive bowels and had cost me the confidence of a potentially great client, all before I had even finished drying her hair.

So angry was I that in between reassuring her I was slicing in for a bit of texture – bullshit, and she knew it – I had no choice but to banish him from the room, sending him to tidy my session bag. Sod being the caring, concerned boss, his bollocks were mine, sliced, roasted, hung, drawn and quartered. I couldn't imagine what I would do to him when we got outside.

Miraculously, I got through the cut without any further glitches, and she was very kind, sweet and polite – until we opened her bedroom door to find the little git crouched, listening at the keyhole. Needless to say, he was history, as was my brief time as her hairdresser.

I tell Mr Pop my little story and he's amused.

'I know her really well, Shaun. Let me ask her if she'll give you another chance.'

'Forget it. Very kind of you, but I know what she'll say, and I can't blame her.' We laugh and start our usual banter about where he's been touring, which hotels he's been staying in and who we both know in common. Mr Pop is a rare breed, our celebrity has spiralled together, so there is empathy and understanding. When I first did him, he was a relatively unknown pop star, struggling to make an impact on the music industry, just as I was in hair-dressing.

I'm just enjoying my chat with Mr Pop, fascinated to hear about the very different world that he inhabits, when an angry-looking woman forces her way under my nose, her hair still wet and her Shaun Lockes logoed gown flapping in the breeze. She is steamingly cross. The salon manager is running after her, desperate to keep her away from me and, above all, Mr Pop.

'Well, what have you got to say for yourself?' she storms, shaking with rage.

'Please calm down, let's talk about this, shall we?' My manager soothes, hands on her rapidly rising and falling shoulders, steering her eagerly away from our famous client.

'Would you excuse me?'

Mr Pop smiles and nods. He's cool and ushers me to go and sort out the situation, picking up his espresso and the latest copy of *GQ*.

'What seems to be the problem here?' I ask, trying to sound concerned and doing my best customer-service bit, hoping desperately that my anger at her outburst isn't showing.

'*You* are!' she thunders.

'I was booked in with you for a bridal trial. I can't believe that this really happens – I mean, you read about it in the papers, normal customers being cancelled for celebrities, but I didn't really think it happened. And at the bloody hairdresser's of all places. How dare you!'

I can't say I blame her. She's right – I shouldn't have cancelled her. I offer her the world – free lunch, free glass of champagne, free hair, free everything – and sit there, shame-faced while she lays into me, having to take everything she says on the chin. Sometimes, and this is one of them, women do have genuine complaints. I've been caught red-handed. Soon, after another glass of bubbly, she's giggling about it, loving all the attention she is suddenly receiving from just about everyone in the entire salon. At least she's being stood up for

Mr Pop, I dare to venture. I even offer to take a picture of him with her on her mobile, knowing that he will kindly oblige, no doubt for the umpteenth time that day. Sometimes, complaints go like that and you can turn the situation round so the client becomes one of your best.

And sometimes it doesn't. Sometimes, people try it on, big time. We've had women calling to complain about their colour six weeks after it was done – funny that, just as the roots need retouching. One even insisted she couldn't call to register her dissatisfaction because she was abroad. Don't they have telephones abroad? I ventured cheekily. But really, it's they who are being cheeky.

Our policy, in line with most respectable salons I presume, is that if anybody is unhappy with anything, we need to know pronto. And that means before they leave the salon, ideally. The analogy is simple – if you're in a restaurant enjoying a meal and are unhappy with your steak, you don't wait until you get home to tell the waiter. Granted, sometimes it's *only* when you get home, wash it and look at it in your own bathroom mirror, or even try and do it yourself, that your realise you're unhappy with it. If so, call and let us know – ASAP. Come back, let us see it and we'll talk about it. We will re-do it as many times as is necessary until you are happy, with our compliments. Or, if it is too short or you want to leave it for a while, we'll give you some credit and promise that we'll make you happy. But only after we've seen it, talked it through, found out what you asked for and analysed the contents of your consultation. What we won't do is issue a refund over the phone without even seeing it. No way, never, ever, ever. You wouldn't complain about a pair of shoes and expect them to refund your credit card without taking them back to the shop, would you? If we weren't so stringent on our customer policy, we would be the losers and our clients would go somewhere else, tell their friends about it, and the money would go in someone else's till. Much better for us to win them over, restore their faith and get them telling their friends how well we dealt with the misunderstanding. For misunderstanding it will most certainly have been. It won't be shoddy work, just maybe us not listening enough to establish what was wanted. Hence my consultation training. Don't use vague words which could be open to misinterpretation, like warm or red – firm it up by checking on the colour chart. Be visual – bring in pictures and photos. Establish your boundaries, agree to the maximum and stay under it, colour-wise, or length-wise.

Sometimes, however hard I try, I just can't connect with someone. This, thankfully, rarely happens, but it does sometimes, and not just to me, to all hairdressers. It's not just a personality thing, it's an I-don't-know-where-you're-coming-from thing. Sometimes, your techniques and your method of working just don't suit the client, who would fit better with somebody else. If this ever happens to you, don't give up on the salon. After all, reception has a tough job trying to match the client to the right stylist/colourist/therapist/manicurist. It's like a dating agency; most of the time, they'll glean some information from you – it might be how you dress, or the little they can judge of your personality from your mannerisms, etc. – and try and matchmake you with your dream hairdresser. Most of the time they get it right, but one man's meat is another man's poison. Sometimes, the least likely of pairings seem to come together to form a rock-solid allegiance, however surprising it may be to everybody else, and a life-long, trusted client/hairdresser partnership can be born.

I wonder whether I would have clicked with my bride, who now seems to be calming down and is faintly amused by the whole thing. Luckily, one of my guys has worked their magic and she's happy. Thank God.

I go back to Mr Pop, finishing off his new look with a scrunch of wax and some careful tweaking and shaping into place. He likes it – it's quite a different look for him and the colour works well. Great, at least I've got one satisfied client. He is very easy, it has to be said. Actors are a different kettle of fish. One very famous one I do actually measures the length of his famous crop with a ruler. Stressful? You bet. Nothing does it for me like the 'I'm watching what you're doing so intently I can't even speak to you' clients. One media darling even brings her make-up artist – who doubles up as her stylist during filming and when I'm not around – with her for her six-weekly cut with me, just so the poor, inferior girl can watch the maestro at work and familiarise herself with my blow-drying technique. Not a very pleasant experience for either of us, I can assure you.

Q: Why aren't there more redhead jokes?
A: Someone told them to a redhead.

Film producers are the strangest, though. Notoriously superstitious when a project is in production, I've known them to come up with all sorts of weird and wonderful reasons for giving me a miss. One I do grew his hair and refused to cut it until his film was released and in the box office top 10 – when he'd been a TV actor, he'd done that with his first film and it had gone on to become a huge success; a crew cut followed swiftly. Another lady film producer refuses to come into the salon until a film is over, blaming any focus on herself as a possible blight on the project's success. I think she just uses the set hairdresser to save a few quid, myself. Mr Pop is far less complicated.

As I wave him off, I watch the *Big Issue* guy papping him blatantly. He's no longer simply tipping off the paparazzi, he now appears to have a camera of his own.

'Yes, Shaun, the cheeky bastard even suggested we might like to go halves with him – it's his new passport to success. He's cutting out the middle man,' my salon manager tells me.

There's enterprise for you, I think, quite impressed with his bold new venture, even though the slimy git's still got it coming from me after this morning.

The now squiffy bride-to-be leaves, hair looking amazing in a perfect chignon, her pearl and diamanté hair slides glistening in the early evening sunshine.

It's been a long day, and I'm still not sure what to do about the guy from the rival salon – he called earlier and has offered to come over at the end of the day and perform a trade test, my secretary tells me. She didn't dare interrupt me in the middle of all the kerfuffle, as she knew she'd be for it for causing the situation in the first place. He'll be here shortly, and I need to gen up on him and his mob quickly. I decide it's time for a drink and ask Paco, who is still cowering in his kitchen, staying firmly out of my way, for a beer. Looking at my watch and anxiously awaiting his return, I am enormously relieved to see my senior (and their ex-stylist) walk through the door, exhausted from his shoot with our rather demanding Little Miss Diva.

Approximately £45 million is spent per year on colour services in the salon.

'For God's sake, Shaun, since when do we have to do Muffin as well? Who do you think I am, Rolf bloody Harris? What is it, Animal Hair Hospital? She asked me to wash and blow dry his fucking ears, the loony bitch.'

Muffin is Little Miss Diva's pooch. She never goes anywhere without the scruff of brown dachshund. She's even started to look like him since going for russet-coloured extensions, a point seemingly lost on everybody but *Heat* magazine. She's a little high maintenance, it has to be said. Recently, when she was in the salon having her weekly – yes, I did say weekly – root retouch, entourage in tow, all busy on their mobiles, Muffin was sitting on her lap, his ears being brushed by the junior, when she said to the manicurist, 'Everybody's *looking* at me. Why won't they leave me alone?' Of course, nobody was looking at her, but the fact that she was complaining was drawing attention to her, and this, of course, was the object of the exercise. It would be tears and tantrums, all to ensure she had the whole salon's undivided attention.

No wonder he'd had a day of it. I get him a beer and leave him to calm down for all of ten seconds before excitedly telling him my news and asking him for a low-down.

'Well, as far as I remember he was all right, but I think you may find them all too bitchy for here, Shaun. They can be an evil bunch of witches, that lot. I'd trade test him, too. His work was OK when I was there, but he was only a junior then. I don't know if he's improved as much as he should have done – after all, they don't believe in retraining there. You're lucky if they even speak to you. Anyway, I think he's here, because I'm sure I saw him at reception just now. Maybe he's done a runner already . . .'

I start to deflate, mentally withdrawing the extra £10k a week of turnover from my cash flow and coming down to earth with a bump. I knew it sounded too good to be true. Still, he's here, and I might as well take a look. You never know, with a few refresher courses and some careful people-management skills, we might just turn him and his motley crew around after all.

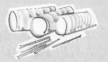

Top Tips

On changing your style

* Have a thorough, detailed consultation with a reputable stylist – recommendation by word of mouth is best.
* Think about your lifestyle – how high maintenance can you go? For instance, if you swim every day, couture blonde highlights are a no-no. Work out if you have time to 'do' your hair every day and if not, opt for something low maintenance.
* Analyse your face shape – if you are unsure, get a photograph and draw round the outline of your face with tracing paper and look at it from a distance. This will give you a guideline on what to avoid. If you have a heavy jaw line, for instance, avoid geometric bobs, or if you have a long forehead, soften it with a fringe.
* Research shows we change something radical about our appearance every three years – it could be style of dress or frames of glasses. The best, and often most cost-effective, way of instantly updating your image is through a hair change. (Think of the makeover shows – the hair sometimes gets more of a response than the clothes or plastic surgery.)
* Have the confidence to know what suits you and your hair and don't be a fashion victim or a slave to the latest styles. You know your hair and what it can do better than anyone else, so communicate this to your hairdresser!
* Bring in photographs of the best your hair ever looked, the worst, and your dream hairstyle. Give your hairdresser lots of information and make sure you input as much as possible.
* Set a boundary with your stylist, i.e. the shortest you are prepared to go, the most drastic a change you'd want to see, etc. And communicate visually so the boundary isn't open to personal interpretation.

The cheat's guide to getting a salon blow-dry

Use a pure bristle brush and always section as follows:

1. Divide your hair into four quarters, as if cutting a cake or an orange — fringe to nape and ear to ear. Then, tackle it as two halves — front and back. Use jaw-clamps to roll up and neatly clip away all the hair you're not working on.

2. Start on the back half by blow-drying each side in three sections taken horizontally from the bottom (the nape) to the top (the crown).

3. Now tackle the top half. Split this half into thirds. Left ear to temple, right ear to temple, and fringe to crown.

4. Blow-dry the sides first by sectioning into two from ear to temple on the left, and repeat on the right.

5. Now work on the remaining section — the one that runs from your fringe to your crown. Section this into three and blow dry from the back, leaving the fringe as your last section, wetting down if necessary.

Chapter 9

6.00 p.m. —
Trade test

There's something about hairdressers that makes them easy to spot. There's a built-in radar, hairdresser to hairdresser, that makes them instantly recognisable to other crimpers. They stand out from the crowd so obviously that I can recognise one a mile away.

First, there is the confident and extrovert body language. Hairdressers are so self-assured they rarely have an insecure day. They'll chat animatedly on their mobiles, while simultaneously smoking and eating a sandwich. This dexterity comes from their ability to do three things at once in the salon, and the fact that hairdressers seldom get a lunch break – they're usually quite thin because of a bizarre mix of starvation and adrenaline. They're normally to be found in gaggles – my collective noun for hairdressers – and there's normally a 'team leader', who will be screaming, guffawing and generally behaving in a weird extrovert fashion. They tend to dress in a high-street meets couture clash of inappropriate daywear – Karen Millen for the women and Diesel for the men. Their hair is always ahead of the game and out there – subtlety doesn't come into it. They bitch and gossip, point and stare, giggle and shout. They are oddly fascinating, holding court in their groups and bewitching whoever happens to walk past. They may be completely over the top, but they are never, ever dull, and I love them for it. If the Scissor Sisters weren't a pop group, they'd make fabulous hairdressers. Now we know where they got their name from . . .

I spot my possible new recruit a mile off, for he is all of the above. We have a brief chat – there's no such thing as a CV with people like him, he's far too grand – and I try to piece together his sketchy past and get to the bottom of his reason for leaving. I'm not at all sure I like him – he's cocky and full of himself, and he swears a lot. I'm no prude but using the 'c' word in an interview is hardly appropriate. He tells me that his friend, another technician, is coming along later. He, too, is fed up and looking to make a move.

My first candidate proves to be a tad petulant. He tells me the new floor manager is an arsehole, and that after an argument with him about a booking he has walked out. Why? I ask, surely he'd see him off soon enough, like countless others before him? He seems vague and ambiguous in response. There are several top salons I know of where the team is so solid they're impervious to any managerial changes. They bide their time, knowing that whoever is temporarily in charge will never out-live their longevity and wait for the new boss to make a monumental cock-up or realise that he or she can never compete or win them over, and take their leave.

20 million women in the UK pay to have their hair done at least once a year, which is 9/10 of the female population. 69 per cent of these women prefer to go to a salon.

Moving swiftly on, I ask him why he left the numerous other salons he has worked at. It makes me a little uneasy. He's supremely confident and very full of his own importance. I decide that I'll reserve judgement until I've seen his work, and set him up in the colouring department with the client he's brought along with him, giving me five precious minutes – the first I've had to myself all day – to ponder my potential new recruit.

It also gives me just enough time to carry out a little professional espionage.

A new salon has opened around the corner, mainly beauty, granted, but they are also doing hair extensions and barbering. It's a strange mix and I can't understand the business ethic. It's like going to Starbucks to buy some toothpaste. Then again, what do I know? Who would have thought years ago that you would be able to buy a sandwich in a pharmacy or flowers from a petrol station? Still, they are too close for comfort and I need to check it out. Some clients have mentioned it to me and I like to know what's going on.

One of my favourite tasks before I became relatively famous was to visit my competitors as a mystery client. It's the only sure-fire way to ascertain how good the service is, or how well the spin doctors are hyping it up. I've been for haircuts to snoop about expensive new salons and to have massages – all just to see how we compare. One over-hyped spa I tried made me gag as the sullen-faced beautician's hands stunk. Health and Safety would do well to remind them about basic hygiene regulations and ensure she washed her hands after the loo with some Carex.

Nowadays, unfortunately, it's increasingly difficult to travel incognito, so I have to rely on my wife's friends to go and do a recce for me. I also pay people to come into my salon and act like real customers, particularly if I am taking on somebody new and I'm not sure whether they're going to cut it. Would you come back and pay full price for what you've had? I ask them, and furthermore, is he or she good enough to make you want to leave your own hairdresser? It's a telling question. The results are frequently discussed by my management team, and in the individual's appraisal if necessary. If the report is unfavourable, it's not good news. New clients are precious, and there's no point in employing somebody who doesn't have the ability to retain them.

I find the salon and peek from the relative safety of across the road. There's a guy sitting in the window having a manicure. That makes a nice change – they have a client! According to reports, there haven't been too many of those. My bitchy camp colourist told me there were *two* customers in there the other day, 'Quite a little *flurry* they were having,' he remarked bitchily, with a giggle.

He also told me that it's hideously overstaffed; and bored employees hanging around is bad news – the more time people have to spend moping about in the staff room, the bitchier the place will be. And that means nasty vibes going out to the clients. Who wants that when you've come to be pampered? Not only that, but the wage bill only checks out if the turnover is coming in – there's no point in paying people to sit on their arses.

A client of mine runs one of London's premier casinos and let me into a little-known secret. The reason people never seem to get tired when they're gambling on the tables is that the atmosphere is pumped constantly with pure oxygen. Ever wondered why those little businessmen with the dandruff and PVC shoes never seem to want to go home, even when they've got enough chips to build themselves their own empire? Well, now you know. They feel fresh as daisies, their tiredness kept at bay by the air they're breathing in. Perhaps our empty rivals should think about that one. A little fresh O_2 circulating round the air conditioning and the despondent staff might perk up a bit.

The guy in the window looks familiar: I'd recognise that hat anywhere. And the camp way his long, lanky legs are crossed. It's one of my senior stylists! Cheeky sod! How could he pay to have his manicure done in a rival salon when he should be giving his custom to his loyal employer! Drastic action is required, so I cross the road and decide to pin myself against the wall of the salon. I wait until a few people have passed by, eyeing me suspiciously, then I leap out, glueing myself like a starfish onto the window in front of him. I can't resist childishly poking out my tongue and making weird googly eyes at him. Through the glass I see him jump out of his skin, then he can't help but giggle, even if it is an embarrassed must-keep-my-cool snigger. He knows he's got some explaining to do when he gets back to work.

We all do this – nosey about each other's salons – especially after a refurbishment or a relocation. I bumped into a rival hairdresser at a trade do recently. We made polite conversation, then he coolly informed me, 'You've got a great salon. I came in for a facial and head massage a few months ago. Had a good look around – your staff are nice, too.' I had to hand it to him, at least he didn't beat around the bush and came straight out with it. I felt relieved he hadn't asked for a discount; it wouldn't have surprised me.

He continued, 'In fact, I'd love to show my business partner around. Can I give you a call sometime?'

The audacity of it!

'Sure,' I replied, knowing I would never allow it. I'd merely forget to return his calls, and make up a bullshit excuse the next time I bumped into him.

That wasn't going to stop him, though. Two days later he turned up on the doorstep, walked straight in and caught me red-handed at reception, with no means of escape. Feeling like a deer in the headlights, I had no option but to give him a guided tour.

'One minute, Shaun,' he said, holding up a hand and hurrying outside excitedly.

'You can come in, now,' he bellowed.

To my amazement he wasn't alone, he had an entourage in tow. Not only had he brought his business partner, who had a face like a smacked arse, but their architect and project manager. Whippet thin, gaunt and sunken looking, the business partner's notorious partying was starting to take its toll and she looked like a Prada-clad Grim Reaper. Not only did she neither smile nor introduce herself, she marched boldly through the salon, rummaging in her bag as she went. Two seconds later a scrawny Cartier-clad arm pulled out a tape measure from her Mulberry Roxanne. No, surely not. I was rendered speechless. She proceeded to measure my backwashes, giving a running commentary of, 'Of course, *we* wouldn't get them in the black . . .' and, 'Make sure you take the model down. Have you got a pen, David?'

The look of incredulity on my face didn't seem to put her off. Her partner, now puce with embarrassment, whispered through gritted teeth, 'Darling, I don't think that's appropriate . . .' and began a non-stop embarrassing one-man monologue of compliments on how beautifully and tastefully furnished my gaff was. Miss Skeletor, however, clearly did not feel it worthy of a mention. Not once, during the entire tour, did she deign to heap one morsel of praise on me or my business, though I knew she'd copy every last detail.

I bumped into him a few days later and he profusely apologised for his business partner's lack of manners. I wasn't impressed, that was obvious. Flowers followed the next day. Oh well, I suppose imitation is the sincerest form of flattery.

I return from my James Bond mission – noting that they have very nice monogrammed towels; I wonder where they got them from? Shit, I'm doing it now . . . – my senior stylist soon follows. By now I've told everybody in the salon where he has been and what he's been up to in the rival nail bar, and we are all desperate to take the piss out of him.

He arrives, flush and panting, he apologises instantly when I berate him for wasting his money on the salon we have christened The Morgue.

'Waste of money? Bloody right, look what the cow did to my cuticles,' he presents his two, normally beautifully groomed hands for inspection.

The skin around his nails is broken and bleeding where a clearly inexperienced college leaver has dug into his precious digits with what looks like a meat cleaver.

'Bugger me! What was she, a cannibal?' I laugh. We all stare at his nails, knowing that they will be the butt of our jokes for the coming week, and also that he is mortified at their now shameful state.

* * * *

*M*y head technician buzzes me from the colour room – the trade test isn't going well.

'What's up?' I sigh.

'It seems we've got a primadonna on our hands, mate. Mr Twinkle-Toes over there isn't prepared to wash off his own colour.'

This is particularly bad form – one should always show willing on a trade test or interview, even if in the real world the chances of a seniors doing anything at the backwash apart from wash their hands between fags is minimal. Squealing pink pigs would fly overhead before such a sight could be seen. They would rather run a stressful forty minutes late all day waiting for a junior to be free to do it than shampoo themselves. Going back to the backwash just isn't an option. But in an interview you're meant to pretend to be a team player. Not sit in the staff room with a cappuccino and your feet up, for God's sake.

This is bad news, and my head colourist knows it. The significance is it shows he has a 'Sod everybody else, I'm all right Jack' attitude – his latest workplace was notorious for this Diva-type behaviour – and it means my lot won't like him. We don't do divas nor selfish gits. Oh, dear. My dreams of improving my takings by an instant 10 per cent seem to be fading into the distance.

He has a long way to go if he thinks he can get away with that kind of behaviour here. It's hardly surprising when you consider the salon he came from, though. The work ethic, if there is one, is very different from ours, as is the culture. They also deal with a celebrity clientele, which can be very demanding, but the bosses hardly set an example, if the stories I've heard are true. The two male bosses don't speak to any of the staff, barely managing to say hello to the team who've made them successful, and they have been rumoured to have had several dalliances with the juniors on the team, which is also a no-no – quick fondles behind the backwashes, apparently, and more than a little foreplay in the VIP room. Mind you, they also have a clientele that has its fair share of Eurotrash royalty with bad coke problems, too, and it's hard to keep your feet on the ground mixing with that lot. They're also notorious for being a hard-partying salon; the majority of them are often hungover for their 9 a.m. appointments – if they arrive at all – and their staff parties are legendary – nearly as revered as the ones from my training days.

Their salon Christmas party was the event of the season, and the inter-salon copulation was the stuff of legend. Everyone was at it with everyone, everywhere. Even the most reserved gay tinter once said to me drunkenly during a mad party night, 'Shame you're not gay, Shaun, because my fantasy is to rip my plastic gloves off, bend you over in the middle of the salon and give you a damn good seeing to . . .'

Sorry to disappoint, mate. I never could look at him in the same light after that. If you were a little confused about your sexuality, you'd be positively baffled after mixing with that lot for a decade.

As a boss, I used to detest the staff party. Don't get me wrong, I loved having a good craic with the staff, but in the past I used to allow other halves to come along, which is never a good idea. I learned my lesson, as it invariably ends up with some pissed-up fiancé or husband bemoaning their loved one's lack of recognition, or worse, pay. And it always starts with the immortal words, 'I know it's the staff party, but . . .' Or, 'She wouldn't want me to tell you this, but she really feels *unappreciated,* you know . . . she doesn't think it's fair that so-and-so charges more than she does . . .' Or, 'He wouldn't want me to say this, but it has been at least twelve months since he's had a salary review . . .' Nightmare! And it always seems to be the partners who are earning less, or are students relying on their other half's salary, who have the biggest grievances. What they should really be saying is, 'I want to have a year out to study my tantric yoga, so couldn't you whack the commission rate up, Shaun?' I can't be doing with all that in my spare time, so it's simpler to ban the partners altogether – and much more fun for me.

Now I enjoy the staff party, even though I regularly get my ears chewed off by my team. They think that if I'm pissed I'll agree to a price increase, which I invariably do. Still, I need to let my hair down sometimes and get away from the PR-frenzied world I increasingly inhabit.

One of my actress clients called me recently and, bearing in mind I haven't seen her for six months while she's been very publicly sampling the delights of one of my rivals, asked me to drop every-thing at two hours' notice and get over to her house to style her hair for the Brits and a party she's host-ing for her new Sky series. Normal people wouldn't behave like this; they'd be far too embarrassed to act like a petulant child if you hadn't seen hide nor hair (liter-ally!) of them for months on end. Somebody had clearly let her down, and she'd suddenly remembered me. I might have been sorely tempted if we were talking about one client, but half a day's worth?

Red wine and coffee
Great for adding to vegetable colour or henna to give more depth and good colour tone.

Of course, she would blame such uncompromising demands on her secretary, and the next time I bumped into her no doubt she'd be charm personified. I felt quite righteous about saying 'No!' for a change. There comes a time when you have to put these divas in their place, and she'll probably have more respect for me for doing so. No doubt it may even make her want to come back. After all, nobody likes a doormat, do they?

But even her shoddy treatment can't compare with the Hollywood diva I did recently in her hotel suite. Constantly fussed over by four assistants she managed to keep me waiting for two hours in the lobby while she took her pre-premiere nap. Not that I was told this vital piece of information; I was just fobbed off with the excuse that she was 'out to lunch'. The sycophantic team just pandered to her every whim by dis-agreeing with my suggestions for her red carpet look; that was, until she thought my ideas were fabulous, when the turncoats quickly changed their tune and started to respect my hairdressing prowess. No wonder she's rumoured to be a bit of a headcase. Who'd want to be surrounded by yes men all day? It's not exactly good for the soul, I would imagine.

My head colourist comes to find me while I'm sitting in the office skimming the latest issue of *Salon Weekly*. It's a bumper edition sponsored by one of the product companies and is guaranteed to piss off their counterparts. I bet the editor's phones are ringing off the hook today. I'm pleased to say I am in it, a full-on mug shot of me accompanied by an article about my creative inspiration. There is also one on Antoine, announcing his new position. My cordless intercom phone buzzes again.

> Hair style is the final tip-off whether or not a woman really knows herself.
> Hubert de Givenchy

The trade test result is not good. For all his cockiness, Boy Wonder is unable to come up with the goods and can't even do a simple colour to the level of one of my graduates. It's deflating news, even if I have already decided that he is an arsehole who won't fit in with the team.

I go outside to see for myself as he arrogantly nods towards his model's head, while rudely chatting into his mobile. A basic colour-match root tint and a few lights look distinctly patchy and uneven. Even if he's never used our product range before, there's no excuse for his colour selection. I can see the lights aren't flush to the root, which already gives the illusion of three weeks' regrowth. It's crap work: slap-dash and uncaring, just like him.

'I'll call you,' I mouth, thinking the rude bastard probably expects me to buy him a drink and offer him the job on the spot.

My head colourist and I go back to the office for a debrief. He doesn't need to go into the technicalities, I can see for myself the hideous fuck-up he's made. Too cock sure for his own good, that one. Still, his friend is coming along soon and, ever the optimist, I tell the team to keep an open mind, even if I'm secretly beginning to wonder exactly how my so-called rivals have managed to gain such a reputation for themselves.

I must admit, though, it makes me feel great, and very proud of my own standards. There am I always wondering whether the grass is greener, and believing the hype that their staff are better technically than mine, only to be pleasantly surprised that they aren't a patch on them. I silently admonish myself for being greedy. That's karma for you – not appreciating what you've already got. I wouldn't book him a precious new client if he was the last hairdresser on earth. Years ago, I might have taken a punt on someone like that, knowing that I could just get rid of him if it didn't work out, but with the increasingly complex employment laws weighting so heavily in the employee's favour, I can ill afford to take a gamble. I have to cover my arse, not just with him, but also when it comes to insuring the salon against any complex legal stitch-ups. We had a case recently where a woman client blamed an overzealous session under the hood dryer for a broken nose – eighteen months after the event, which she never reported at the time. Society is becoming more and more litigious and salon owners need to be on their toes.

We are lucky to have a very low turnover of staff, thanks to the lessons learned in my training days. If somebody does leave the salon, I make a point of filling the position as quickly as possible. Normally I have a couple of CVs on file that I am interested in. It's important to send out a message to the team: as much as I value them, nobody is indispensable. It's always great to open a CV in the post and it's a comfort to know that people want to join us.

Reception buzz me to tell me the second interviewee has arrived. With a sinking feeling in my heart, I head to the sofa where he is waiting to meet me and start the process all over again. He is not what I expected. He isn't flashy or trashy, in fact, he looks quite normal and very nervous.

I show him into the office, but the interview doesn't go well at first. He's edgy and defensive and seems to be interviewing me, rather than the other way round. What are our prices? Why aren't we more expensive? What colours do we use? How many clients can we feed him? It's a totally me, me, me, one-sided conversation.

Hey, hold your horses, I think, time to get this back under my control. Who's the bloody salon owner here? I decide to pull in the reins and get my own back.

What sort of clients is he used to doing? Isn't it all ladies who lunch over there? Does he know that we've worked enormously hard to make our clientele much younger, less boring and more diverse? How well does he cope with pressure? What does he do when he doesn't have a junior? How well does he work in a team environment? Then the real stinger, when was the last time he went on a training course?

He quietens down a little, relaxes and listens to me. He tells me, without slagging off his old salon too much, what his reasons are for leaving. He has been through fifteen changes of management in the course of his career, but this one is making him really unhappy. People are leaving the salon like drowning men leaving a sinking ship. He has lost colleagues he liked working with and wants a new start. He wants something long term. And no, he doesn't think the previous candidate would be what we are looking for. He is certainly older, more experienced and hopefully more accomplished. I warm to him, deciding that he's just nervous as he hasn't been for many job interviews – his technique is bound to be a little rusty. He's been incarcerated in one salon and is set in his ways. Can he change, though? He gives me a good, cohesive argument for giving him the job and starts to win me over. Now it's a question of whether or not he can cut it professionally.

I show him through to the technical area and introduce him to my head colourist. He has some models lined up, so sets to work. I'm resigned to the fact that he may be too set in his ways and am fearful that his work won't be up to much. Bloody Frankie.

While the results spoke for themselves with the other guy, this one seems much more grounded. He's certainly been loyal to Austin & Harte, having been with them since his training days. Perhaps all this talk about the new floor manager and people leaving really is making people like him unhappy. He's the type who hates change, I decide, and perhaps that's the reason for his blunt questions.

I head to the kitchen, anxious to catch Paco before he locks up. I have yet to have it out with him, and he'll be aiming to scurry away to avoid me, hoping I'll let him off the hook and forget about his almighty faux-pas by the morning.

Too late, he's beaten me to it. And the little sod has even had the audacity to cut out the picture of Antoine from *Salon Weekly*, draw on some drops of blood dripping from one ear with red pen, and stick it on his kitchen door, with a bubble caption reading, 'Shaun Lockes – hairdresing's leeding cutta' I can't help but laugh. I decide to draw a sandwich in Antoine's hand, with a big black hair coming out of it, and another bubble caption: 'Paco – Michelin star, nil; Michelin tyres, 4.' I chuckle to myself, knowing all the staff will see it tomorrow morning and give Paco shit all day.

27 per cent of eight- to twelve-year-old girls wish they had different coloured hair.

My potential new guy comes over and catches me like a naughty schoolboy, pen in hand, and asks me where he might find some conditioner as all the backwashes are empty. It's a good sign – at least he's not asking to nab a junior to assist him: they're all dying on their feet and desperate to go home.

He grins, looking at the caption and laughing. His model is nearly ready to be washed off, do I want to have a look at his foil insertion? I wander over, where my head colourist is inspecting his work closely. He nods and smiles; his foils are a work of art. They are the most precise, beautifully inserted highlights I've seen in ages. The excitement starts to well inside – we may be onto a winner.

He shampoos his client at the basin to remove the colour and, better still, tidies up after himself. He even takes the conditioner and starts refilling the backwash pumps while his model goes to the loo. Something tells me this isn't just for show. When she returns, I watch him as he starts rough-drying her hair, then my phone buzzes.

I can see that it's Ms Editor; I put her direct line into my mobile earlier when I was cutting her hair in the hope that she might be true to her word and decamp to the Shaun Lockes client list.

'Shaun? I've got news . . .'

Shit, she's going to tell me she doesn't like her cut, or worse, she's going to turn into a stalker and expect me to nip over to her desk and touch up her hair every bloody minute.

'About three weeks ago the supermarket chain Costcutters called me asking who I thought was the hottest thing in hairdressing, as they were looking to venture into the designer hair care market. Of course I said Lucas at the time – as you know, before that bloody hair guru screwed up my hair, he was my regular stylist . . .'

'Yes, I know, but what's . . .'

'Listen, listen. Anyway, they said they weren't interested in Lucas as he was doing electricals with somebody else. They wanted someone of their own, so I told them I'd have a think and get back to them. Well, after the wonders you've done with my hair today, I called them to let them know I've found my new Vidal, and theirs, too! They're desperate to meet you; the MD has asked me to pass on his number. I told him you'd call him first thing in the morning. Got a pen, darling?'

With one little turn of events, it looks as if all my hair dreams are about to turn into a reality. I frantically scribble down the number and thank her a million times before she whizzes off the phone and on to some painfully trendy gallery opening.

Perhaps it's my turn after all. At last, I may get my own product range. The years of research I have quietly done on bottle shapes, packaging, colours, fragrances and, most importantly, ingredients, may not have been in vain. My product line may come to fruition after all.

As for ingredients, as hairdressers we're perfectly placed to judge whether something is a magic formula or not, and I fully intend to do my homework with any product that bears my name. I can't afford to mess this opportunity up.

My mind is already working overtime on how my range will look. If they're going to invest in me, they might even blow me a mould. This means that instead of buying a bottle shape from a manufacturing company, I could come up with my own bespoke design. Perhaps I'll go for something phallic, like one of my rivals did. Strangely enough, women seemed to like that one . . .

My phone buzzes, waking me up from my daydream. It's my secretary again, but she has something to tell me before I can spill my own beans.

'Do you want the bad news or the bad news?' she asks, listening for my sigh.

'Carl has just called and let me know he's coming down with a horrendous cold and will be off sick tomorrow and he was fully booked. He had two colour changes and three full heads. What do you want me to do?'

'Little gob-shite! I heard him in the staff room earlier telling everyone he's going to that boy-band reunion party. Bollocks he's ill! He's just telling his lies now because he knows he'll be too shit-faced tomorrow morning to call!' I thunder.

'I know, I know. But it could be a great trial day for your interviewee, Shaun, could it not?' she suggests cheekily. 'Make your mind up – I'd rather get on with cancelling them now if we've got nobody to do them. Get the stress out of the way tonight instead of piling it all up for a bad start in the morning.'

My mind is racing. I go over to the finished model and the colour is gleaming – glossy, rich and lustrous. The roots match the ends seamlessly and the subtle highlights are perfectly woven and beautifully close to the root.

I look over to my head colourist and he gives me a slow smile with a nod of his head. We've found a great new team member, and with a little careful shaping, he might prove to be dynamite. He even has all his numbers, although with this standard of work, we'll have no trouble filling his column.

Just one little question. Very unethical, but why not? OK, so he'll have to either pull a sickie or get back over there and hand in his resignation tonight – they'll never make him work his notice. Salons never do, they can't. If they allowed any of their staff to work when they're planning to leave, they'd have at least two precious weeks to tell all their clients, and worse, the other team members, where they're going. They may even get in with a receptionist and plot to get a list of their client's numbers off the salon database. Some salons frog march the defecting staff number straight out of the salon minutes after opening the dreaded envelope. No, they'll never make him work his notice, which would mean he'd be on gardening leave and free to work tomorrow . . . which would save me cancelling all that precious turnover.

'Welcome on board. How soon can you start?' I ask excitedly.

You know you're in trouble when . . . . A guide to avoiding possible hair disasters

Your technician says: 'I'm just going to dry it off a bit and put a toner on.'
Your technician means: Your colour has not come out to the target shade. It has gone wrong and if you knew how badly, you might cry. Particularly serious if you are at the backwash and they won't sit you in front of a mirror for fear that you might see it. You can now officially panic.

Your stylist says: 'Who cut your hair last time?', then goes quiet.
Your stylist means: The last cut was so dreadful whoever did it should be shot. However, if the client says somebody who works here I will say nothing — if she says she went to a lesser salon I can bore her for ages about what is wrong with it.

Your technician says: 'We'll just give it a little cleanse to get rid of the colour build up.'
Your technician means: The colour they have used may have grabbed or become patchy and needs to be stripped out. Don't look in a mirror until it's all over or you'll cry. This is possibly the worst-case scenario.

Your stylist says: 'You've got lots of new hair growing at the front.'
Your stylist means: Your hair may be falling out. Lots of searching questions will follow about your diet, stress levels, pregnancy, medication, etc.

Your stylist says: 'Do you have school-age children?'
Your stylist means: You may be about to be told that you have nits. This normally happens after the shampooist and stylist stand over you at the backwash examining your hair. You are going to die of embarrassment. Your gown and towel will be whisked away to be incinerated and you will be asked to leave even if your hair is wet. Die of shame here and now.

Your stylist says: 'Your hair is very sensitised.'
Your stylist means: Your hair is absolutely knackered and if you, or I, do anything else to it you'll be taking it home in a brown paper bag.

Your stylist says: 'I want you to be really sure about making such a huge commitment'
Your stylist means either: I'm not sure either about such a radical change of cut/colour. If I say this it gets me off the hook.
OR: Stop fanny-arsing about and hurry up and decide what you want me to do. You've wasted half of your appointment time already, so whatever we do is going to be a rush job, and you're not even sure if you want a shit, shave or haircut.

Chapter 10

7 p.m. — Locking up

I love the salon when everybody has gone home as it has a peaceful eeriness to it.

The reception, which was just a few short hours ago a hive of buzzing phones and clients checking in and out, is still and silent. There are no women changing notes for coins so they can tip, or admiring their new coiffed look in the full-length mirror. There are no stylists running to check their schedules or juniors hovering around to check their tip boxes to see if they can afford lunch or whisk the frantic latecomers over for a quick shampoo before their hurried fit-in. Even the once-frenetic backwash is now tranquil; used towels and empty shampoo bottles are strewn around the basins and the bins are full of moulted wet hair and crumpled foils.

The kitchen is full of empty, lipstick-stained coffee cups, and the magazine racks are once again stuffed full with the well-thumbed issues, all crinkled and used from a day's heavy duty cover to cover reading by an endless stream of clients.

The stylists' sections, which were buzzing with animated gossip, rollers and hairspray are quiet and still; the binfuls of hair clippings the only evidence of the activity the salon has witnessed during the course of the day. The manicure bars are depleted of their usual rainbow-stacked nail polish, the beauty rooms still, calm and customarily fragrant, and here, in the tranquillity of closure, my team will re-stock and replenish for tomorrow's bookings. The phones will start ringing at 8.30 a.m. and we will all put on our smiles and start over again, whatever we may be feeling inside.

It's time for me to take stock of what has happened and reflect on the working day, as I mooch about the salon, remembering the countless conversations that peppered my day.

As I wander around, I can't help feeling like Arkwright the shopkeeper from *Open All Hours*, thinking through the day that has been. I have a system to closing the salon, readying myself for whatever tomorrow may bring.

First, I do a reccie around the salon, ensuring that everything is where it should be – the chairs are all in the right areas, the pedicure bowls have been returned to their rightful place, the price brochure racks are full and everybody's stools are back in situ. Some stylists can't work without a stool and others never use them. Some even use them like the colourists use their trolleys. But like everything in hairdressing, ownership of such items is strangely territorial. The last thing I need tomorrow is one of my seniors going ape because somebody's swiped their stool. Especially the tall ones. Most above-average height hairdressers are prone to a spot of sciatica – it's all to do with the slouching when we cut – and simply can't function without their stool, even if it's only used as a resting place for their dryer.

By 2008, the men's grooming market will be worth £1.5 billion per annum in the UK.

Next, I check to make sure we have towels for tomorrow, for although the juniors will all arrive to do their jobs – washing, drying and folding the towels is the most crucial. unless we have clean, dry towels ready for the first clients, the day is bound to start stressfully, and that's the last thing I need.

I want to walk into a spotless, fully prepped business model; a marvel of efficiency, a tight, well-run ship, at 8.00 a.m. tomorrow. Some nights I feel too exhausted to even attempt to get things straight and sometimes I enjoy being here on my own, pottering about. I care about this baby, this salon I have created from nothing. I mother and nurture her, she is my golden goose. I feel a strong desire to pet her and thank her for putting up with us all, day after day, without complaint. She, like the chairs, couches, mirrors and basins, has more than performed her duty. She has done me proud and never let me down. I have a strange urge to do her justice by taking some time out to treat her with the respect she deserves, silently promising her a new lick of paint and a thorough spring-clean when time allows.

One thing's for sure, hairdressing is never groundhog day. How could I possibly tire of it? Who knows who will be sitting in my chair next, or what delicious secrets they may spill? I know I could never be happy sitting in an office, without the full-on witty banter, gossip and fun. My soul would be destroyed. If only my salon's walls could talk. What stories they could tell.

But who will take over my little empire when I finally decide to hang up my scissors? I worry about this constantly. Nurturing your chosen protégé can be a dangerous business – too much encouragement and you create a monster; not enough praise, financial reward and motivation and inevitably they'll open their own salon and vow to treat their protégés with more respect. The ironic thing is, they never do treat them any better. For when they become a salon owner, they'll finally understand the pressures and complexities of being the boss.

Once people have a taste for it, glory is not something they are good at sharing. I've seen it happen too many times with other salon owners. They develop one particular member of staff, hoping to pass the hairdressing mantel on to them, introducing them to their contacts, throwing

Experience is a comb which nature gives us when we are bald.
Proverb

a little show work their way, creating an ego, a level of importance within the trade, perhaps even giving them some share
options; then there's a spectacular fall-out and their carefully
cultivated plans go tits-up. The fledgling leaves the nest, possibly even adding insult to injury by taking a few others with
them, or goes to work for a rival in an elevated position. Then
the circle of hairdressing life starts over, and the next best thing
is created again. As much as I'd love my children to be bankers
or lawyers, if you keep it in the family you've got a built-in suc-
cessor to your crown. Blood is thicker than water, as they say.

It's taken me two and a half decades of slog, learning,
watching and practising to feel that I'm good enough to lead
and head up a huge team of equally talented and creative people. I've cultivated a calm, self-assured stance that at times
hasn't mirrored the insecure emotions inside. I have pushed
myself relentlessly to get better and better, more confident and
more creative, striving to become a better hairdresser, a better
people manager and a better businessman.

Sometimes I envy my clients, those who are free from all
these nagging doubts. Those who work for somebody else,
free of the hassle and pressures of owning their own business.
Those who close their office door and don't have to give it
another thought until they arrive back the next day.

Take my last client: a city boy who seems to earn in one
annual bonus what I will take a lifetime to achieve. He sat in
my chair, Blackberry buzzing and mobile vibrating, and his
scalp was peeling and flaking so badly into my comb that I
couldn't cut his hair without taking off six layers of red-raw
skin. Although I may fleetingly envy his new Porsche and the
trappings of his success, I look at men like him and see them
for what they really are: stressed, hardly able to enjoy their
lives and burnt out at forty. Is that what I really want? Is that
what I want for my children? Would I be that disappointed if,
even after their expensive private education, they chose to follow me down the hairdressing career path? I often wonder, as
I snip away, secretly envying him his Val D'Isere ski chalet, his

Tuscany summer retreat and his Kensington penthouse, if it's him who envies me? Who has got it right, and who has got it wrong? Can he ever leave his stress at the office door when his working day is over? Or is the cut-and-thrust of his competitive work environment more alopecia-inducing than mine?

My relationship with my career is like the one you have with your partner's parents. It's OK for me to criticise it, but if anybody else says a word, even in jest, I become strangely defensive. We are more than just hairdressers. We are therapists, life-coaches, social workers and miracle workers. We give people a feel-good factor, all via our carefully trained, well-honed hairdressing technique.

Hearing my mother tell me about her hairdressing days, I realise that her pensioner clients, who admired her so much and had such a good time in her salon, saw their weekly visit as a lifeline. They probably didn't speak to anybody else for days on end, and having their hair done was the high point of their week. It was important to them, as it is to so many women. It's not just about the hair, it's about human contact. If you happen to be a good hairdresser and have the power to transform a person's hair, you can transform their self-esteem too. It's a powerful drug, and it's what keeps us hooked to our profession. Nurturing women and making them feel good. We are just as much a public service as those performed by health-care workers.

HAIR FACTS

Greasy hair is caused by the scalp producing too much sebum – shampooing with lukewarm water so as not to over-stimulate the sebaceous glands will help reduce greasiness.

Hairdressing has given me twenty-five fabulous years of privilege and experience and I've loved every minute. Would I change a thing? No, I don't think so. I've had my share of luck and misfortune, but I've worked hard to accomplish what I've got, and ultimately my job is good fun. As demanding, physically knackering and emotionally trying as it can be, it is *always* enjoyable. No wonder it's been championed as *the* profession of the twenty-first century, or has been celebrated as the most happy, stress-free job, with the salon being voted the best environment to work in.

I turn off the salon lights, knowing that tomorrow I'll be back, bright and early, ready to face another set of challenges.

Q: What do you call a redhead with an attitude?
A: Normal.

Who knows what will happen tomorrow? My new guy has agreed to start and do Carl's column, and more may follow from Austin & Harte once he settles in. The salon will be buzzing; the new broom that will sweep into the colouring department might just cement the existing team in the colouring department. Having somebody new around keeps everyone on their toes. And the salon owner is not the only one who will benefit, the clients will too. Everybody will be on their toes, and their work, standards of service, takings and retail sales are bound to improve as a result. And that will make me very happy. All is right with my world.

Maybe the next big look or hair trend will be effortlessly created by me during the course of the following working day and I'll be the toast of the trade. I'll create something timeless, iconic and ground-breaking that will make me even more of a household name. It will be copied in salons up and down the country and all over the world. It may even turn into the defining image of the decade. It will make some actress's name and give her a look the magazines will die for. I'll be feted for my artistic ability and envied for my amazing profile. I wish . . .

Perhaps someone will even come along and offer me a fortune to sell out, so I can spend the rest of my days sitting on the balcony of a beautiful Spanish villa, reading about the next hairdressing new boy in town in my Spanish edition of the *Daily Mail*. And perhaps not. Perhaps I will remain happy in my salon, snipping away and making a good living, still trying to figure out what makes women tick.

The most important people in my working life will always be my everyday clients; the women and men, teachers and nurses, housewives and bankers, who sit in my chair and let me snip away. It makes me feel proud that they have chosen to come to my salon and I am forever grateful for their custom. They call me a 'celebrity hairdresser' these days; but celebrities are only 2 per cent of my clientele. It may be a useful title, but I never forget who has put me where I am.

What was that? What did I hear you say? What would I do with your hair? Give me a break, it's home time. Of course, you could always book in and then I'll tell you . . . I may even create that new iconic look on you.

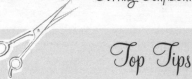

Top Tips

On choosing your colour

✳ Decide if you are warm-toned or cool-toned. If you are unsure, scrape your hair back in a turban and stand in the daylight. Wrap a warm-toned piece of fabric (a peachy colour, for instance) around your face, then a cool one (lilac is good). One will bring your face to life and make your eyes sparkle and the other will make your skin look sallow. Let the warm/cool principle guide you in all the colour you wear – make-up, clothes and hair.

✳ After thirty, our skin tone naturally lightens, so you should always aim to go two or three depths lighter than your natural base. Think fifty-year-old with jet black dyed hair and you'll get the picture! Lighter pieces in the form of subtle highlights around the hairline soften the face and can make you look younger.

✳ Experiment with colour if you are a colour virgin by going for a vegetable colour (not literally made of vegetables but large, conditioning colour pigment). Not only will it cover greys, but it will add shine and lustre without damaging the hair.

✳ Protect your colour investment – couture colour isn't cheap and you must help prevent fade by looking after your hair. Avoid salt water, chlorinated water and sun as they will all damage and fade your colour. Think of it like Scotchguarding your Manolo Blahniks!

✳ Dark hair will always shine more than light hair as there is more pigment and so more light is reflected. Artificial blonde hair means natural pigment has been removed by bleaching, that's why only natural very light blonde hair shines well.

✳ Be realistic about how far from your natural base your target colour is. The more depths (lighter or darker) between the two, the more risk to the condition of your hair the technical work will be, especially if you're going lighter, as you are removing pigment not adding it) and the more commitment you will have to make to your hair looking good. Don't do anything radical if you don't want high-maintenance colour.

✳ The only way to make hair lighter is by using bleach or permanent colour. To make hair lighter you have to remove colour pigment. Temporary or semi-permanent colours can only add depth and tone, not remove it.

* Artificial red is the hardest colour to achieve staying power with, to prevent fade, and ironically, to remove. If you want to go red, be prepared to really invest in looking after your colour.

How to colour your own hair

DON'T even think about it. Go on the game rather than not be able to afford a professional job. It will always, *always* look like you've done it yourself.

Most frequently asked top 10 questions

Is it worth buying an expensive brush?

Yes. Like everything, you get what you pay for. It's not necessarily what the bristles are made of — nylon can be as good as bristle — but as synthetic brushes are normally manufactured cheaply, the ends are not finished well and are rough and scratchy so the bristles can rip the hair, which is very bad when blow drying, as the hair is in a weaker and more fragile state when wet. Pure bristle is normally well made and therefore would be much less damaging. Buy a good professional brush from a reputable salon.

Do you need to wash your hair twice with shampoo?

If it's relatively clean already, for example, washed the day before, no. If left longer, yes. Many people use far too much product in one shampoo, whereas it is better to use more sparingly and deep cleanse with two shampoos; emulsifying each time with a splash of water before massage helps to ensure it is evenly distributed across the scalp. When we shampoo at the salon, the first wash is like a pre-cleanse, whereas the second is the ultra-cleanse. Using salon professional products that are highly concentrated will not only give better results, but may work out cheaper in the long run, as you will use less. The size of a ten-pence piece is ample for highly concentrated products. It is far better to get into the ethos of cleansing and conditioning really well, and therefore less often, than washing every day and not taking the time to do it properly.

Will anything stop the frizz?

Yes, getting your hair into amazing natural condition. Hair is much more prone to frizz if it is damaged or chemically treated. If you can't go without the colour, at least cleanse and condition it really well. Blow-drying in proper sections will not only help keep the frizz at bay, your style will last longer. Don't be tempted to rough dry for speed and reach for the straightening irons — take your time and blow dry like the professionals do; otherwise it's a false economy! Lots of de-frizz products contain silicone derivatives which, if not used sparingly, can overlap and cause build-up. Finish your blow dry with a slick of serum (warmed through your hands first to aid application) and remember the golden rule: one product is ample. Don't be tempted to overload or you will actually create product build-up, which may result in more frizz. Don't over-wash either; allow the natural oils (sebum) to work their Mother Nature magic. Hair is generally better the second day — less static and easier to work with, so get to 'know' your hair really well and make the most of its natural state.

Humidity and dampness in the air is the biggest problem for frizzy hair, but it should frizz less if you follow the above guidelines.

How do I get salon-beautiful hair every day?

Blow-dry your hair properly at least two or three times per week, in sections the same length and width as the barrel of your brush, starting at the nape of your neck and finishing at the fringe area. On in-between days, simply go over your style with a good medium-barrelled bristle brush and hairdryer. There's no need to damp down, just re-blow dry the main sections, taming any frizzy new hairs around the hairline, and re-sleeking your hair until it looks like it's freshly blow-dried. When you can't get away with it any more, you know it's time to shampoo.

How do I keep my curls fresh?

Take some time to put them in properly. If you want large, wavy curls, the best way is to spritz some mousse or a volume booster onto freshly washed hair, then take a section the same size and width as your chosen roller (the smaller the roller, the tighter the curl; the more twists on the roller; the tighter the curl) and pop in a Velcro roller, which will stay in place. If you want curly ends only, wind the roller loosely halfway along the length, if you want curl to the root, wind it all the way up. Blast with the dryer or leave to dry naturally. Shake out by raking through with fingers. Heated rollers are also great, but use sparingly as they can damage your hair. The more careful the sectioning and the more rollers used, the better the result. If using heated rollers, leave to dry until the rollers feel completely cool for extra hold.

What's the worst thing you can do to hair?

Although hair is naturally quite strong, it is a dead protein. Some people just assume their hair is invincible and heap the damage on until it fights back. Think of colour chameleons like Kelly Osbourne and Madonna, who are platinum blonde one minute and ebony the next, then back to blonde. Hair needs to go through a variety of chemical processes and pigmentation removal for so drastic a change. You cannot change your hair so dramatically without serious problems such as hair loss, temporary alopecia, etc. Treat your hair kindly and don't expect too much of it. If you are unsure about what colour you want to be, experiment with some wigs and hairpieces, not the dye bottle. (Go to www.trendco.co.uk for more information about where to find wigs you can try on.)

How do I break the habit of my straightening irons?

Most women use straighteners because they are convinced they save time. Untrue. It would take the same amount of time to blow-dry from scratch in proper sections as it would to rough dry and re-straighten with irons. And the blow-drying result would be much better. If this doesn't work for you, you're using the wrong dryer. Invest in an 'AC' salon professional dryer (not like the ones you buy in the high street) and you'll find that blow-drying your hair is a breeze. They are slightly heavier, but once you get the hang of them, they take half the time. Invest in some clamps too, and section your hair properly, following my blow-drying guide on p.227.

How do I get volume in my hair?

Getting volume when you blow dry is all in the brush action. Think of the direction the roots are growing in naturally. To get root lift, you need to get the roots moving away from their natural directional growth. Instead of blow drying with 'root drag', you need to lift the brush up above the section and dry from underneath to get volume and lift. Careful use of products can give extra oomph, too. Spritz some root activator onto the roots of towel-dried hair before you start styling, and be careful not to weigh down with the wrong products, like using a shampoo for dry hair if your hair is normal. Hair should always squeak after washing, denoting it has been thoroughly cleansed.

Is home colouring really damaging?

Home colour products have improved drastically over the years — the technology leading the way in the professional field has really advanced the home care market. However, it is the choice of colour where salon expertise cannot be compromised. How can Joe Public ever expect to get it right when even with all our technical training we sometimes screw up? We have to take so much into consideration: percentage of grey, natural pigment, target level of lightening, arriving at the correct undercoat, natural tone present, sensitivity, tensile strength, porosity, age of hair, lifestyle and skin tone, degree of fade and colour history, to name but a few. Colour isn't simply a case of picking a shade and getting it, like painting a wall, there are lots of 'scientific' matters that can affect the result, and that is what you are paying for — our expertise. And that's before we even take into account skilled application — most women colouring their hair at home overlap on previously coloured hair, which not only causes colour 'banding' but can cause irreparable damage to the hair's condition.

How can I get the best out of my hairdresser?

Like everything, you get out what you put in. If you are happy with your hairdresser, keep them on their toes and stop them from getting complacent by being open to subtle changes and suggestions. If you are too dismissive, eventually they'll stop trying, which is no good for either of you and ultimately the biggest reason why women leave their hairdresser. If you change the subject and natter on about your partner when your stylist is trying to talk about your hair, don't complain when they never suggest anything new. Don't be tempted to socialise or get too personal with your stylist and then be surprised and disappointed when they stop treating you like a client and get too personal with you.

Don't use vague words — be specific. Bring in pictures of colours and styles you like so there is no room for misinterpretation. Set boundaries too — how short you are prepared to go, for instance. That gives no excuse for the stylist to cross them! Communicate well — tell them what you like and what you don't. Ask them to show you how to style your hair at home, and listen to their recommendations. They're not always just trying to sell you something — for instance, a salon dryer is an excellent investment, as is the right brush. If you aren't happy, and want to go elsewhere, word of mouth is by far the best recommendation. Find a friend whose hair you admire and ask her where she goes, then get yourself booked into a stylist she recommends.

The latest survey says we change our hairstyle on average twenty times between the ages of eighteen and twenty-four and just four times between the ages of fifty and eighty. So, what are you waiting for?

Should I change my shampoo regularly – will my hair 'get used' to a product?

This is an urban myth. Hair does not become immune to a product working, yet most women I know have showers and bathrooms that have more hair products than Boots. By all means experiment, but be aware that if you find a product that really suits your hair, stay with it.

Does hair have different needs at different times of the year?

Yes. Weather, temperature and pollution all affect the way our hair feels. For instance, in the winter, central heating can dry out hair and skin. If you work in an air-conditioned building, this may affect your hair, too. Humidity causes frizz, due to increased moisture levels in the atmosphere, so hair has different concerns in a hot, sticky summer. April showers and drizzly autumn days also will affect frizz control. Just a normal two-week summer holiday can do untold damage if hair is subjected to intense sun, salt water or chlorine.

Is there any truth in the old wives tale that 100 brushes every day is good for my hair?

In some ways, yes. The benefit 100 brushes with a soft, natural bristle brush is the stimulation of the blood supply to the scalp, which could encourage healthy hair growth. Scalp massage would be just as good.

Is it worth splashing out on a fancy hairdresser? Do I really get a better haircut?

In my opinion, yes. Although there are some excellent hair-dressers working in thousands of salons up and down the country, the cream, as they say, always rises to the top.

Will lemon juice on hair make it lighten naturally?

First, we need to define naturally. By natural, we mean that it is a natural product which has caused the bleach-ing effect, so sitting in the sun with lemon juice on your hair will lighten it. However, just because it is 'natural' doesn't mean it isn't going to result in roots — so be warned!

Why do I always leave the salon feeling a little disappointed?

Be realistic! Know what your hair is capable of. If you've got spindly, fine hair you'll never look like Catherine Zeta-Jones witohut a hell of a lot of high-maintenance help and a head full of hair extensions!

Glossary

Average age of hair before it falls out
4 years (or bra-strap length).

Backwash
Hair-washing station.

Bag of crisps (i.e. her hair's like a bag of crisps)
Hair that has been seriously chemically damaged, possibly beyond repair and hopefully not by your salon.

Baristas
Servers in coffee bars.

Batty boy
Gay man – Jamaican slang meaning 'bats for the other side'.

Bob
A one-length hair cut, normally considered to be bobbed if it is worn jaw length to shoulder length.

Clean sectioning
Tidy sectioning of hair essential to obtain an accurate haircut.

Colour cleanse
An over-sanitised term meaning to strip a disastrous colour out of the hair with bleach-based colour stripper, which could inevitably cause further chemical damage.

Column
See 'Running a column'.

Cooked (as in 'Is my lady cooked yet?')
Is my client's hair dry yet, or has her colour completed its time processing.

Dandruff
Comes in two forms, dry or greasy. Dry is greyish and can be itchy, greasy is yellowish and can be sticky. Both need pharmaceutical treatment if severe.

Depth
How light or dark a client's hair is. Most salons use an international numbering system that all product companies conform to, from 1, the darkest, to 10, the lightest. It makes up the first part of the product code, before the point or dash – 10.3.

Dirty mare
Client who comes in with very unclean, greasy hair at every appointment. No good if you're having your colour done as excess sebum or dirt can cause a barrier to the colour process – far better to have colour on clean hair for a clearer result.

Dispense
Short for Dispensary, the room where all the chemicals are mixed. Always keep out of client's sight in case of hushed discussions if an emergency occurs.

Diva
A gay, male stylist who is demanding, creative and difficult to handle, but also a gay male hairdresser.

Dry scalp
Commonly thought of
as being dandruff. Can be caused
by using over-strong, harsh shampoos,
and ironically anti-dandruff shampoos can
therefore sometimes exacerbate the problem.

Dusting
A technique used after the hair is blow-dried after cutting. The scissors glide over the cut to gently take off any endy bits or straggly hairs.

Elfin
A term to describe a tapered cut – think Mia Farrow's famous sixties crop or Kylie's recent take on it.

Fag hag
Female hairdresser who has a lot of gay male friends and therefore doesn't get to have a lot of heterosexual relationships.

Fairies
Fake clients normally booked in without the boss's knowledge and usually scheduled to allow for either a later start or to leave early. i.e 9 a.m. client: Betty Swum fails to arrive when stylist knows he won't be able to make it on time after heavy night out. Or 5.30 p.m. Ben Dover doesn't turn up for his gents haircut allowing knackered hairdresser who hasn't stopped all day to get home early.

Frizzy pubes
Hair that is coarse, frizzy and difficult to straighten.

Gent (as in 'Your gent's in)
Male client who has arrived for an appointment.

Geometric
The famous Sassoon sixties cut – a bob cut at a diagonal angle.

Graduated bob
A bob where the hair is cut shorter at the nape and longer around the front – think Posh's Bob, or the Pob as it is now known.

Graduated layers or cut
Layers cut at an angle from shorter to longer, with the weight and length normally left around the perimeter or baseline of the cut.

Hair loss – average
Between 50 to 100 hairs per day are shed naturally. Expect seasonal variations – more likely to shed in the autumn, for example. Pregnancy, diet and stress can also affect hair loss.

Harrod's helmet
A term to describe a coiffed-to-death unmoving hairdo, so perfectly set that it resembles a hat. Much beloved by the elderly Ladies-Who-Lunch, tweed-suited, quilted handbag brigade that frequents Knightsbridge. The hair is set rock-hard by regular bursts of Elnett and is designed not to move for a whole week between appointments.

'I'm not a miracle worker'
What your hairdresser says about their client in the staff room if they feel you have unrealistic expectations.

'I'm not a plastic surgeon'
What your hairdresser says in the staff room if confronted with a moose.

Inverted bob
Popular in the eighties – hair is shorter at the mid point of the nape, graduated longer towards the ears, and there is a cropped underneath section at the back, which is sometimes V-shaped.

Junior
Apprentice hairdresser assisting a stylist or colourist.

Knife and fork (as in 'Looks like it's been cut with a knife and fork')
A very poor haircut.

Landing strip
Colour regrowth, more commonly known as roots.

Layers
When hair is cut to the same length at angles all over the head so it appears to be falling into layers.

Maison Flo/Sweaty Betty's/Dead Fly in the Window and Net Curtains
A derogatory term for a suburban salon.

Marrying section
When some hair is taken from the previous section and used as a guideline for the next section to be cut.

Moose (as in 'She's a moose')
Client not too blessed in the looks department expecting to be totally transformed into a raving beauty by the hairdresser's scissors.

Moving across the park
Reference to Hyde Park. Stylists moving from the two main

London areas where top salons are located – Mayfair and Knightsbridge – often at the risk of losing clientele, who are notoriously prone to stick firmly to one or other location.

My lady (as in 'Is my lady ready?')
Female client who is being shampooed.

Natural base
The natural depth of a client's hair, referred to using the numbering system – 6 is dark blond to us, while you would call it mouse

On the floor (as in 'She's just gone on the floor')
Newly qualified apprentice taking paying clients for the first time.

Over-direction
When the hairdresser combs hair too far from the section he is working on so it isn't flush but pulled too far over, resulting in an inaccurate cut. Sometimes hair is over-directed deliberately for a different cutting result, or for when a build-up of weight is required.

PIA
A code describing a particularly difficult client, meaning pain in the arse.

Pigment
Can be granular or diffuse (large or small particles). The amount of pigment makes up the natural depth and tone and varies depending on hair type and texture.

Point cutting
The blades are kept firmly together and the point where they meet takes away weight by nipping into the hair.

Porosity
The hair's ability to absorb moisture. Dry or damaged hair will absorb moisture or product faster, but may not have the ability to retain it, hence fading colour.

Primadonna
A stylist who is demanding, creative and difficult to handle.

Privates
Clients who have been poached away from the salon for home visits by cunning staff. The bug-bear of every salon owner who has to make the salon environment ever more fabulous to ensure that customers stay out!

Rate of hair growth
Hair grows about 1.5 cm a month on average.

Razoring

Texture is created by removing bulk from the hair's mid-lengths and ends and forming a shape with the razor. Whole haircuts can be done like this, but be warned, hair can be difficult to manage afterwards, particularly if it's curly or frizzy.

Rent a chair
A self-employed stylist – salon takes half, hairdresser takes half. Not much beloved by the tax man and on the decrease.

Repeat rate
Percentage of clients returning to or requesting a particular stylist/colourist.

Root drag
A styling term that means working with the natural growth direction of the roots to achieve smooth, sleek roots.

Root lift
A styling term that means working away from the natural growth direction of the roots to achieve volume and bounce at the root.

Running a column
Working a busy clientele column of appointments.

Scissor over comb
An expert technique for cutting hair very short without using clippers. The comb is placed directly on the hair or scalp and the hair is cut through its teeth. Requires lots of practice.

Sensitivity
The technical term for damage to the cortex – the internal, main structure of the hair – through heat (electrical styling equipment), technical processes, sun, sea and chlorinated water.

Slicing
When hair is chipped into using a pointing motion, with the blades positioned almost together to remove bulk and weight.

Slide cutting
Blades are slid through the mid-lengths and ends of hair to create texture and movement. Often used to get a subtle graduation between two lengths.

Sparkle
To insert some fine, random weaves of bleached highlights amongst your regular colour in order to look sun-kissed.

Suicide fringe

When a client has attempted to cut their own fringe without following the rules resulting in a short, wonky or too-high fringe.

Tapered cut

A cut where the hair is at its shortest around the hairline and nape and is heavily graduated in reverse, so hair is left longer on the top.

Tensile strength

The elasticity of the hair. Hair stretches over a third of its length when wet, so it's at its most fragile, and returns when dry if healthy. Seriously damaged hair breaks when stretched.

Texture

The size of the follicle of each individual hair, not how much hair a client has. Larger follicles mean thicker hair, though the amount of hair depends on the individual. Normally there are between 100–150,000 hairs per head. Smaller follicles mean finer hair, but hair can be fine and there can be lots of it (many follicles).

Texturising

Subtle cutting into the root area of the hair to remove weight and bulk.

The hairdresser's inch (as in 'I'll just take an inch off')

Not an accurate tool of measurement as it can be anything from 2 cm to the length of a very long thumb. Remember, many hairdressers failed miserably at maths at school.

Thinning
Weight removal on bulky, coarse hair, normally done with serrated-edge scissors.

Tight as a gnat's chuff
A term for clients who never tip.

Tone
The colour that you see – red, gold, copper, blue, ash, etc. – whether natural or artificial. Also conforms to the international numbering system, and is the number after the point or dash – 10.3 is lightest blonde, with gold tone.

Tone-on-tone colour
A demi-permanent, ammonia-free permanent colour that lasts twelve to sixteen weeks and gives only a subtle regrowth.

Trim
An extremely vague term, completely open to personal interpretation, as it has no technical meaning to hairdressers – be warned.

Two hairs and a nit (as in 'She's only got two hairs and a nit')
A client with extremely fine hair.

Vegetable colour
Non-permanent colour which washes out after six to eight shampoos.

Virgin head
Natural hair that has undergone no chemical processes.